James Fitton

Sketches of the Establishment of the Church in New England

James Fitton

Sketches of the Establishment of the Church in New England

ISBN/EAN: 9783337092672

Printed in Europe, USA, Canada, Australia, Japan

Cover: Foto ©Lupo / pixelio.de

More available books at **www.hansebooks.com**

The First Catholic Church in Boston.

[Dedicated September 29, 1803.]

SKETCHES

OF THE

ESTABLISHMENT OF THE CHURCH

IN

NEW ENGLAND.

BY

REV. JAMES FITTON.

BOSTON:
PATRICK DONAHOE.
1872.

Entered, according to Act of Congress, in the year 1872,
BY PATRICK DONAHOE,
In the Office of the Librarian of Congress, at Washington.

Stereotyped at the Boston Stereotype Foundry,
19 Spring Lane.

PREFACE.

THE object contemplated in this small volume of Sketches, was, to give as succinct an account as possible of the introduction of our Holy Religion, and the foundation of its early churches, to assist, at least partially, the future historian, who will write of the several Dioceses, of which there are already five, where a few years ago there was but one, embracing the six New England States.

To the honor and glory of God, and to the spiritual advantage of thousands, as already seen, has been the erection of these Dioceses, in which so many churches, academies, convents, schools, confraternities, and other religious, literary, and benevolent Institutions have been introduced.

The Editor acknowledges his indebtedness to

the "Journal" of Right Rev. Bishop Fenwick, to Dr. J. G. Shea's "History of Catholic Missions," to the "Catholic Observer," and "Boston Pilot," wherein several interesting events here mentioned have appeared, or been alluded to, as well as to those gentlemen who assigned dates to facts herein published.

The parents of the Editor were of the congregation of one hundred, who assembled for divine worship, at the close of the last century, in the small rented building originally occupied by the Huguenots on School Street. Baptized by the venerated Reverend Dr. Matignon, confirmed by Right Rev. Dr. De Cheverus, and admitted to Holy Orders by the illustrious Right Rev. Bishop Fenwick, are events mentioned, as far as they may have weight, in authenticity of what has been here compiled, as his name or pretensions, otherwise, he allows to be of no consideration.

CONTENTS.

	PAGE
THE DISCOVERY AND EXPLORATION OF AMERICA	7
THE CHURCH IN NEW ENGLAND	34
BRIEF VIEW OF THE MISSIONARY LABORS OF THE EARLY JESUIT FATHERS	63
INTRODUCTION AND PROGRESS OF THE CHURCH IN BOSTON	74
HISTORY OF THE CHURCH IN BOSTON	80
CONSECRATION OF RIGHT REV. JOHN DE CHEVERUS	110
CONSECRATION OF RIGHT REV. BENEDICT J. FENWICK	121
DIOCESE OF HARTFORD	188
DIOCESE OF BURLINGTON	239
DIOCESE OF PORTLAND	259
DIOCESE OF SPRINGFIELD	286
CONCLUSION	333

SKETCHES,

ETC., ETC.

THE DISCOVERY AND EXPLORATION OF AMERICA.

The continent of America includes an extent of territory equal to one half of the continents of Europe, Asia, and Africa, and constitutes about three tenths of the dry land on the surface of the globe. It is bounded east and west by the great Atlantic and Pacific Oceans. On the west, the Pacific separates it from Asia, and at Behring's Straits, in the north, the two continents come almost in contact. On the north is the Arctic Ocean, divided by huge frozen islands into bays and inlets. On the east, the Atlantic separates it from Europe and Africa. On the south, it presents a storm-beaten cape to the expanse of the Southern or Antarctic Ocean.

When, in the designs of Divine Providence, the time had arrived for opening a communication between the two worlds, a man appeared, who was born for the achievement of discoveries of incalculable importance to mankind, as implied by the name recorded at his baptism: Christopher Columbus — the

Christbearing Dove. He was born at Cogoleto, in the republic of Genoa, in 1446. His father's name was Domingo Colombo, a citizen of the same republic.

Having cultivated the sciences at a tender age, and made such rapid progress in the Latin language and the rudiments of the mathematics, Christopher was soon enabled to understand the cosmographic writers, of the reading of which he was particularly fond.

At the age of fourteen, he returned from the University of Pavia to his native country. He learned navigation, and pursued it three and twenty years successively, with such zeal and perseverance, that he remained at sea for a long time, in order to gratify his unbounded and praiseworthy curiosity. He made voyages on the seas frequented by Europeans, full of desire to sail farther than other navigators had ventured. He sailed through the Northern Ocean, a hundred leagues beyond Iceland, the *Ultima Thule*, or the boundary of what had been thought navigable up to that day. At every place where he landed he endeavored to open a trade with the natives, in order to obtain information of these countries. He compared the knowledge he acquired in this way with the accounts then in existence relative to those regions, and enriched them with his own observations. In this judicious practice, he was aided by his knowledge of the sciences auxiliary to navigation, — the use of sound astronomy, extensive geographic learning, and an able hand in delineating maps, and in making spheres and other instruments.

The western world still unknown, the intercourse between Europe and India was carried on through the Red Sea. The spirit of maritime discovery received its first impulse from the kings of Castile. These monarchs, in following up their conquests and settlements in the Canary Islands, led the way to further navigations into the Atlantic, in search of new islands in the west. Hence, also, arose the traffic with the African coast, and the splendor and wealth of the city of Seville; and hence the extraordinary zeal for nautical adventure along the coast of Andalusia. The Portuguese, emulous of the glory of their neighbors, entered into the same career, and pursued it with such vigor and perseverance as to outstrip their precursors, by improving naval science and extending their commerce in a surprising manner. Their ships sailed along the western coast of Africa, and at length reached the Cape of Good Hope. Curiosity received a new stimulus from these discoveries; the boundless ocean of the west offered a wide field for speculation; the time had arrived for the achievement of the grand enterprise, — the knowledge of a New World.

On Friday, August 3, 1492, when the Catholic religion alone flourished throughout the world; when nought was known or heard of Episcopalians, Unitarians, Calvinists, Baptists, Methodists, Shakers, Quakers, Spiritists, or other modern sectaries; under Ferdinand and Isabella, the Catholic, encouraged by Fray Juan Perez, Guardian of the Convent of La Rabida, at the little seaport town of Palos, in Andalusia, the scene was interesting to behold!— where faith was kneeling to ask protection; where confidence was drawing new strength from devotion to God and Mary; where the adventurers, their commander at their head, were preparing, by Confession and Holy Communion, to enter, like Christian men, upon the perilous undertaking.

The mass over, out from the church, grave, resolute, and calm, walked the Admiral at the head of his crew. A few moments were allowed for farewells. Then the brief orders were given, and the sailors, to the number of one hundred and twenty, entering the boats, rowed out to their respective vessels, the largest of which was named Santa Maria, the second the Pinta, and the third Nina.

Then the report of the culverin sounded from the bows, and the standard of Castile swung out to the breeze from the peak of the SANTA MARIA; and the crew cheered, and the crowd on shore responded, as the Admiral stepped on board. A few moments more and the anchors were weighed, the yards were trimmed, the sails filled, and the flotilla stood out to sea.

Christopher Columbus thus committed himself to an ocean, whose bounds were unknown, and steered his course directly to the west. Every schoolboy is familiar with the scenes and incidents that daily and nightly took place on the decks of the little vessels, in which the heroic Admiral and his men sailed the trackless sea. Matin and vesper song alternated with the murmur of the wind and the sea, and when the

Atlantic tempests threatened to sink the frail crafts, the terror-stricken crew would beseech the Star of the seas to shine out upon the storm-riven ocean and guide them safely, for compass failed, and no sun, or moon, or stars illumined their darkened path.

On the morning of the 9th of October they breathed a fresh and odoriferous air, such as is felt at Seville in April. Every moment exhibited fresh marks of the neighborhood of land; and the soundings, the clouds, the varying winds, and other infallible appearances revived their drooping spirits. On the evening of the 11th they were all transported with joy, when they discovered a green rush, a kind of fish that is usually found among the rocks; a small plank, a cane, a stick artificially worked, a grassy turf, which appeared to have been wafted from the shore, and a thorn-bush, bearing red berries. When the night approached, and Columbus was persuaded that they were near land, he assembled the crew, and reminded them of the unspeakable obligations they were under to Almighty God, who had granted them such favorable weather, and who, notwithstanding their murmurs and despondency, had not deserted them till He had conducted them to the great object of their adventurous voyage. About ten o'clock at night, as he was making observations with his usual attention, on the quarter-deck, he saw a light, somewhat like a torch, carried from one place to another. At first he called Pedro Gutierrez, a royal page, and afterwards the superintendent, Rodrigo Sanchez, who saw it likewise. It was remarked that this light rose, sunk, vanished, and instantly appeared again; it was concluded, therefore, that it was carried by hand.

Near two o'clock in the morning land was descried by the Pinta, at about two leagues distance. The captain of the Pinta communicated the joyful news by the discharge of guns. The ships came together, and as soon as it was broad daylight, a flat and pleasant island appeared in view, full of limpid rivulets, and abundance of green bushes. This was one of the Bahama Islands. The crews were filled with the liveliest transports of joy; the Admiral lifted up his heart and eyes to heaven, and poured forth ejaculations of thanks and praise to God. The whole crew joined in the *Te Deum Laudamus*, which he intoned; and as soon as they had paid their early vows to the Divine Author of all blessings, they gave themselves up to joy and congratulations.

In the mean time, as soon as the vessels had reached the wished-for shore, they landed, fell on the ground, kissed it, bedewed it with tears of joy, and repeated their thanks to the Blessed and Adorable Trinity, the Father, the Son, and the Holy Ghost. Columbus then rose from his knees, and with a loud voice, pronounced the word *Salvador*, as the name of the island, and as a testimony that he dedicated the first of his discoveries to our Adorable Saviour.

Having passed three days at St. Salvador, he shaped his course to another island, which seemed to be larger, and about ten leagues to the west. He there cast anchor, and took possession of it, by the name of *Santa Maria de la Concepcion*.

Thus did the great Columbus, — the Christbearing Dove, — the pious and devoted son of the Church, consecrate to Jesus and Mary the consummation of all his toils, the first of his discoveries in the New World. The prayer of Columbus on reaching San Salvador, preserved by Washington Irving, evinces the humble and reverent spirit in which the great event was, as all things should be, consecrated to God.

"Domine Deus, æterne et omnipoteus, sacro tuo verbo cœlum et terram et mare creasti; benedicatur et glorificetur Nomen tuum, laudetur tua majestas quæ dignita est per humilem servum tuum ut ejus sacrum Nomen agnoscatur et prædicetur in hac altera mundi parte."

"O Lord, eternal and omnipotent God, Thou hast, by Thy holy word, created the heavens, the earth, and the sea; blessed and glorified be Thy Name; praised be Thy Majesty, who hast deigned that, by means of Thy unworthy servant, Thy sacred Name should be acknowledged and made known in this new quarter of the globe." — *Irving: Columbus*, i. 156.

Upon the return of Columbus, March 15, 1493, after the accomplishment of the grand momentous enterprise, several of the European nations fitted out small fleets to sail to the continent of North America, and as early as 1517 the English, French, Spanish, and Portuguese had so far made their discoveries in the New World useful, that they had established a successful fishery at Newfoundland, in which they had fifty-seven vessels engaged.*

In the latter part of 1523, Francis I., of France, a monarch deeply captivated with the love of glory, fitted out a squadron of four ships, the command of which he gave to Giovanni Verazzani, a Florentine navigator of great skill and celebrity. Soon after the vessels had sailed, three of them were so damaged in a storm that they were compelled to return; but Verazzani proceeded in a single vessel, with a determination to make new discoveries. Sailing from Madeira in a westerly direction, he reached the coast of America, probably in the latitude of Wilmington, North Carolina.

After exploring the coast for some distance, north and south, without being able to find a harbor, he was obliged to send a boat on shore to open an intercourse with the natives. The savages at first fled, but soon recovering their confidence, they entered into an amicable traffic with the strangers.

At one place, by the desire of Verazzani, a young sailor had undertaken to swim to land, and accost the natives; but when he saw the crowds which thronged the beach, he repented of his purpose, and, although within a few yards of the landing-place, his courage failed, and he attempted to turn back. At this moment the water only reached his waist; but

* For the early exploration of the southern portion of America, and the missionaries in Mexico, Florida, Texas, and California, see J. G. Shea's History of Spanish Missions, from 1529 to 1854.

overcome with terror and exhaustion, he had scarcely strength to cast his presents and trinkets upon the beach, when a wave threw him senseless on the shore. The savages ran immediately to his assistance, took him up in their arms, and carried him a short distance from the sea. Great was his terror, when, upon coming to his senses, he found himself in their power. Stretching his hands towards the ship, he uttered piercing cries; to which the natives replied by loud yells, intending, as he afterwards found, to reassure him. They then carried him to the foot of a hill, stripped him, turned his face to the sun, and kindled a large fire near him.

He was now fully impressed with the horrible thought that they were about to sacrifice him to the sun. His companions on board, unable to render him any assistance, were of the same opinion; they thought, to use Verazzani's own words, " that the natives were going to roast and eat him." Their fears, however, were soon turned to gratitude and astonishment; the savages dried his clothes, warmed him, and showed him every mark of kindness, caressing and patting his white skin with apparent surprise. They then dressed him, conducted him to the beach, tenderly embraced him, and, pointing to the vessel, removed to a little distance, to show that he was at liberty to return to his friends.

Proceeding north, Verazzani landed, probably near, what is now the city of New York. Continuing his journey, he entered, it is supposed, the haven of Newport, Rhode Island, where he found the natives liberal, friendly, and confiding, and the country the richest he had yet seen.

Verazzani proceeded still further north, and explored the coast as far as Newfoundland; but he found the natives of the northern regions hostile and jealous, and unwilling to traffic except for weapons of war. He gave to the whole region the name of La Nouvelle France, and took possession of it in the name of his sovereign.

The celebrated Jacques Cartier succeeded Verazzani. He explored the north-east coast carefully, and, passing through the Strait of Belle Isle, traversed the great Gulf of the St. Lawrence, and subsequently went to Gaspé Bay, where he erected a cross thirty feet high, with a shield bearing the three fleurs-de-lis of France, thus taking possession in the name of Francis the First.

In his second voyage he entered the great river of Canada, which he named the St. Lawrence, because he began to explore it on the festival of that martyr. Continuing his voyage, he moored his vessels safely in the river of St. Charles, which he named " Port de Ste. Croix," or Port of the Holy Cross. He here received a visit from the chief, " The Lord of Canada," who lived at Stadacona, attended by five hundred warriors, who came to welcome the strangers.

Having heard that there existed, far up the river, a large settlement called Hochelaga, he determined to advance in quest of it. Previously to his setting out he caused his men to let off twelve cannons, charged with balls, into the wood near them. " At whose noise," says Hakluyt, an old historian, "they were greatly astonished and amazed, for they thought that heaven had fallen upon them, and put themselves to flight, howling, crying, and shrieking."

Leaving his vessels, he proceeded in two boats and the pinnace as far as Lake St. Peter, where, on account of the shallowness of the water, he was obliged to leave the pinnace, and proceed in the boats. Here they met with five hunters, "who," says Cartier, "freely and familiarly came to our boats without any fear, as if we had even been brought up together." Everywhere he seems to have been received with kindness, for the chief of the district of the Hochelai, now the Richelieu, paid him a visit, and presented him with one of his own children, about seven years of age, whom he afterwards visited while Cartier was wintering at St. Croix.

Delighted with his journey, Cartier proceeded, and soon came to Hochelaga, which he found to be a fortified town, on a beautiful island, under the shade of a mountain. On his landing, he was met by more than a thousand of the natives, who received him with every demonstration of joy and hospitality. He was delighted with the view from the mountain, which he named Mount Royal, which time has changed to Montreal.

The inhabitants were of the Huron tribe, and seem to have regarded Cartier as one of a superior order, as they brought to him their sick, decrepit, and aged, with an evident expectation that he would heal them. Touched by this display of confiding simplicity, he did all he could to soothe their minds. The French historians relate that he made the sign of the Cross upon the sick, distributed *Agnus Dei's* amongst them, recited with a loud voice the sufferings and death of the Saviour, and prayed fervently with them.

On his return to his boats, he was accompanied by a great number of the inhabitants to the landing-place below St. Mary's current. They even carried on their shoulders some of his men who were fatigued. They appeared to be grieved at the shortness of their stay, and followed their course along the banks of the river with signs of kindly farewell.

Cartier, having returned to France, made no subsequent voyage. He died soon after his return home, having sacrificed health and fortune in the cause of discovery. He evidently was a man firm in the faith, a devoted Catholic, and piously disposed, as we learn from the festivals and saints' names he gave to his discoveries, wherever made.

Sieur de Champlain, the distinguished naval officer, who was the destined founder of the principal French settlement in the north, was, in 1603, the worthy successor of Cartier. His Catholic, Christian character is learned from those memorable words which history records: "The salvation of a single soul is worth more than the conquest of an empire, and kings should seek to extend their dominions in countries where idolatry reigns, only to cause their submission to Jesus Christ."* He undertook his

---

* The first words of the Sieur de Champlain's voyages.

toils and labors with patience, in order " to plant in this country the standard of the Cross, and to teach the knowledge of God, and the glory of His holy Name, desiring to increase charity for his unfortunate creatures." *

Thinking that he would " commit a great fault if he employed no means of bringing the savages to the knowledge of God," he earnestly " sought out some good Religious who would have zeal and affection for God's glory." Such as these are always discoverable by those who are really in want of them, and Champlain soon found them,— men " who were borne away by holy affection, who burned to make this voyage, if so, by God's grace, they might gain some fruit, and might plant in these lands the standard of Jesus Christ, with fixed resolution to live, and, if need were, to die, for His sacred Name." † So, when the ship is ready, we naturally expect the next record, that " each of us examined himself, and purged himself of his sins, by penitence and confession, so best to say adieu to France, and to place himself in a state of grace, that each might be conscientiously free to give himself up into the keeping of God, and to the billows of a vast and perilous sea." ‡

When the voyage was thus undertaken, what won-

---

* " Planter en ce pays l'estendart de la Croix et leur enseigner la cognoissance de Dieu et gloire de Son Sainct Nom, estant nostre désir d'augmenter la charité envers ses misérables créatures."—Voyages et decouvertures depuis 1615.

† Voyages depuis 1615, p. 3.   ‡ Ibid. p. 8.

der that we find, along the first discovered coasts, names so purely Catholic: St. Mary's Bay, St. Mary's Isle, St. Mary's River; that Montreal is called *Ville Marie;* that the first grant of land from the Duc de Ventadour to the Jesuit fathers is the seigneurie of Our Lady of Angels; and that then, by Mary's Lake, and missions of Assumption and Annunciation, we sweep away westward to the mysterious river of the Conception?

Thus were Catholics the first discoverers of America, the first to announce the glad tidings of salvation to the red men of the wilderness.

We do not wish to draw any invidious distinction, but we do wish the truth of impartial history to be known. With rare exceptions, all the writers of our so-called American histories have ignored many important facts, and the readers of these histories would conclude that America had been explored, built up, and developed by Protestants, and that our free institutions are due, solely and entirely, to Protestant minds and Protestant love of liberty! whereas, who but our Catholic ancestors were the first to enthrone liberty on the European continent? Who formed the republics of Venice and Genoa, of Switzerland and San Marino, long before the religious persuasions of those who revile and misrepresent our creed had either a name or existence? And were they not the first who, in this western hemisphere, formed a constitution in the colony of Maryland, in 1632, which proclaimed that she alone was the beacon rock of civil and religious freedom? Let the friends of civil and religious liberty read the oath of the governor of this colony. Here it is; and it is the best legacy which can be bequeathed to generations yet unborn: "I will not, by myself or another, directly or indirectly, trouble, molest, or discountenance any person professing to believe in Jesus Christ, for or in respect of religion; I will make no difference of persons in conferring offices, favors, or rewards for or in respect of religion, but merely as they should be found faithful and well deserving, and endowed with moral virtues and abilities. My aim shall be public unity; and if any person or officer shall molest any person professing to believe in Jesus Christ, on account of his religion, I will protect the person molested, and punish the offender."

And regarding the form of our government, and its free institutions, let it not be forgotten that the *Magna Carta*, that embraces all the essential principles of American liberty, chief among which are the right of trial by jury, and the writ of *habeas corpus*, and, in fact, our bill of rights, were planned and drawn up by the Catholic barons of England, and enforced, centuries before modern *isms* had an existence.

CATHOLICISM IN ACCORDANCE WITH POPULAR INSTITUTIONS.

In connection with this brief sketch of the discovery and exploration of America, we would add a few words on Catholicism and its polity, spoken as long ago as 1832, by that illustrious scholar and divine, Most Rev. Francis Patrick Kenrick, D. D., on those words of our Saviour, " Render to Cæsar the things that are Cæsar's, and to God the things that are God's." (Matt. xxii. 21.)

In a country like this, observes the great divine, enjoying free and popular institutions, wherein the most elevated man is but the chief servant of the people, it might seem superfluous to urge the former part of this divine precept. Here no Cæsar sways the imperial sceptre, or exacts from subject millions subsidies to sustain his power, and increase the pomp of majesty. But though the words of the Redeemer regard Cæsarean authority, they imply a maxim of order applicable to society under every form, namely, that the established government should be respected and supported. They contain no peculiar sanction of imperial domination; they warrant no abuse of power; but merely declare that our duties towards the civil authorities may be discharged without offence to God, or interference with religious obligations. St. Augustin[*] beautifully observes that the Church, or City of God, is composed of men of all nations, with perfect independence of the various forms of civil polity. To these she is indifferent; and with wise condescension, she respects and sanctions the national usages and institutions, however diversified, wheresoever they come not into collision with the divine doctrines of her Founder, or the general interests of piety. Thus she adapts her children

---

[*] City of God, lib. xvii.

to every state of society, and enables them to coalesce with men of every character, uniting and cementing all hearts in all things whereby social order and happiness are promoted. Others may investigate abstract questions in regard to the excellence of particular systems of civil polity, the immediate origin of power, and the limits wherein it is circumscribed. She attends to practical lessons, applicable to established order, and teaches the exercise of those virtues which, under every form of government, are calculated to render men good and happy. Whether popular choice confer a presidential chair, or ambition grasp a crown, or victory brandish the sword of power, she regards the vicissitudes of human things as subordinate to Divine Providence, and considers every just exercise of established authority as sanctioned by Him from whom all power emanates. "For there is no power but from God, and those that are, are ordained of God." (Rom. xiii.)

It has been alleged, that the Church is essentially allied to monarchical governments, and that her own constitution is an absolute monarchy. Others have maintained that she is, at best, a monarchy tempered with aristocracy; while some have discovered her principles to be highly democratic. The Church is evidently distinct in her constitution from every form of civil polity, and yet bearing characters similar to each, and combining all their perfections. She is a kingdom, though not of this world, and meek and lowly is her sovereign. The vicegerent of Christ, however high his prerogatives, lords it not over our faith, and can do nothing against the truth, but for the truth. The power which the Lord has given him is for edification, not for destruction. "The kings of the Gentiles lord it over them, and they that have power over them are called beneficent; but you not so," said our Saviour to his apostles. "But he who is the greatest among you, let him be as the least; and he that is the leader, as he that serveth." (Luke xxii. 25, 26.)

The dignitaries of the Catholic Church are not those whom descent from renowned ancestors has ennobled, without personal merit; but they are the children alike of the mechanic or of the prince, whom virtue has exalted. Their lineage is derived from the Apostles, by the divine rite of ordination. Their honors impose on them the duty of rivalling their virtues; and they are charged to communicate their powers to those only whom merit shall have distinguished. The Church may be styled a Republic, as St. Augustin observes,* for the obvious reason that she is intended for the true happiness of the people; but we must never forget that Christ is her founder and her ruler, and that the powers of her ministers are derived from Him who alone could communicate them. "We are of God." "We are ambassadors for Christ, God, as it were, exhorting by us." "Let a man so look upon us as the ministers

---

* "Vera autem justitia non est, nisi in ea republica, cujus conditor rectorque Christus est: si etiam ipsam rempublicam placet dicere, quoniam eam rem populi esse, negare non possumus." — Aug. l. ii. de Civ. Dei, c. 21.

of Christ, and the dispensers of the mysteries of God." (1 John iv. 6; 2 Cor. v. 20; 1 Cor. iv. 1.)

The congeniality of the constitution of the Church with free institutions, and the consequent aptitude of her members for the rational exercise of the rights of free citizens, may be easily discovered on comparison. The principle of equality is justly regarded as the basis of republican institutions. Every man who has breathed the vital air in this happy government, is equal, in the eyes of the law, and entitled to the privileges of citizenship. The child of the cottager and the king were equally recognized as creatures of the same God, formed to His image and likeness, and when born anew to the baptismal font, were entitled to the same Christian privileges. The factitious distinctions whereby society marks her members, from the peasant to the sovereign, though respected by the Church, which always regards order, give no prerogatives to the great of this world, in the solemn rites of religion. All hear the same Gospel, all kneel before the same altar; and all participate of the same sacraments. The lowliest amongst the faithful, in the extremity of life, summons the minister of God to his bed of sorrow, to dispense to him the sanctifying mysteries; and the summons is obeyed equally as if the lord of vast dominions had sought the succors of religion. Every office and dignity of the Church is accessible to all her children, without any distinction but that which arises from merit. The youth who, in the humblest walks of society, toiled for a scanty subsistence, and who was indebted for his education to the bounty of some friend to talent and virtue, may in mature age rise to the altar of the living God, or even sit among the princes of his people; nay, he may rise to the pinnacle of Church authority, and govern an empire far greater than ever owned the power of the Cæsars. Virtue, not birth, is with us the true title to distinction. Let republics boast of greater equality than this.

The elective system is another feature in popular institutions. It is, however, even in several States of the Union, circumscribed by conditions required in the voters; and it is, in many instances, confined to the representatives and chief officers of the people, whilst a far greater number of inferior offices are created by appointment. The Church, from her foundation, under the absolute sway of the Cæsars, cherished the principle of election. St. Chrysostom justly remarks, that the Prince of the Apostles doubtless possessed the power of filling up the vacancy in the apostolic college, by appointing one to occupy the place of Judas; but that through a spirit of condescension and conciliation, he allowed the assembled multitude interference in the appointment. In the same spirit, so worthy of the meekness of their Master, the twelve bade the multitude to look among them for seven men of good reputation, whom the Apostles might appoint to the office of Deacons. The power and right strictly belonged to the apostolic college, and not to the laity, because the Apostles alone had been sent by Him to whom all power was given in heaven and on earth. It was discretionary with them to make the appointment without the interference of others, and to judge of the qualifications of those who might be presented; but it was in no way derogatory from their high authority to receive the testimony of the faithful with regard to the merits of the candidate, particularly whilst the purest zeal for the interests of religion was common to the great body of believers. Their example was imitated by their successors in the Christian Prelacy, and to this day the solemn ceremonial of ordination points out the wise motives that determined her earliest pastors to adopt a system so conciliatory.

The elective form is preserved in regard to the dignity of Bishop in many portions of the Church, wherein the clergy elect the prelate that is to govern them, or the Bishops of the province make the choice, dependent on the sanction of the Roman Pontiff. The highest ecclesiastical dignitary is chosen by the votes of two thirds of the College of Cardinals, most solemnly sworn to regard only the general good of Christendom in the choice of its chief ruler. The many precautions that are taken to guard their integrity against bias, or intrigue, or any species of undue influence, and the happy results of the election, which, in a few weeks, generally gives a Pontiff of exalted merit to the Christian world, prove the freedom and wisdom of the system. Elections, therefore, are coeval with the Church, and are congenial to her spirit of conciliation.

Deliberative assemblies, which are so characteristic of popular institutions, are particularly congenial to

Christianity, and as ancient as the Church herself. When doubts arose among some of the first professors of the faith, in regard to the necessity of exacting the observance of the Jewish ceremonies from converted Gentiles, the dispute was decided in a solemn assembly convened for the purpose. "The Apostles and ancients came together to consider of this matter." (Acts xv. 6.) The advocates of both opinions were heard, ere Peter arose to terminate the discussion, and James concurred in judgment; when a decree was drawn up in the name of the Apostles and ancients, and by the authority of the Holy Ghost, determining the controversy. Subsequent ages were not inattentive to the precedent. Each Bishop regulated the chief affairs of his diocese in the assembly, and with counsel of his brethren, the clergy, over whom he presided. The Bishops of each province semi-annually assembled to deliberate in common on the means of promoting truth and piety throughout the flocks committed to their charge; and when the doctrines of faith were assailed, or other general interests of the Christian world were at stake, the representatives of the whole Church were congregated to testify the faith, and legislate for the general good of Christendom. The tyranny of the Cæsars, and the fury of their persecution, could not entirely prevent assemblies so congenial to Christianity, and when Rome saw her Constantine raise the victorious banner of the cross, Nice soon beheld the most sublime spectacle the world had witnessed, the assembly of three hundred and eight Pontiffs, venerable for their learning, sanctity, and sufferings, all concurring in proclaiming the faith of the universe, the Divinity of the Saviour of mankind.

In these assemblies, the most perfect freedom of discussion is admitted, and moderation and condescension mark the decisions, which generally are made with unanimous suffrage. No doctrine is defined, unless, on examining the Scriptures, and consulting the monuments of the faith of preceding ages, it is clearly ascertained to belong to the original deposit of Revelation. No law is enacted, except such as the majority deem expedient for the purity of Christian morals, and the advancement of piety. In them we have the freedom and moderation, without the instability, of popular institutions. Hence, though the government of the Church may appear absolute and arbitrary to one who regards the high powers of her functionaries, it will be found to be moderate and just, since the canons, or laws of those assemblies, direct and restrict each Bishop in the exercise of his authority, so that he is scarcely more than the executive of their decrees.

In the Religious Orders, which the Church regards as states of perfection, we discover the same equality, the same elective system, the same deliberative bodies, and even the popular and democratic principle of rotation in office. The young Noble who figured in the courts of Princes, and the Monarch himself who directed the destinies of nations, are, after their entrance within the gates of the cloister, undistinguished from the peasant and the mechanic. Their former dress and decorations are exchanged for the simple habit worn by every member of the Institute. Their titles are forgotten, and the affectionate appellation of brother is alike addressed to the peasant and the noble. An Aloysius of Gonzaga, and a Francis Borgia, are distinguished in religion, not by the titles and honors of the Princedom or Dukedom which they once bore, but by the heroism of their virtue. No one is incorporated in the Order, or admitted to the solemn profession, unless a majority of the actual members approve his merit. None are elevated to the most responsible offices, unless by the suffrages of a like majority. The son of a cottager may be chosen to govern a body wherein courtiers are enrolled, if learning and virtue ennoble him. The powers of the Superiors are confined within the limits of the rule and constitutions. In many important affairs they need the consent of the Chapter or Council of the Order, wherein the majority of votes prevail. A term is likewise fixed to the duration of their authority. Many centuries before the American Constitution was framed, the humble Francis of Assisium formed the rule, that the General of the Order should be chosen for the term of four years; and other founders of religious Institutes have added, that after their re-election for a second term, they should not be capable of being chosen a third time, unless all danger and appearance of perpetuity was removed by the intervention of another superior between the second and third terms of service. Compare these provisions with those of the Constitution of the Union, and say with candor whether it might not be conceived that its framers, those Statesmen of their day, had borrowed largely from our Religious Institutions?

In thus exhibiting the accordance of the Constitution of the Church and of her Institutes with that system of civil polity for which we entertain a predilection, it is not with the view to demonstrate that she is a democracy. The will of the people is the immediate source and supreme law of democratic institutions; the will of Christ our Lord is the source and rule of all Church power. The truths of religion must emanate from the unerring wisdom of the Deity: the grace whereby the souls of men are sanctified must be a communication of divine sanctity and justice. Scripture is positive on this point. "How can they preach, unless they be sent?" (Rom. x. 15.) "Neither doth any man take the honor to himself, but he that is called by God." (Heb. v. 4.) Nevertheless, the power thus divinely conferred is not directed to the aggrandizement of the individuals who are clothed with it, but to the welfare of the whole Christian Commonwealth. We possess the most striking advantages of the democratic system, without the defects that are inseparable from every system of human polity. The divine Constitution of the Catholic Church exhibits the infinite wisdom of her Founder, combining, in an admirable manner, the excellences of each system, and excluding their imperfections. We have in it Monarchy without despotism, Aristocracy without hereditary entailment,

Democracy without fluctuation. Our Sovereign Pontiff is but the servant of the servants of God; our Bishops and Priests are the fond fathers of their flock; the faithful at large are the mystical members of Christ our Lord. In the variety of grades there is nothing to flatter human pride, or debase a single member of this great family. All are children of the same God, aspirants to the same bliss, and responsible at the same tribunal. In the similarity of features which the whole system exhibits, when compared with each form of civil government, we have incentives to the discharge of our social duties in every state of society.

The Catholic Church is everywhere the friend of human happiness. With the various forms of civil polity it is not her province to interfere. To none of them is she allied, to none is she hostile. Oppression, tyranny, injustice, and disorder of every species, are by her condemned; but yet she mingles not in the strife when an indignant nation struggles to wrest from the tyrant's grasp the sceptre of iron wherewith he rules them. All the calamities of licentiousness and anarchy present themselves to her mind when she sees subjects maddened by oppression into revolt; and whilst she hears the crash of falling thrones, her heart bleeds, not so much through sympathy for the misfortunes of the great, as in anticipation of the evils which the licentious may perpetrate in the abused name of Liberty.

The sceptre of the Cæsars, which the early Christians were taught to respect, has long since been broken; the fragments of the vast Empire have been divided among Barbarian conquerors. Dynasty after dynasty has passed away. Republics have risen, flourished, decayed, and perished: but the Church still remains, the imperishable monument of the wisdom and power of her Divine Founder. The gates of Hell have not prevailed against her.

THE CHURCH IN NEW ENGLAND.

CATHOLIC France, the eldest daughter of the Church, zealous for the growth of the religion, which through so many changes her devoted hierarchy had so tenderly preserved, claims, and with justice, the honor of the permanent foundations of Catholicity on the soil of what we at present know as New England. The sons of this truly Catholic Power had, long before the settlements of Port Royal and Quebec, sailed along the rocky coast of its northern boundary; and the many islands and headlands, graced by the names of the sainted personages of history, bear testimony to the sterling worth and true piety of the commanders of the several expeditions, the Cartiers, the Champlains, and others.

In 1604, Pierre de Guasts, Sieur de Montz, laid the foundation of French power by beginning a settlement on St. Croix Island, a delightful spot at the mouth of the river of Holy Cross. Here Rev. Nicholas d'Aubri erected a small chapel, the ruins of which could have been seen till within a short time since, and from its rustic altar proclaimed the solemn truths of religion to the infant congregation of aborigines and colonists. The year following, Port Royal, now

Annapolis, was settled, and Rev. Jesse Fleche ministered to the spiritual wants of the settlers.

In 1611, Father Peter Biard, a native of Grenoble, and Father Enemond Masse, two members of the Society of Jesus, whom the bigotry of the Huguenot ship-owners and the secret hostility of Jean de Biencourt, Sieur de Potrincourt, the new Seigneur of Port Royal, had long detained in the ports of France, arrived. Their object was to evangelize the native tribes, and they devoted themselves to their missionary labors with great success, converting among others the almost centenary chieftain Memberton, and many of his people. The colonists, however, many being poor, were in great distress, and for a time the Jesuits might be seen laboring for the general good of all, becoming carpenters, fishermen, and everything, in a word, that charity could suggest or devotedness inspire, which endeavor on their part, however, instead of melting seemed to harden the hearts of the bigoted even more and more against them, so much so that at length, from the brutality of Biencourt and a young and headstrong son of Potrincourt, they resolved to leave Port Royal and return to France, which attempt their oppressors equally prevented, and they were compelled to remain.

The report of their suffering and persecution reaching France, their friends sent out other Fathers, with emigrants, and all necessary supplies, to commence a settlement elsewhere. Mount Desert, at the mouth of Penobscot, was selected, and hither the Sieur de la Saussage, the commandant, having taken Fathers

Biard and Masse on board, steered in the month of March, 1613. Landing on the eastern shore of the Island, they planted a cross, and traced out a fort on the west side of the "Pool," a part of the sound which runs into the centre of the Island.* Religious in its design, the settlement bore the name of the "Holy Saviour." Here the Fathers daily offered the holy Sacrifice at the foot of the cross, expecting soon to see a rustic chapel rise on their Island. On a certain day Father Biard, accompanied by one of the officers, proceeded to the mainland to visit the natives. The wailing of distress in the distance soon satisfied them that an Indian village was not far off. In a short time they entered it; and imagine their surprise when seeing a poor Indian holding a dying child in his arms, surrounded by the tribe ranged in a double row! The scene touched the tender chord of pity in the heart of the good missionary; hastily drawing near, he took the infant and baptized it. The healing water of the sacrament restored, not only spiritual, but bodily health; the child recovered, and the natives looked upon the new comers as envoys of heaven.

While the natives were thus being won over to the truth, and the mission seemed destined to effect immeasurable good, it pleased the Almighty to allow it to be arrested in a moment, and all its hopes to be dashed to the ground. A fleet of fishing smacks from Virginia, escorted by one Argal, already noted for his lawless acts, and known at a later date as the

* Williamson's History of Maine, i. 206. 76.

tyrant and scourge of Virginia, reached the coast of Maine. Hearing of the French settlement, Argal resolved to destroy it, and sailing up, opened a brisk fire on the unprepared French, few of whom were in their vessel. De Saussage made what resistance he could, but was soon compelled to surrender, with all his party. In this skirmish, a lay-brother, named Gilbert du Thet, was mortally wounded, and expired soon after his removal to the shore, rejoicing with his latest breath at his happiness in being permitted to shed his blood for the faith. He was buried at the foot of the mission cross, and the missionaries were compelled to bid a last farewell to the spot whence they had hoped to spread civilization and Christianity throughout the land of the Abenakis. Two of them, Fathers Biard and Masse, were carried off to Virginia as prisoners; the other two, Fathers Lalement and Quentin, were allowed to leave for the nearest French port.

Such was the close of this celebrated mission, destroyed by violence and injustice. Argal's atrocity did not end here; seizing de Saussage's commission, he treated him and his comrades as pirates, and almost succeeded in having them hanged in Virginia as such. The bloody penal laws of England, which darken with their awful atrocity so many a page of the colonial statute-book of Virginia, were also held in terror over the heads of the Fathers. But God was still with His own, and after being taken back to Acadia in a new plundering expedition, they owed their lives only to a storm which drove them to the

Catholic Azores. Here the captain was in their power; but disdaining to repay evil by evil, they forbore to disclose their character and sufferings to the authorities at the Island, and allowed him to depart in peace. They subsequently reached England, and after a little delay, proceeded to France: one to die soon after in the midst of his labors, the other to return to America, to toil for years before receiving the reward of the just.*

Although the Virginians destroyed Port Royal, the French soon returned to the coast of what is now the State of Maine, and in 1619 two associations were formed at Bordeaux, one for trading purpose on the Acadian coast, the other for the fisheries. Not to be deprived of religious succor on that lonely shore, the members of these associations applied to the Recollects of the Province of Aquitaine for three Fathers

---

* Peter Biard, a native of Grenoble, was a Jesuit of learning and ability. After his American mission, he was for a time professor of theology at Lyons, and afterwards a chaplain in the French army, in which post he died at Avignon, November 17, 1622. — See Louvenay, Historia Societatis Jesu, 324.

Enemond Massé was born in 1574, and entered the Society of Jesus at the age of twenty-two. When chosen for the Acadian mission, he was Socius of the Provincial, Father Coton. His misfortunes in Maine did not quench his apostolic spirit. He was one of the first Jesuits sent to Quebec in 1625, and though again taken by the English in 1629, he again returned in 1633, and labored chiefly among the Montagnas and the French till his death, which took place May 12, 1646. — Shea's Hist. Cath. Missions, 134. — Bressani, Relation Abrégée, 174.

and a lay-brother, whom they promised to support as long as their companies lasted. Several Fathers came and established a central mission on the River St. John, whence they extended their labors to Miscou, near the mouth of the St. Lawrence, on the one hand, and the Penobscot, apparently, on the other. Their labors were not fruitless, the Indian, no less than the French trader and fisherman, reaped the advantages; and in the discharge of their duties they shrank from neither peril nor hardship. One of them, Father Sebastian, was, above all, noted for his intrepidity, and he penetrated to Quebec overland, and wintered with the Recollects there. In 1623, however, setting out from Miscou for the mission on the St. John's, he sank beneath his labors, and perished from hunger and misery, closing a three years' apostolate by a death which, though unseen by men, yet perhaps before God, from its peculiarity, was as precious as the martyrdom of a Brebœuf or a Chabanel. The next year his surviving companions, Father Jacques de la Foyer, Louis Fontinier, and Jacques Cardon, in consequence of orders from their Provincial, left the mission, and penetrated by the Riviere du Loup to Quebec.*

The English swept over Acadia, and the French settlements fell into their hands; but the conquerors did not secure possession. As early as 1630, Charles St. Etienne de la Tour was on the Acadian coast, and extended his stations to the Penobscot. Three Recollect missionaries attended him, and soon restored

* Champlain's Voyages, p. 282. Charlevoix, ii. p. 195.

their missions in Maine. Champlain tells us, in 1632, that they were still there; and as the French, in that year, seized the last English post on the Penobscot and at Machias, the mission probably lasted for some years, but of which we have no details.*

The commander De Razillai, who owned this part of Acadia, died in 1635, and his portion passed to d'Aulney de Charnisy, who made Biguyduce his post. More devoted to the religious wants of the French on the coast of Maine than La Tour, who was a Protestant, he established a Capuchin mission on the Kennebec in 1643. To the old fort on the Penobscot, near to the present town of Castine, the Superior often sent his missionaries. The good Fathers, wherever stationed, whether on the coast, keeping alive by daily exhortation the faith of their countrymen, or in the interior, warning the traders of the severe justice of God when directed towards the unjust buyer and seller, forgot not in the "all for all" in the Scripture, the no less important monition of St. Paul, to beware of the danger of a "reprobate and castaway," while engaged in preaching and laboring for others.

Missionaries had thus labored for years, when Catholicity was now to take a firm hold in the land, not in the stranger from afar, but in the children of the soil, the red men of the forest.

The Jesuit Fathers had not abandoned the mission ground where Du Thet lay, at the foot of the broken

---

* Charlevoix, i. 436. Rel. 1646-7. Hildreth's United States, i. 299. Williamson's Maine, i. 71, 322.

cross; their eyes were often turned longingly towards it. In 1642 they had gathered, at St. Joseph's, on the St. Lawrence, a number of Algonquins and Montagnais, won from their nomadic life to Christianity and civilization. This settlement was the charitable work of the pious Knight Noel Brulart de Sillery, and under the name of this valiant chevalier, its events have passed into history.

Like all the mission settlements, its early annals show examples of high and heroic sanctity. Among the Christian warriors of Sillery, none is more illustrious than Charles Meiaskwat. When the Abenakis of Maine and Algonquins of Canada were on friendly terms with each other, word reached his ears that some of his Algonquin brethren had revived old animosities, and delighted in torturing the Abenakis who had fallen into their hands. In company with Nicolet, the great explorer of the west, this true child of faith set out to rescue them. Nicolet perished in a rapid, but the generous Charles, nowise discouraged, pressed on, met the torturers and their victims, and after administering a justly merited rebuke to the heartless wretches, provided for the wounded in the Convent of the hospital nuns of Sillery. There cared for with a tenderness which the good Sisters knew well how to bestow, these poor Indians soon became convalescent, and with strength came the desire to return to their homes. Charles accompanied them, and before arrival at the mission ground of the Abenakis, the story of his devotedness and affection had been noised through the tribe. His reception was cordial, for gratitude lingers long and prompts to good in the savage breast. The occasion was profited by, for our hero at once acted the catechist towards these long neglected children of Maine, and with signal success. Returning to Sillery, Charles was accompanied by a sagamore, or chief, who remained at St. Joseph's, and was soon followed by others.

Ere long an embassy came, in the name of the Abenakis, to invite the black-gown to come and reside in their midst. As soon as the fearful Iroquois war, which desolated Canada, lulled, so as to enable the missionaries to attempt a new mission, Father Gabriel Druilletes was sent, in 1646, to found the mission of the Assumption. He set out on the 29th of August, with a party of Indians, and after a painful and laborious journey through the wilderness, reached the village of the Abenakis in safety. His uncomplaining endurance had won all hearts, and he found a rude chapel raised for his use about three miles above the present town of Augusta. This became the centre of his labors, and in a few months he had acquired their dialect so far as to be able to converse in it. His people were docile and attentive; they were soon won to the faith, and numbers implored baptism; but this he prudently deferred. He came to prepare the ground, to learn their dispositions, leaving the superstructure to be raised by others, requiring, however, their immediate renunciation of their superstitions, their quarrels, and intemperance.

The English at Augusta, and the French to the eastward, warmly encouraged the good work, as did also the Capuchin Superior, Father Ignatius, who extended to him the most cordial greeting. His stay, however, was limited, as, in accordance with the orders of his Superior, he was to return to headquarters, where he was to hand in his report. The grief of the Abenakis, at hearing of his departure, was intense, till alleviated with the promise of his speedy return.

About the time of which we write, the New England Colonies had made proposals of amity and alliance with Canada, and the Governor of the latter chose Father Druilletes to proceed to Boston to discuss the matter with the General Court.*

Before entering on his embassy, we shall glance at the early history of Plymouth and Massachusetts Bay Colonies. The French had, as we have seen, explored all the coast, but made no attempt to settle west of the Kennebec; yet, in 1617, a French vessel was wrecked near Cape Cod, and all who reached the shore were massacred by the Indians, except three, who were sent from one Sachem to another in triumph. Two soon sank victims to disease and violence. The third, supposed to have been a priest, lived longer, and endeavored to convert the Indians and win them from vice; but their obdurate hearts were proof to all his appeals, and he frequently held up to them the terrors of eternity and the wrath of an offended God. Soon after his death, a pestilence

---

* Convers Francis's Life of Eliot, p. 219, and authority there cited. Hildreth's History of United States. Winthrop's New England, pp. 59–67, Boston edition, 1853.

swept over the land, which they looked upon as the result of his prayers, and as their tribes were reduced to a mere handful, they repented of their obduracy, and resolved to listen to the white men who should tell them of the Great Spirit. Thus was the field prepared for the future labors of Eliot.*

In 1620, the May Flower bore to the rocky shore, which had already received the name of Plymouth, the gloomy Separatists, — men of iron will, intolerant, tyrannical, and self-righteous. Discarding the forms and creed of the Church of England, they assumed the divine right of forming a new church; in this they enrolled the more mature as members, and admitted others only on their giving such proofs of personal religion and due submission as pleased them. Such is church membership. But these zealots not only thus narrowed down the number of those who were to share in the benefits of the church of their own creation, but enriched church membership with the exclusive privilege of an elective franchise. None but a church member could vote, much less be elected to office. Massachusetts, soon after founded, followed the example thus set. No Protestant even, who differed from their views, was permitted to stay within their territory; — Roger Williams, the Baptist, was driven out; Gorton, another Baptist, dragged into their territories and flogged; Mrs. Hutchinson, exiled; and the Quakers hanged. As might be supposed, Catholicity was unknown, except as an object

* Hildreth, i. 222.

of horror and dread. In 1631, Sir Christopher Gardiner, on mere suspicion of being a probable "Papist" (for such in those days was the common term for Catholics), was summarily seized and sent out of the colony without the least form of trial.*

Three years after, led by Williams, so often held up as the father of toleration in America, they declared the Cross a " relic of antichrist! a Popish symbol savoring of superstition, and not to be countenanced by Christian men," and, accordingly, in the height of their zeal they actually cut the cross out of the English flag, refusing to march or live under anything that bore the " sign of the Son of Man."

In 1646 D'Aulney visited Boston with some troops, to get aid, if possible, in his war with De la Tour, and exceedingly alarmed the Protestant town. That same year, as we have seen, Father Druillctes reached the English settlement at Augusta. This increased the alarm : in their fervid imaginations New England was already in the hands of Catholicity. They resolved to check its inroads: in 1647, while the simple-minded Druilletes was still laboring to regenerate the red man, of whose salvation these self-righteous men

---

* In the same year Mr. Phillips, the minister at Watertown, and Mr. Brown, one of his elders, expressed the opinion that the Church of Rome was a true Church of Christ. So terrible did this doctrine appear to the Puritans, and so important to the State, that the General Court, or Legislature of Massachusetts, took the matter in hand, and wrote a letter denouncing such an opinion. — General Laws and Liberties of Massachusetts Colony, p. 67.

scarcely thought, the General Court of Massachusetts met, and took the matter into consideration. They resolved to pass an act forbidding Jesuits to enter their domains. The preamble is curious, as showing the degree of enlightenment then prevalent in New England. "The Court taking into consideration the great wars, combustions and divisions which are this day in Europe, and that the same are observed to be raised and fomented chiefly by the secret underminings and solicitations of those of the Jesuitical order, men brought up and devoted to the religions and the Court of Rome, which hath occasioned divers states to expel them their territories, for prevention whereof among ourselves;" &c., to enact that all Jesuits should be forbidden to enter their jurisdiction, be banished if they did, and be put to death if they returned. With a degree of humanity, quite remarkable in men who thus charge on others their own seditious principles, they kindly added, that if a poor Jesuit should be shipwrecked on their shore they would not hang him.*

Such was the province to which, in 1650, the Rev. Jesuit Priest, Father Druilletes, was sent as envoy.

Father Druilletes in Boston and at Plymouth in 1650.

The United Colonies of New England having made proposals for a kind of alliance, Father Druilletes

---

* General Laws and Liberties of Massachusetts Colony, p. 67.

was chosen, in the summer of 1650, to repair to Boston, to confer with the Commissioners. With full letters as plenipotentiary, he set out from Quebec on the 1st of September, with a companion, John Guerin, and several Indians, and after losing their way and suffering greatly, reached Norridgewock. On the 28th of September he arrived at Augusta, then called Coussinoe, where Noel, the Indian chief who accompanied him, addressed Winslow, the commandant of the post, in Indian style, giving him presents, and committing the Father to his care.

The commandant, John Winslow, entertained the highest esteem for Druilletes, and promised to treat him as a brother. He kept his word, and there sprung up between the Plymouth Puritan and the French Jesuit such a degree of friendship, that while the former styled the missionary his Xavier, the latter bestowed on his friend the name of Pereira, in remembrance of Xavier's devoted friend.

After meeting a deputation of the Sokakis, or Saco Indians, to whom he proposed an alliance, Druilletes and his companion, with Mr. Wilson, proceeded to Merry Meeting Bay, where they embarked on the 25th of November.

Passing Damariscotta, where a Catholic church in later times was to rise, the voyagers at last, on the feast of the Immaculate Conception, reached Boston.

The principal men of Charlestown immediately waited on him, and Major General Gibbons, being informed of the character in which he came, invited him to his house, and, says the good Father, " gave me the key of a room where I might, in all liberty, pray and perform the *other exercises* of my religion; and he besought me to take no other lodging while I was in Boston."

Father Druilletes does not state in his own narrative that Guerin attended him, or that he carried his missionary chalice with him; but as this is by no means improbable, we may infer that the Holy Sacrifice of the Mass was offered in Boston, in December, 1650.

He began his negotiations with Governor Dudley and the Boston magistrates, but as the Abenakis lay in a territory claimed by Plymouth, they referred him to that colony. The missionary accordingly started on the 21st December for Plymouth. On his arrival there he was very courteously received by Governor Bradford, who invited him to dinner, and very considerately had a dish of fish prepared, as it was Friday.

The Plymouth people, more interested in the French trade than others, readily consented to give the aid which the Governor of Canada asked against the Iroquois as a condition of an alliance.

Returning to Boston, he stopped on the way at Roxbury, and spent a night with the Protestant minister, John Eliot, the celebrated Apostle of the Indians. Here, too, he won esteem, and the New England missionary urged his French fellow-laborer to pass the winter with him.

At Boston, Druilletes found the officials more inclined to aid the French, now that the Governor of Plymouth had expressed himself favorable, and having, by conferences and visits, gained all whom he could to vote in his favor at the next meeting of the Commissioners, he sailed from Boston on the 3d of January, 1651, and putting in to Marblehead on the 9th, left a proxy with Mr. Endicott, to act for him at the meeting.

By the 8th of February he was again at the Kennebec, prepared to resume his missionary labors.* Such was the first visit of a Catholic priest to Massachusetts. There is not a word in his narrative to show the existence of a single Catholic at Boston, Plymouth, Roxbury, or Marblehead, and indeed the only Catholic whom he met in his voyage was a French sailor, whom he found at York, Maine.

The great mass of his Catechumens on the Kennebec, in spite of his long absence, had persevered; their dying children had been baptized, and buried beneath the cross-surmounted graves. His neophytes had even become catechists, communicating to the less fortunate the knowledge which they had acquired. His labors in this happy tribe were soon repaid with abundant fruits, and he continued his mission till March, 1652, the only interruption being a visit to Quebec and another to Boston, in 1651. The Abenakis had adopted him as a Chief, and revered him as their best and most devoted Father.

With his departure, the Abenakis mission ceased for

* Druilletes, Narr. l'un Voyage, MSS., privately printed for Mr. Lenox, after Shea's copy. For a translation, see Collections of the New York Historical Society, series ii. vol. III., or the Proceedings of the Mass. Historical Society for 1855.

a time, and for some years, it would seem, no Catholic priest stood in the territories of New England.

Father Druilletes returned, indeed, in the latter part of 1656 to his former station at Norridgewock; but in the following spring bade a last farewell to his Abenakis children.*

Missionaries are said to have resumed his labors there in 1659; but this is uncertain, and many of the Catholic Abenakis, despairing of obtaining a resident missionary, emigrated to Canada, and joined the Algonquin mission at Sillery.

Phips's war also induced many to strike towards the St. Lawrence, and in the summer of 1675 a large party of Sokotis proceeded to Three Rivers, and a large party of Abnakis to Sillery, which they reached in the spring of 1676, after undergoing the utmost extremity of famine during the winter. Here the missionary Father James Vaultrer received them with all cordiality, and after providing for their tem-

* Father Gabriel Druilletes was born in France in 1593, and after entering the Society of Jesus, was sent to Canada in 1643. He was immediately sent to the missions of the wandering Algonquins, and after losing his sight, which was miraculously restored, continued his labors amongst them for nearly forty years. He evangelized the Montagnais, Algonquins, Knistineaux, Papinachois, and Abenakis, on the St. Lawrence and Kennebec; and proceeding to the west in 1666, labored among the Ottawas and Chippeways at Sault St. Marie for several years. He died at Quebec, April 8, 1681, at the age of eighty-eight. He was highly esteemed for his sanctity; and even miracles were ascribed to him. — Shea's History of the Missions, 141.

poral wants, began to instruct them in the faith. They showed every disposition that he could desire, and their chieftain, Pirouacci, was a model of fervor and piety. Several were soon baptized, and the Abenakis Christians began to form the majority at Sillery. Old and young attended the missionaries' instructions, and afterwards repeated them to each other in their cabins. The medicine men were unheard of, intoxication unknown, while purity reigned for the first time among them.*

In 1677 a mission was also established on the Riviere du Loup, for the Penobscots and Passamaquoddies, many of whom were gained to the Faith by the zealous Father Morain.† A few years later, in 1683, we find Father James Bigot and Father H. F. Gassot stationed at Sillery, now almost exclusively an Abenakis mission, and the centre of Christianity for the tribes of Maine. As this spot, however, was no longer fit for an Indian village, the soil being completely exhausted, Father Bigot resolved to seek a new site, and as a charitable lady, the Marchioness de Bauche, had given means to found another settlement, he purchased a tract on the River Chaudiere, just by its beautiful falls. Many settled here, and in 1685 all that had remained at St. Joseph's or Sillery, proceeded to St. Francis, as the new mission was called, in honor of the holy Bishop of Geneva, and the cradle of the Algic Church was deserted. The new mission flourished, and, though

---

* Rel., p. 107.

† Charlevoix, ii. 676. New York Colonial Documents, edited by Dr. O'Callaghan, ix. 440.

it subsequently was transferred to another spot, bears to this day the name of St. Francis.

Scarcely had the zealous Father Bigot thus established the Abenakis mission in Canada, than the government urged him to renew the work of Druilletes on the Kennebec. With his brother Vincent, he set out for the village of the Abenakis, where, notwithstanding the opposition of a French fishery company, and a war which the Indians were waging on the English, these two missionaries induced no less than six hundred to leave Maine and join the mission at St. Francis.*

Almost at the same time the Rev. Peter Thury, a secular priest connected with the Seminary of the Foreign missions at Quebec, left his newly-founded mission at Miramichi to plant the cross at Panawaniske, or Indian Old Town, on the Penobscot.†

Here he was invited by the Baron Vincent St. Castin, who, having built a fort there, and married the daughter of the Sagamore Modockewando, had acquired great influence among the Indians. He was a man of deep religious feeling, and offered to support the missionary at his own expense. M. Thury accordingly founded, in 1688, the mission of St. Anne, and as the church he gathered there subsists to this day, it is the oldest Catholic settlement in New England.

N. B. Without destroying the thread of our narrative, we would here introduce, what is rather

---

* New York Colonial Documents, ix. p. 57.
† Charlevoix, i. 416.

lengthy for a marginal note, a few simple little traits of the devotion of the Indian Christians to the Blessed Virgin, Mother of our Lord. Asking the family names of the women at baptism, to distinguish in their registers one from another, they often found the greatest difficulty in procuring them. "My name is Mary," they would say. "But I want your Indian name — your Abenakis name;" and the answer would be, "I have no other name; Abenakis name no good; *my* name is Mary!" Almost every woman was a Mary; if they did not receive that name in baptism, they took it in confirmation, or they would go and ask permission of their pastor to be called henceforward by the beloved name. Or, after Mass, they would linger in the church, even in the depth of winter, to recommend, in an especial manner, their resolutions and good thoughts to her.

An Indian, who desires to reach a point in argument, has a way of going straight at it. Not remarkable for syllogistic abilities, he has a shorter method of reaching correct conclusions. The Mohawk, when the Dutchman sneered at her for honoring Mary, asked to whom he prayed. He said, to Christ, his God. But she, shaking her head gravely, said, "Guess not pray much; no have no honor for Mother, no have much for Son."

One of the Kennebec chiefs, of Father Bigot's time, was taunted with the errors of his creed, in his visits to the English settlements, and urged by the people to adopt theirs — Protestant Principles. "Which of them?" asked the red man, "for no two of you have the same." Of course they must deny the power of the Blessed Virgin; for they could see the scapular on his swarthy chest, or the beads and medal twisted into his head-dress; but he fought the usual battle with them, and gave himself as an example to prove his doctrines. "You have known me long enough," he said. "You know that I was as big a drunkard as ever lived. Well, God has had pity on me; and I can defy any one to reproach me with having tasted wine or brandy for many years. To whom am I obliged for this but to our Lady, to the Mother of Jesus. For to her I had recourse, in my extreme feebleness, for grace to conquer my inveterate habit of drunkenness; and by her help I conquered it. After that, will you tell me that the saints do not hear us? that it is useless to address ourselves to the Mother of God? I believe none of your words; you are deceivers. My own experience convinces me; and know you this," — and the brave, a renowned one, drew himself up, and his dark Indian eye kindled, — "know this, that I will love and bless the Holy Virgin to the last breath of my life. For I am sure that she is glad now, and that she will recompense me for defending her cause against you."

The war still continued to desolate the State of Maine. In 1689 the Penobscots, before engaging in battle, the men, women, and children of the tribe together approached the Sacraments, and while the braves were marching against the common enemy, the mothers, and wives and children, kept alive affection, by the daily recitation of the Rosary for their success.

The English were now, under Sir William Phips, preparing to ravage the Acadian settlements, and M. Thury soon after retired to Port Royal, but fortunately returned to his mission; for on the 25th May, 1690, Phips took Port Royal, and carried off the two clergymen there, the Rev. Louis Petit and the Rev. Claude Frouve. The former was carried to Boston, which the Rev. Mr. Geoffrey, one of his associates, visited in 1687, on his way to France.*

Between the epochs of the visits of these two priests to Boston, the witch mania had broken out in New England, and an Irish Catholic woman had perished its first victim. Mrs. Glover, for such was her name, was probably one of the unfortunate women whom English barbarity tore from their homes in Ireland, to sell as slaves in America. English she could scarcely speak; and, on being accused as a witch, by a certain Miss Goodwin, for whom her daughter had worked, she was arrested and put to the usual tests, one of which was the repetition of the Lord's Prayer: she repeated it in Irish, but as it was not understood, they required more. She repeated it next in Latin, but not quite correctly: in English she could not, as she had never learned it. This, however, corroborated the testimony of the girl, her accuser, and the poor Irish woman was hanged, because she could not pray in a language to her foreign and unknown! and, strangely enough, for not praying in pure Latin! †

* Bancroft, iii. 65-6. Chandler's American Criminal Trials, ii. 76. Hildreth's History of the United States, i.

† New York Colonial Documents, ix. 567.

The defeat of Phips, at Quebec, enabled the French to recover the ascendency in Acadia. M. Petit returned to Port Royal, or Annapolis, while the Bigots at Norridgewock, and M. Thury at Old Town, continued their labors among the Indians.

In 1693 Father Julian Binneteau succeeded Father Bigot on the Kennebec, but retired to St. Francis the next year,[*] and was succeeded by the celebrated Fr. Sebastian Rale.[†] M. Thury continued at his mission at Panawaniske, Old Town. He was joined in 1696–7 by the Rev. Henry Honore F. Deschambault, whose talents, youth, and vigor rendered him one of the hopes of the mission; but he expired on the 29th of August, 1698, and was soon followed by M. Thury, who closed his career on the 3d of June, 1699. His death was a severe blow, for he was not only a priest of great zeal and piety, but a man of great ability and

---

[*] Before Father Rale, Father Joseph Aubery and Peter De la Chasse were also there, but we have no means of ascertaining the precise time. Of Father Binneteau, we only know that he was at St. Francis in 1694, and soon after in the west, where, while attached to the Illinois mission, he followed the hunters to the prairies of Missouri, and contracted a fatal fever, of which he expired in the arms of Father Gabriel Marest, as that Father tells us in a letter dated 1711.

[†] Peter Thury, born at Bayeux, was ordained at Quebec, December 21, 1677. He was sent to Acadia in 1684, and founded a mission at Miramichi in the following year. — Taschereau: Memoir on the Acadian mission.

Louis H. F. Deschambault also belonged to the Seminary of Quebec. He was ordained in 1694. — Taschereau: O'Callaghan's Colonial Documents, ix. 696.

discretion, well fitted for the trying circumstances in which he lived. He was interred in his chapel, where so recently another missionary of the tribe, Father Kenneth Kennedy, of the Society, had been laid to moulder beside him.

On the death of this excellent man, the Seminary of Quebec sent the Rev. Mr. Raylot, and subsequently the Rev. Micael A. Gaulin, to Indian Old Town, or Panawaniske, where they remained till 1703, when the mission was transferred to the Jesuits. Father Stephen Lauvergat seems then to have taken up his residence there, and we find him at the spot for several years. A Recollect, Father Simon, about the same time erected a mission at Medoktek, on the St. John's.*

The war between the Indians and the New Englanders continued, or was revived, after brief intervals. In 1700 Massachusetts passed a new act, levelled at the missionaries, condemning them to perpetual imprisonment, and death if recaptured; a renewal of the act of 1647, in almost the same terms, and with a preamble equally replete with untruth. Like the New York Act of 1700, it charges the missionaries with having *lately* come into the province, but, as our readers have seen, CATHOLIC MISSIONARIES PLANTED THE CROSS IN MAINE BEFORE THE MAY FLOWER SAILED FROM ENGLAND. Even Rhode Island, with all her boasted toleration, now specially excepted Roman Catholics.†

---

* 12 William III. chap. vii., Old Colony Laws, p. 134.

† The Rhode Island Act bears date 1663-4, but the penal

58   SKETCHES, ETC.

The Abenaki mission on the Chaudiere, was on the same year removed to its present site, and many Indians emigrated thither from Maine.

The New Englanders, inflamed by the law, and encouraged by a reward offered for the head of Father Rale, sent an expedition under Captain Hilton, against Norridgewock.* The missionary and most of his flock were absent, but returned only to find their church and village in a heap of smoking ruins: Hilton had profaned the sanctuary, plundered and fired all.

The missionary soon after fell on the ice and broke both legs, so that he remained a cripple for life.

The treaty of Utrecht restored peace in 1713; but

---

clause was introduced subsequently, probably about 1669. The question has been frequently discussed, and will be found treated at some length in An Appeal from the Judgments of Great Britain respecting the United States, by Robert Walsh, p. 428. Walsh, long consul at Paris, is a Catholic, and was one of the first graduates of Georgetown College.

* Rev. Sebastian Rale was born in 1658, in Franche Comte, where his family occupied a distinguished position. He came to America, and arrived at Quebec, October 13, 1689. He was first stationed at St. Francis, then among the Illinois, but from 1695 to his death, August 23, 1724, was missionary at Norridgewock. He was acquainted with several languages, and his Abenaki Dictionary, carried off in 1722, was published in the Memoirs of the American Academy of Arts and Sciences. The original is still preserved as a treasure at Harvard College.

A monument was erected to his memory by Bishop Fenwick, in 1833, an account of which will be found under the historical sketch of the PORTLAND DIOCESE.

as Maine had been yielded up to England, many of the Abenakis again emigrated to Canada, and founded the mission of Becancour; but Father Rale remained, rebuilt his church, and when a Protestant clergyman was sent to seduce his flock, the faithful missionary, by his ability, soon rendered the intruder's efforts of no avail.

His position, however, became daily more dangerous. The French government wished all the Indians to emigrate to Cape Breton; the missionaries urged a convention between the two crowns; but meanwhile the Indians, roused by repeated injuries, took up arms. In 1722 Father Rale's mission was again attacked and plundered, and his flock reduced to utter want: his life was in constant danger, but withal was cheerful and undaunted. Father Loyard, who had succeeded the Recollect Father on the St. John's, was in similar distress, and sailed to France in 1723, to obtain relief.

While peace was negotiating in 1724, the English resolved to make one more attempt on the life of Father Rale. On the 23d of August, 1724, a force of English and Indians attacked the village during the absence of the braves. At the first report of musketry the heroic missionary rushed from his chapel to offer himself to the enemy, anxious to lay down his life for his flock, to draw on himself the wrath of the enemy, and enable his neophytes to escape. He was the object of the hatred of the foe: no sooner was he seen than every musket was turned upon him, and he fell at the foot of the cross, riddled with the small shot of the enemies' firearms. Rushing on him, the infuriated men then hacked and mangled his palpitating corpse, clove open his head, broke his legs, and in their rage trampled upon him. Proceeding to the church, they rifled the altar, profaned the Adorable Host, and fired the sacred edifice!

No missionary occupies a more prominent part in our early history than Sebastian Rale. The reverence of the French and Indians for him is only equalled by the bitter hatred of the English, as seen in their many, and at last successful, attempts on his life. Learned, zealous, and laborious, Father Rale was careless of his own ease and comfort, unwearied in toil, eager for martyrdom, and most devoted to the religious progress of his flock.*

The other missions were undisturbed, and when peace was restored, we find the Abenakis of the Kennebec soliciting a successor to their missionary, and a chapel service to replace that carried off to Boston. The King ordered presents to be made to them, " to cover the body of the missionary," that is, to condole with them for their loss; he also directed their chapel to be suitably furnished. The Superior of the Jesuits at Quebec chose for the dangerous post Father James Sirenne; who made them a visit in 1729, and took his permanent residence among them in the following year.† He remained here for some years, although we cannot positively state the duration of his mission.

---

* E. B. O'Callaghan's Colonial Documents, ix. 1002, 1004.
† Williamson's Maine, i. 465, 606; ii. 259, 297.

Le Bean, a rambling traveller, found him still there in 1731; but the tribe was rapidly disappearing: the Sokokis had mostly repaired to Becancour, near Three Rivers, the Wawenocks and Androscoggins had indeed joined the tribe at Norridgewock, but war and emigration had greatly reduced the village. A missionary is said to have been there in 1774, but it is doubtful. Before the loss of Canada, it had become the abode of merely a few straggling families, and soon after was entirely deserted. The monument of Father Rale is now the only trace of the once celebrated Indian village.

At the time of Father Rale's death, Father Lauvergeat was still on the Penobscot, but as he was greatly opposed by the young Cassines, he returned soon after to Medoktek, leaving the Penobscots without a missionary in 1732.

On the St. John's, the Recollect Father Simon had been succeeded by the Jesuit Father Loyard, who visited France in 1723 to solicit aid for his flock, and remained there till about the period of Father Lauvergeat's mission.

The war of the Spanish succession, which broke out in 1744, desolated what is now Maine, New Brunswick, and Nova Scotia. The Catholic missionaries were again deported, or compelled to seek refuge in the woods; but acting as mediators, they at last gained the confidence of the English colonists. The peace of Aix la Chapelle, in 1748, enabled them to renew their labors in peace; but six years after war again broke out, and gave a death-blow to the Catholic establishment in Maine and its borders.

Father Germain, of the Society of Jesus, was the last of the old Jesuit missionaries in Maine. His chief station was the mission of St. Anne, on an island in the St. John's, the old Medoktek, whence he visited the various tribes in Maine, leading a life of laborious usefulness amid the general respect. As the fatal war advanced, he deemed his post unsafe, and retired to Canada. The missions of Maine thus became deserted, and the fall of Quebec seemed to forebode difficulty and danger to the Abenaki church.

BRIEF VIEW

OF THE

MISSIONARY LABORS OF THE EARLY JESUIT FATHERS.

THE members of the Society of Jesus, founded, as we have seen, at Quebec, radiated throughout all New France, carrying the light and warmth of salvation to every part of its territory. Checked for a while by the success of the British arms, it was only to commence again with renewed fervor. By 1633 no less than fifteen priests of their order were at work in Canada, "and every tradition bears testimony to their worth. Away from the amenities of life, away from the opportunities of vainglory, they became dead to the world, and possessed their souls in unutterable peace. The few who lived to grow old, though bowed by the toils of a long mission, still kindled with the fervor of apostolic zeal. The history of their labors is connected with the origin of every celebrated town in the annals of French America. Not a cape was turned, nor a river entered, but a Jesuit led the way." *

They followed the shores of the lakes to the Bay of

---

* Bancroft's History of the United States, iii. 122.

Saguenay, and pierced into the heart of the Huron forests. St. Mary's rose upon the Niagara River. The Marquis de Gamache gave himself to the Society, and endowed with his ample fortune the first college at Quebec. From 1641 to 1644 the remoter Huron missionaries received no supplies. Their clothes fell to pieces; they had scarce flour to make bread enough for the Holy Mysteries; they themselves pressed the necessary wine from the wild grape that sprang in the woodlands. And yet, before 1647, forty-two members of the order had visited and labored in these lonely wilds, counting their lives as nothing, if only they could win souls for the kingdom of Christ.

Before 1690 thirteen had baptized the pagan land with their blood. Others had fallen victims to starvation or exposure.

Father Anne de Noué, after years of terrible toil, died, frozen stiff and cold by the wild February blasts, upon the banks of the St. Lawrence. They found him, kneeling upright, with crucifix clasped to his breast, and calm eyes open, and fixed on heaven, on the Feast of the Purification of her whom he loved and served so well (1646). Charles Garnier, pierced by three Iroquois musket balls, when about to die, perceived a poor Christian Indian in the act of expiring. The sight awakened all the priest within him; he staggered to his feet, only to fall again. But though he could not rise, he could, and did, drag himself along the blood-stained ground, and, as he gave the last absolution, a tomahawk clove his skull, and he died on the eve of the Immaculate Conception, which gracious mystery he had early bound himself by a vow to defend, even unto death (1649).

Anthony Daniel fell at the Iroquois sacking of St. Joseph's, in 1648. The braves were all absent at the chase. There were none at home but the old priest, the women, and the children, when the savages burst through the palisades. Swiftly he rushed to the wigwams to baptize the sick; a crowd of others demand that sacrament; he had no time for even shortest ceremonies; he dips his handkerchief in water, and baptizes them by aspersion. Then he gave general absolution to all who sought it, and, entering the chapel, he vested, and stood prepared to meet his death. " The wigwams are set on fire; the Mohawks approach the chapel, and the consecrated envoy serenely advances to meet them. Astonishment seized the barbarians. At length, drawing near, they discharged at him a flight of arrows. All gashed and rent by wounds, he still continued to speak to them with surpassing energy, now inspiring fear of the Divine anger, and again, in gentle tones, breathing the affectionate messages of mercy and grace. Such were his actions until he received a death-blow from a halbert. The victim of the heroism died, the name of Jesus on his lips. The wilderness gave him a grave, the Huron nation were his mourners." * It was in the Octave of the Visitation of Mary, Mother of God.

* Bancroft's History of the United States, vol. iii. 139.

Noel Chabanel receives his death-blow upon the banks of a stream near St. Mary's, from the axe of an apostate Huron, on the 8th of December, the Feast of the Immaculate Conception.* Réné Goupil, so livid and mashed with club bruises that his features were undistinguishable, had his thumbs cut off while repeating "Jesus, Mary, Joseph." Tied to the ground upon his back, at night the savage boys poured coals upon his breast until his flesh was charred. Six days tormented thus, he and his companion, Father Jogues, too weak to escape, were left at liberty. But one day, when they had retired apart to pray, two young men followed and ordered them back. "Dear brother," said the Father, "let us recommend ourselves to our Lord, and to our good Mother, the Blessed Virgin, for these men have some evil design." They walked back, telling the beads of their rosary. They had said four decades, when a tomahawk crashed into the brain of Réné, and he died, uttering the holy name of Jesus.†

Bressani (1644), captured by the Iroquois, marched, chained, in their procession, whereof the banner was the head of a Huron Catholic, whose heart he saw torn from the body to be eaten in bravado, — marched fearlessly in that dread procession; for "I was filled," he says, "with confidence in the intercession of the Holy Virgin." Six days they advanced through the forest, he being compelled to act as their slave, fetch-

* Marie de l'Incarnation, p. 148.
† Shea's Narrative of the Captivity of Jogues.

ing the wood and water for the night encampments, cooking for his savage captors, and repaid by blows. He slept, tied to a tree, uncovered, in the night air of the early northern April. Arrived at the village, they prepared him for running the gantlet, by splitting his hand up between the ring and little fingers, and then beat him, as he moved between their barbarous lines. They forced him then to dance and sing for hours; they ran splinters into his flesh, and burned him with brands; they covered sharp points with hot ashes, and compelled him to walk thereon; they tore out all the nails of his fingers with pincers, or with savage teeth. One night they would tear out a nail, the next, cut off or burn a joint; and all this, and more, lasted for a month. His wounds at length swarmed with worms, and he could say, with holy Job, xvii. 14, "Unto rottenness, thou art my father; unto worms, ye are my mother and my sisters."

Finally, the sentence was passed, that what life lingered in him, it should be burned out at the stake; and then he says, "I prepared my soul, and commended myself unto the Mother of Mercy, who is, in truth, the Mother most amiable, most admirable, most powerful, most clement, and the consoler of the afflicted. She, after God, was the only refuge of me, a poor sinner, abandoned by all creatures, in a strange land."* Then they reversed the death sentence. "For such," he says again, "was the will of God and of the Virgin Mother. To her I owe, not my

---

* Bressani, Relation, pp. 116-139.

life only, but the strength to support my pain." It was the Hollanders of New York who saved him at length, purchasing him from the barbarians for some forty dollars, and he says, "I sang with the Israelites" (Ps. cxiii.) "my coming out of Egypt on the 19th of August, in the Octave of the Assumption of the Virgin, whom I consider the bestower of my freedom."

Well, this at least was enough for one man! he surely left his mission! On the contrary, the same year saw him on his way to the Hurons. Four times he made that voyage, and thrice he fell into the same bloody hands, and was covered anew with wounds, yet God and our Lady delivered him out of all. What wonder that those mutilated hands can record among the reverers of Blessed Mary, as the fruits of thirteen years, *Twelve Thousand Indians!*

There was yet another of these missionary priests, the last we shall cite, who came in 1625, and won the crimson crown of martyrdom. When he came to the Hurons, he found not a single Christian; when he left them for eternal glory, they numbered eight thousand. It was the noble Jean de Brebœuf, the heroic, impassioned servant of Mary. It was he who "once, imparadised in a trance, beheld the Mother of Him whose cross he bore, surrounded by a crowd of virgins, in the beatitudes of heaven."*

This was his vow: "What shall I render to Thee, O my Lord Jesus, for all that I have received from

---

* Bancroft's History of the United States, iii. 124.

Thee? I will accept Thy chalice; I will call upon Thy name. And now I vow, in presence of Thine Eternal Father, and of the Holy Ghost, in presence of Thy most holy Mother; before the angels, the apostles, and the martyrs, my sainted fathers, Ignatius and Francis Xavier, that if, in Thy mercy, Thou shalt ever offer unto me, Thy unworthy servant, the grace of martyrdom, I will not refuse it. So that if any occasion to die for Thee occur, I promise not to shun it (unless Thy greater glory so demand), and even to receive the mortal blow with joy. Now, from this hour, I offer unto Thee, with all my will, O Thou my Jesus, my body, my blood, my soul, so that, by Thy permission, I may die for Thee, who hast deigned to die for me. So let me live that I may merit such a death! So, Lord, will I accept Thy chalice, and invoke Thy name, O Jesus, Jesus, Jesus." *

St. Louis, St. Mary's, and Conception were attacked by a thousand Iroquois in the winter of 1649. Among the prisoners taken was John de Brebœuf, who, when seeing the stake destined for his torture, kissed it with respect. So earnestly did he exhort his companions to be firm, that the brutal savages, in anger, cut off his lips and tongue. Continuing still his exhortation by signs, they gave him the first preference in the torture. "Thou wert wont," they said to him, "to tell others that the more they suffered here, the greater would be their recompense in the new life.

* Relation de Bressani, p. 260.

Now, thank us, for we only brighten thy crown." Then, having made a necklace of red-hot hatchet-heads, they hung it about his neck. In mockery of baptism, they poured boiling water upon his head. They pierced his hands and breast with red-hot irons; they tore his flesh away in strips; they cut his scalp into the semblance of a crown, then tore it from his head. He was a strong man, yet he died in three hours, while his comrade, Gabriel Lallemant, young, delicate, and frail, lived seventeen. Yet his first torture was to be stripped, enveloped from head to foot in bark, saturated with rosin, and set on fire.*

With this brief sketch of the last days of the heroic martyred Brebœuf, whose memoir will be found more in detail elsewhere,† we will conclude, with the historian of the missions:‡ "Fain would we pause to follow each in his labors, his trials, and his toils; recount their dangers from the heathen Huron, the skulking Iroquois, the frozen river, hunger, cold, and accident; to show Garnier wrestling with the floating ice, through which he sunk, on an errand of mercy; Chabanel, struggling on for years in a mission from which every fibre of his frame shrunk with loathing; Chaumonot, compiling his Indian grammar, on the frozen earth; or the heroic Brebœuf, paralyzed by a fall, with his collar-bone broken,

---

* Bancroft's History of the United States, iii. 140.
† Catholic World, August, 1871.
‡ Shea, History of Catholic Missions, p. 183.

creeping on his hands and feet, along the frozen road, and sleeping, unsheltered, on the snow, when the very trees were splitting with cold."

But we must turn from these advance guards of God's army in North America, to the secular and regular clergy, bishop, and priest who are in the heat of the fight, — who live to battle in the day we live.

Bancroft, the historian, to whose testimony we have more than once referred, after a tribute to the zeal of the missionary, says: "And yet the simplicity and the freedom of life in the wilderness had its charms. The heart of the missionary would swell with delight as, under a serene sky, and with a mild temperature, and breathing a pure air, he moved over waters as transparent as the most liquid fountain. Every encampment offered his attendants the pleasures of the chase. Like a patriarch, he dwelt beneath a tent; and of the land through which he walked he was its master, in the length of it and in the breadth of it, profiting by its productions without the embarrassment of ownership. How often was the pillow of stones like that where Jacob felt the presence of God! How often did the aged oak, whereof the centuries were untold, seem like the tree of Mamre, beneath which Abraham broke bread with angels! Each day gave the pilgrim a new site for his dwelling, which the industry of a few moments could erect, and for which nature supplied a floor of green, inlaid with flowers. On every side clustered beauties, which art had not spoiled, and could not imitate." *

"He has the rough, hearty life of a soldier, and the triumph of the discoverer; and he has to teach the true God to those who have worshipped demons.† But the priests, in the midst of a more or less perfect civilization, have not this. Their fight is against the vices of civilization, very unpoetic, very unromantic; against the love of money, the cheatery of trade, the permitted dishonor and dishonesty of the world; against the influence of the drinking-shop and the low gambling-table; against the serpent of liberalism and godlessness; against the temptations of impurity and false doctrine; against the ever-changing phases of sin in individuals; against dangers which confer no glory, and poverty which is not picturesque. They are in the heart of the army, in the midst of the ranks; they are the unnoticed fighters, who fall, and are succeeded by others, who fall in turn; who combat, all their lives, to gain one foot of·ground, or, perhaps, only not to lose one foot; and whose record is only on the page of the book of the Great King on high.

"For them the steaming walls of the hospital replace the dark green, arching aisles of the stately, immemorial wood. For them the rush and roar of the hot and narrow street must be a substitute for the

---

* Bancroft's History of the United States, iii. 153.
† Rev. X. D. Macleod: Devotion to the B. V. Mary in North America, chap. i.

fresh, free leap of the wild and beautiful river. The skulking convict and the drunkard, the brazen harlot and the apostate Catholic, must be their dark-skinned warrior tribe. The idols they must shatter are the human passions; the temples they must renovate are human hearts."

INTRODUCTION AND PROGRESS OF THE CHURCH IN BOSTON.

Under the strict rule of Puritanism, Catholics were so closely prohibited, that none entered the colony as voluntary immigrants; some poor natives of Ireland were sold there as slaves; some, at a later period, came as redemptioners. From a letter addressed by Villebone to the home government, in 1698, it would seem that as these unfortunates occasionally visited the French settlements as sailors or servants, their first question was for a priest, for the French commander asked for an Irish priest, to be stationed at St. John's, for the benefit of the Catholics of Boston.*

This is the last we hear of these poor children of the Faith, till, in 1756, Colonel Winslow and Captain Mallay of New England, by order of government, carried off fifteen thousand Acadians, or French inhabitants of Nova Scotia, after taking them by surprise, burning their village and farm-houses, and plundering them of everything. Most of these people were landed at various points on the coast in a state of utter destitution. Many of them were left in Massachusetts, and at other points of New England. Men reduced from a state of ease and competence,

* Paris Doc. (Boston), iii. 371.

they disdained to become menials, and claimed their rights as prisoners of war, but were quartered on the towns as paupers. The law prevented any priest from entering the colony, and so their prayer for one to bend over their dying kindred, was rejected with scorn by men who boasted of a purer faith! and who, year after year, tell us in their histories that the "Neutrals," as they were called, were "still ignorant, bigoted Catholics, broken-spirited, poor, and ignorant." *

Of these many died of misery, leaving their children to be brought up by men who spoke in a foreign language, and professed a foreign creed; others returned to Nova Scotia, or reached Canada, or Madawaska, where they founded a settlement, which still subsists; others sailed to France, the West Indies, or Louisiana, founding in the latter colony a new Acadia.†

Long justified by the oppressors, this act was first held up to odium by a woman, and now that our poet Longfellow has embalmed the sufferings of these poor Catholics in undying verse, even historians must blush to record the deeds of a Winslow.

A few Catholics may have gathered at Boston, or been scattered through the country, but under the penal laws, deprived of all religious instruction, their

---

* This is the language of Williamson's History of Maine. published (credat Judæus Apella) in the year of grace 1835.

† Garneau's Canada. Some facts may be found in Mrs. Williamson's Neutral French, preface and appendix; the more curious from the queer bigotry of the amiable writer. See, also, Walsh's Appeal from the Judgment of Great Britain, p. 437.

children grew up Protestants. Among these we must number General Sullivan, whose name is blended with so many hard-fought battles of our Revolution, but whose Catholic parents seem never to have taught him to lisp the name of Mary.

With the Revolution, however, a change came. Washington, the long-to-be-remembered Father of his country, unused to the bigotry of the north, had scarcely appeared in the camp at Boston, when he found preparations on foot for burning the Pope in effigy. His order shows at once his mode of viewing the matter : —

"November 5th. As the Commander-in-chief has been apprised of a design formed for the observance of that ridiculous and childish custom of burning the effigy of the Pope, he cannot help expressing his surprise that there should be officers and soldiers in this army so void of common sense as not to see the impropriety of such a step at this juncture; at a time when we are soliciting, and have really obtained, the friendship and alliance of the people of Canada, whom we ought to consider as brethren embarked in the same cause, — the defence of the liberty of America. At this juncture, and under such circumstances, to be insulting their religion, is so monstrous as not to be suffered or excused; indeed, instead of offering the most remote insult, it is our duty to address public thanks to these our brethren, as to them we are indebted for every late happy success over the common enemy in Canada." *

* Washington's Writings, iii. 144. See U. S. Catholic Magazine, viii. 85.

Thus discouraged, the silly custom was suppressed in the camp, but still held undisputed sway in the towns and cities.

Washington wrote, about this time, to the Catholic Indian tribes in Maine, inviting the Penobscots, Passamaquoddies, and St. John's, to join the cause of freedom. Delegates of those tribes at once set out to confer with the Massachusetts council, which met them at Watertown. Ambrose Var, the chief of the Indians from the St. John's, was the spokesman; he was a Catholic — a man of deep religious feeling. "We are thankful to the Almighty to see the council," is his salute.

Convinced by the arguments adduced by the delegates of Massachusetts to show the justice of their cause, these Indians promised to adhere to the Americans in the coming struggle, and aid them to the best of their power. They made but one request: "We want a black-gown, or French priest. Jesus we pray to, and we will not hear any prayer that comes from Old England."

The General Court of Massachusetts expressed its satisfaction at their respect for religion, and declared themselves ready to get a French priest; but truly added that they did not know where to find one. The Penobscots followed the example of the Passamaquoddies and other eastern tribes; they, too, joined the Americans, but a priest should accompany them, was their request; and they, too, obtained the promise of one from the very body which had made the missionaries' life treason, and scarce fifty years before tracked one to death like a wild beast of the forest.

The Indians joined the American cause sincerely. How important their accession was, we may judge from the words of the historian Williamson.*

Numbers of the Abenakis joined the American army, and Orono, the Penobscot chief, bore a commission, which he ennobled by his virtues and bravery. They had long been without a priest, but their church still remained, to maintain their faith. This, at length, fell a sacrifice to the English, who destroyed it during the war. But the Penobscots never wavered in their faith. In all his changes, from the forest and wigwam to the camp and the city, from the society of the Catholic children of the forest to that of the more polished Congregationalist of New England, Orono was ever faithful to his religion. When urged to frequent Protestant places of worship, as he had no longer any of his own, he exclaimed, "We know our religion and love it; we know nothing of yours."

Soon, too, the alliance with France brought whole Catholic fleets and armies across the Atlantic. Count d'Estaing entered the harbor of Boston on the 25th of August, 1778, and remained till November. During this interval many of the Boston people witnessed divine service performed for the fleet, and were favorably impressed with the piety and respect of the officers and crew.

When the fleet arrived at Newport, Rhode Island

---

* See authorities in Shea's History of the Catholic Missions, 155.

hastened to wipe off her statute book the clause excluding Catholics.*

At Boston, too, either on the occasion of the festival of All-Souls, or on the death of some officer, a funeral procession traversed the streets with a crucifix at its head, and priests solemnly chanting, while the selectmen of Boston joined in the ceremony, giving this public mark of respect for the faith of their allies.†

* Williamson's History of Maine.
† U. S. Catholic Magazine, viii. 246.

HISTORY OF THE FIRST CATHOLIC CHURCH IN BOSTON.

WHEN the Revolutionary War had been brought to its happy termination, and the United States of America had gained their independence, there were in Boston a few Frenchmen and Spaniards, and about thirty Irishmen, among whom a clergyman, who had been chaplain of the French navy, resolved to settle. His name was Claude Florent Bouchard de la Porterie; but his stay, however, was limited, as in 1790 he left for the West Indies. He was succeeded by Rev. Louis Rousselet, another clergyman, originally from France, who also, soon after the arrival of an English speaking successor, set out for the same destination. This was Rev. John Thayer, who was born in Boston, and belonged, through his father Cornelius, to one of the oldest and most wide-spread families in Massachusetts.*

---

* See Family Memorial, by Ezra Thayer. He speaks of the illustrious convert on page 125.

Like many others of his family, he studied for the church, and became a Congregational minister. From the position of his family he was soon made chaplain to the Governor, but had not been two years in the ministry when God called on him to leave his country and home. By the signal mercy of Heaven he was to be led to a distant land, to bow in humble and sincere faith to the Church of God, which his ill-starred ancestors had forsaken to grope in the maze of man-made creeds.

"I felt a secret inclination to travel," he says, in an account which he published after his conversion. "I nourished the desire and formed a resolution of passing into Europe, to learn the languages which are most in use, and to acquire a knowledge of the constitution of states, of the manners, customs, laws, and governments of the principal nations, in order to acquire, by this political knowledge, a greater consequence in my own country, and thus become more useful to it. Such were my human views, without the least suspicion of the secret designs of Providence, which was preparing for me more precious advantages."

He sailed for France in 1781. Shortly after his arrival he was taken sick, and so strongly was he attached to his sect, that he gave orders that no priest should be admitted into his room. After his recovery he passed over to England, where he spent three months. He was there asked to preach, and accepted the invitation; but his doctrine was found not to be conformable to that of the country where he was. He justified himself, by stating that he had drawn it from the Holy Scriptures.

Mr. Thayer had nourished a bitter prejudice against Catholicity, and the nations who professed it; hence the Italians were to him objects of a holy horror, his prepossessed mind viewing them in the most odious light, as the most superstitious of men. However, he must see Rome, that great metropolis of the arts; he must visit the tombs of Virgil and Dante; he must drink at that living fountain of letters and science. In his passage from Marseilles to Rome, he was obliged to remain several days in a small harbor, called *Port Creolé*. The Marquis d'Elmoro, mayor of the place, received him with fraternal affection and kindness, though a perfect stranger. His house, his table, his library, all were at his service. At his departure he made him promise to keep a continued correspondence with him. Mr. Thayer, in the account of his conversion, to which we have alluded, and from which we glean these facts, tells us that he afterwards met with many Italians whose kindness and cordiality towards a stranger and a Protestant, dispelled the bitterness of his early prejudice, and prepared his soul to receive the light. As soon as he entered Rome, his first desire was to visit the principal monuments of antiquity which are attractive to strangers. The Rotunda or Pantheon, a temple formerly consecrated to the worship of *all* the heathen deities, and now dedicated to the ONE GOD, under the invocation of the Virgin Mother and ALL the Saints, was in an especial manner the object of his admiration. While he regretted that the superstitions of Catholics should have entered it, the sublime thought of elevating the Crucified over the idols of the nations, and establishing the empire of God on the ruins of the kingdom of the "strong one armed," seemed to him to be truly heavenly, and in the fervor of his heart he prayed for the benighted men who knew not the true gospel of Christ, and remained plunged in the darkness of former errors.

He had of the Jesuits the opinion entertained by many Protestants, deeming them men of deep cunning, political craft, and subtle reasoning. He had never seen a member of the Society of Jesus, and knew the Jesuits but from the calumnies of their enemies. While visiting some of the public monuments, he met two ecclesiastics whose simplicity and conversational charms pleased him exceedingly, and great was his astonishment when they told him they were Jesuits. The Catholic religion was soon introduced as the subject of their conversation by Mr. Thayer himself, who wished to acquire some knowledge of it, as he would have desired to learn what were the tenets of Mahometanism, had he been in Constantinople. The examination of the dogmas of the Catholic Church was long and serious; considering, on the one hand, that unerring sameness through ages of the Church of Rome, on the other, the wavering instability of all the Protestant sects, he became convinced that Protestantism was not the religion of Jesus Christ.

One obstacle still remained. A deeply rooted prejudice caused him, until by ocular demonstration it was removed, to disbelieve in miraculous events since the days of the apostles. During his stay in Rome, the venerable Benedict Labre died in the odor of sanctity; poor and despised during his life, this pious servant of God was glorified after his death. Many miracles, well attested by an entire population, were wrought through his intercession, to several of which Mr. Thayer was himself a witness. Convinced of the truth, he still hesitated, for he must renounce all the ambitious projects of a bright earthly career, dissolve all connection with parents and friends, who would despise the superstitious papist, forget the past, and begin a new life, unlearn all he had been taught, and subject his reason to authority. Faith, however, prevailed, and on the twenty-fifth of May, 1783, he abjured Protestantism publicly, and before a large assembly of former friends, whom he had invited to the solemn ceremony.

He subsequently concluded to embrace the ecclesiastical state, being fully persuaded that he was called to it by the Almighty, for His greater glory, and the salvation of his own soul, as well as of those of his own countrymen. He returned to France, and entered that eminent school of learning and piety, St. Sulpice of Paris, that has given to the Church so many pious priests and pontiffs. After due preparation, he was ordained to the priesthood, and returned to America, where he was appointed, by the Rev. Dr. Carroll, to the mission of Boston.

At that time Boston contained only 18,038 souls; and the Catholic portion of this population did not exceed one hundred. They were in the habit of assembling in the little church on School Street, formerly occupied by a congregation of Huguenots, which, since the death of their minister, Mr. Mercier, had dwindled away to nothing.

In order not to be disturbed or molested, under any pretence, in the exercise of his ministry, he obtained a lease of the building from the Perkins family, to whom the property belonged. Here he continued to collect his little flock, who were overjoyed to have among them a pastor speaking their own language, who in his native city had witnessed their growth, while yet he knew them not, and whom their religious adversaries respected for his independent profession of a faith odious to many. His reception by his former friends and acquaintances, and by Protestants in general, was equally flattering and kind, and led him to form the most favorable anticipation of a successful ministry. The following letter, written to a friend a few months after his arrival in Boston, will show how cordially he was greeted by all classes of citizens: —

"My dear Friend: I reached Boston on the 4th of January last, and have everywhere been received with the most flattering attention. My own relatives expressed the greatest joy at my return. The Governor of the State, whose chaplain I formerly was, has promised to do all in his power to forward my views, and favor the work for which I have been sent to Boston. I have received nothing but kindness and attention from the ministers of the town. Many of them have visited me, and evinced a degree of cordiality which I had little reason to expect. The officers of the custom-house have also carried their politeness so far as to be unwilling to take anything for the many large boxes which I had procured from France and England, having looked upon their contents as things designed for sacred purposes.

"On the first Sunday after my arrival, I announced the word of God, and all flocked in crowds to hear me. A great degree of curiosity is manifested to become acquainted with our belief, and the free toleration allowed here has enabled me to enter into a full exposition of it. But I was not long in a condition to satisfy the curiosity and eagerness of the people of Boston. I had been only a fortnight in the town, when it pleased Almighty God to afflict me with a sickness that kept me confined to my bed for a month. The danger appeared to me so serious on one occasion, that I requested the Holy Viaticum of a French clergyman with whom I am associated in the work of the Lord and of His Church. My health was restored by degrees; and as soon as I had recovered sufficient strength, I availed myself of the privilege allowed me to celebrate Mass in my chamber. When my health was sufficiently restored, I resumed my functions of preaching, confessing and visiting the few sheep that compose our little flock.

"On every occasion the Protestants evince the same eagerness to come and hear me; but they content themselves with that. The indifference and philosophy which prevail here as much as anywhere else, are an obstacle to the fruit of preaching, which it is exceedingly difficult to remove,— an obstacle, however, which does not in the least discourage me. I have had the pleasure of receiving a few recantations, and our dear neophytes afford me great consolation by the sanctity of their life. About one hundred Catholics, consisting of French, Irishmen, and Americans, are what constitute at present our Church. About a dozen of them can attend Mass daily. I am engaged in instructing a few Protestants, whom I hope to restore shortly to our common Mother. I recommend our mission most earnestly to your prayers. We are in want of laborers for the cultivation of the immense field which has been so long abandoned in these United States.

(Signed.) THAYER.

"BOSTON, July 17th, 1790."

Our apostolic missionary had now labored ten months, when, in the ardor of his zeal for the conversion of his countrymen, he was prompted to publish in one of the public papers the following advertisement: —

"Mr. Thayer, Catholic Priest of Boston, fully persuaded that he has found the inestimable treasure of the Gospel, is greatly desirous of imparting it to his dear countrymen. For this purpose, he offers to preach on the evenings of the week-days in any of the neighboring towns. If any persons desire to hear the exposition of the Catholic faith, — of which the majority of Americans have so mistaken an idea, — and will furnish any place for the accommodation of hearers, Mr. Thayer will be ever ready to attend them. He will also undertake to answer the objections any gentleman would wish to make, either publicly or privately, to the doctrine he preaches."

Shortly after the above advertisement, a Mr. George Leslie, a Congregationalist minister, looking upon it as a challenge, declared that he would take up the gauntlet, which he attempted, but soon courage failed him, and he was silent.

In the month of January, 1791, Mr. Thayer opened a series of controversial lectures in his little church on School Street, to which he invited all who loved the truth, and sincerely desired salvation, that they might hear about those great and important things which hitherto had been concealed from them. "It is no vain presumption in my own learning or abilities that prompts me to this step," says Mr. Thayer, "my only motive is the glory of God in the salvation of souls. My entire trust is in the strength of my Redeemer and the goodness of my cause." These controversial lectures were continued twice every week, and the church was crowded by those who, through curiosity or a desire for information, came to hear the exposition of Catholic doctrines. The little flock now began to gain some consideration, and the name of Catholic was no longer synonymous with ignorance, as it had been in past days.

In the meanwhile the enemies of the Church sent forth every now and then some new pamphlet or tract to revile her doctrines, and every attack was repelled by Mr. Thayer alone and single-handed; and as he never suffered any argument to go by unanswered, he effected much good, among those particularly who were anxious to know the truth. The ministers, however, for the most part, finding they could not meet successfully the arguments of the priest, sought by ridicule and misrepresentation to prevent if possible the people from embracing the Catholic faith, or even from examining and investigating its true principles; and in every instance where any conversion should take place under the preaching of Rev. Mr. Thayer, to use every effort to deter others from following their example, by arming their own relatives against them, by depriving them of the society and assistance of their friends, and striving even to deprive them of the means of obtaining a decent maintenance so long as they should persevere. Discouraging as it was under such circumstances to abjure heresy and join the Church, yet many were daily added to the fold.

Additional Laborers. — The Arrival of Rev. Drs. Matignon and Ciquard.

The French Revolution had now broken out, and thousands of the best clergy of France were exiled from their native land. Four eminent priests, victims of the same persecution, landed together in Baltimore on the 24th of June, 1792. Rev. Francis Matignon, Regius Professor of Divinity in the College of Navarre; Rev. Ambrose Marechal, Rev. Gabriel Richard, and Rev. Francis Ciquard, Director of the Seminary of Bourges.

Rejoiced at this accession to his clergy, Bishop Carroll resolved to send two of them to New England; one to Boston, and the other to the State of Maine. Dr. Matignon was sent to Boston, and begun by devoting himself to the study of English, entering on the duties of the ministry on the 20th of August, 1792.

Dr. Matignon was born in Paris on the 10th of November, 1753. Devoted to letters and to religion from his earliest youth, his progress in learning was rapid and his piety truly remarkable. He attracted the notice of the learned faculty as he passed through the several grades of classical and theological studies, in the last of which he was under the guidance of St. Sulpice. Having taken the degree of Bachelor of Divinity, he was ordained priest on Saturday, September 10, 1778, — the very day of the month and week which forty years after was to be his last.

REV. DR. MATIGNON.

His talents and his piety had recommended him to the notice of Cardinal De Brienne, who obtained for him from the king, Louis XVI., the grant of an annuity, which was sufficient for all his wants, established him in independence, and took away all anxiety for the future. But the ways of Providence are inscrutable to the wisest and best of the children of men. The revolution which dethroned his beloved monarch, and stained the altar of his God with the blood of holy men, drove Dr. Matignon an exile from his native shore. He fled to England, where he remained a few months, and then returned to France, to prepare for a voyage to the United States.

The talents of Dr. Matignon, says a writer who knew him well, were of the highest order. In him were united a sound understanding, a rich and vigorous imagination, and logical precision of thought. His learning was extensive, critical, and profound, and all his productions were deeply cast, symmetrically formed, and deeply colored. The early fathers of the Church, and the great divines of every age, were his familiar friends. His divinity was not merely speculative, nor merely practical; it was the blended influence of thought, feeling, and action. The wise bowed to his superior knowledge, and the humble caught the spirit of his devotion. In manner he was an accomplished gentleman, professing that kindness of heart and delicacy of feeling which made him study the wants and anticipate the wishes of all he knew. Born and educated in the bosom of refinement, he had associated with chevalier and nobles, had been the friend of cardinals, prelates, and premiers. Amenity and urbanity has at all times been a distinguishing characteristic of the French people, and the clergy of France has at all times been the flower and pride of the nation. And their scrupulous fidelity to the social observances, and to those duties which man owes to his fellowman, was but a natural consequence of their fidelity to their duties towards their God and their faith; fidelity that made them suffer cheerfully everything for Christ, the loss of their wealth, of their good name, even of their life; and in the days of the monster persecution of infidel philosophy, of one hundred and forty bishops of France, but four were found wanting in integrity and good faith.

When Dr. Matignon came to Boston new trials awaited him. He found the people of New England more than suspicious about the great designs he had in view. Absurd and foolish legends of the Pope and Popery had been handed down from father to son since the first colonization of New England, and a prejudice of undefined and undefinable dislike, if not hatred, to everything connected with Rome, reigned supreme in the minds of the Puritan community. It required a thorough acquaintance with the world to know precisely how to meet these sentiments of a whole people. Violence and indiscretion would have destroyed all hopes of success; ignorance would have exposed the cause to sarcasm and contempt; and enthusiasm too manifest would have produced a reaction that would have ruined the infant establishment. Dr. Matignon was exactly fitted to encounter all these difficulties; and he saw them, and knew the extent of his task. With meekness and humility he disarmed the proud; with prudence, learning, and wisdom he met the captious and slanderous; and so gentle and so just was his course, that even the censorious forgot to watch him, and the malicious were too cunning to attack one armed so strong in his poverty.

Rev. Mr. Thayer rejoiced at the acquisition of a co-operator of such merit, and already began to anticipate from his superior learning and piety the most favorable results to the rising Church in Boston. He received him in his humble mansion as an angel from heaven sent expressly to promote the great cause of the Redeemer by extending His Church in this new section.

The destination of Rev. Mr. Ciquard was different; his mission was to the Indians of Maine. The Kennebec tribe had dwindled away by emigration, disease, and war; but the Penobscots, Passamaquoddies, and the Indians of St. John were still numerous. Although destitute of missionaries, since the withdrawal of their last spiritual guide, — Father Germain, — they had still clung to their faith, and on joining the Americans in the revolution, solicited a priest. Hearing that there was a black-gown at Boston, they wrote to Father Thayer, through their agent, Mr. Allen; and this letter, shown to Bishop

Carroll on his visit, first informed him of the existence of those of his children in Maine. Soon after his return to Baltimore, he received a crucifix from them, a relic of one of their former missionaries, and another letter imploring a priest.

The reply of the Bishop was as follows: —

"BRETHREN AND BELOVED CHILDREN IN JESUS CHRIST: I received with the greatest pleasure the testimony of your attachment to your holy religion, and I venerate it, the sacred crucifix sent by you as expressive of your faith.

"Brethren and Children: I embrace you with the affection of a father, and am exceedingly desirous to procure for you a worthy teacher and minister of God's holy sanctuary, who may administer to your young people, to your sons and daughters, the sacrament of baptism, and instruct them and you in the law of God and the exercise of a Christian life, — may reconcile you to your Lord and Maker, after all your transgressions, and may perform for your women after child-bearing the rites ordained by the Church of Christ.

"Brethren and Beloved Children: As soon as I received your request, and was informed of your necessity, I sent for one or two virtuous and worthy priests to go and remain with you, that you may never more be reduced to the same distressful situation in which you have lived so long; but as they are far distant, I am afraid they will not be with you before the putting out of the leaves again. This should have been done much sooner if I had been informed of your situation. You may depend upon it that you shall always be in my heart, and in my mind; and if it please God to give me the time, I shall certainly visit you myself.

"Brethren and beloved Children: I trust in that good God who made us all, and in His blessed Son Jesus Christ, who redeemed us, that all the Indians, northward and eastward, will be made partakers of the blessing which my desire is to procure for you; and I rejoice very much that you and they wish to be united to your brethren, the Americans. You have done very well not to receive amongst you those ministers who go without being called or sent by that authority which Jesus Christ has established for the government of His Church. Those whom I shall send you will be such good and virtuous priests as instructed your fathers in the law of God, and taught them to regard this life only as a preparation for, and a passage to a better life in heaven.

"In token of my fatherly love and sincere affection, I send back to you after embracing it, the holy crucifix which I received with your letter, and I enclose it in a picture from our Holy Father, the Pope, the head on earth, under Christ, of our divine religion; and this my answer is accompanied likewise with nine medals representing our divine Lord Jesus Christ and His most Holy Mother. I desire that these may be received by the Chiefs of the River St. John, Passamaquoddy, and Micmacs, who signed the address to me. They came from and received the blessing of our same Holy Father, the Vicar of Jesus Christ in the government of His Church.

"That the blessing of God may come down upon you, your women and children, and remain forever, is the earnest prayer of your father, friend, and servant in Christ.

"✠ JOHN, *Bishop of Baltimore.**

"BALTIMORE, Sept. 6, 1781."

Thus the descendants of the flock of the Jesuits, Recollects, and missionary priests of Quebec, passed under the spiritual care of the Bishop of Baltimore. The Rev. Mr. Ciquard was selected to be their spiritual guide, and proceeded to Old Town, on the Penobscot, and soon after his arrival restored the mission founded by Mr. Thury, and labored here with zeal and success for many years. During his stay he instituted very wise rules for the direction of the Indians, and had much to struggle with in order to bring them to anything like regularity. Wishing, however, to join his fellow Sulpitians at Montreal, he passed to the English side, and became pastor of the Indians on the St. John's River. This was a severe blow to Bishop Carroll, as it left an interesting portion of his flock without a spiritual father.

Rev. Mr. Thayer, upon the arrival of Rev. Dr.

---

* Brent, Biographical Sketch of the Most Rev. John Carroll, page 150.

Matignon, was now at liberty to give greater scope to his zeal by taking a wider range and extending his visits to other parts of New England. His excursions, therefore, were more frequent, and he was able to tarry longer in particular places where his services were more required. In this way he continued to labor, announcing the Gospel in every large town and village, and gaining many souls to God by reclaiming them from heresy, until the year 1799, when the Bishop of Baltimore, anxious to provide for the spiritual necessities of all confided to his pastoral care, withdrew him from the New England mission, and sent him to labor on that of Kentucky, a State of which the vast extent and increasing population seemed to require one of his activity and great zeal.

What we learn subsequently of Rev. Father Thayer, is, that while laboring on the mission of Kentucky, and meditating the advantages of a truly Christian education, he conceived the design of establishing in his native city an institution similar to many he had seen abroad in France and Italy, — a convent school for young Catholic females. He therefore, after a few years, left Kentucky, and with the approbation of the Bishop went to Europe, with the view of raising, by eleemosynary contributions, sufficient funds for its establishment. The plan was ridiculed by some, laughed at by others, while even the most friendly to the undertaking thought it never could succeed. Father Thayer, however, persevered in his pious project, and had already collected between eight and ten thousand dollars, when Almighty God called him to Himself, to reward him for his zeal and missionary labors. He died in Limerick, Ireland, beloved and respected by all who knew him, leaving his funds and the completion of his design to the great and good Dr. Matignon. The funds were wisely and prudently managed by him till the sum had nearly or quite doubled itself. At the death of Dr. Matignon, Right Rev. John de Cheverus became sole trustee, and immediately prepared to carry the intentions of his predecessor into effect as far as he could. A lot of land adjoining the church of Holy Cross was purchased, upon which buildings were erected, and on the 16th of June, 1820, at the invitation of the Bishop, two professed nuns and two sisters of the Ursuline Order arrived and took possession of their convent. In a short time a school was opened, of which the advantages were soon felt by the whole community, and which diffused among the pupils a degree of piety and intelligence highly creditable to the establishment.

Should any be inquisitive enough to ask what became of this first Young Ladies Catholic School establishment? and the sisters, what became of them? the history of "Mount Benedict," Charlestown, August 11, 1834, will answer the question, and tell the event till the end of time.

The Arrival in Boston of Rev. John de Cheverus.

Rev. Dr. Matignon was not, however, left long alone. Among the French clergy whom he had left in England was one in whom he had great confidence. This was Rev. John de Cheverus, a native of Mayenne, and rector there when the revolution broke out. He wrote to him in 1795, urging him to come to a field so destitute of evangelical laborers, and adducing every motive which he thought could influence his friend. Rev. J. de Cheverus yielded, and having fortunately found a vessel sailing for Boston, embarked, and reached here on the third of October, 1796, to the great joy and consolation of Dr. Matignon.

"This great and good man," says the writer of his memoir, "was born at Mayenne, in the province of the same name, on the 28th of January, 1768. His family was highly respectable. At an early age he entered the ecclesiastical state. The canons requiring the candidate for the priesthood to be in his twenty-fifth year, and J. de Cheverus not yet being twenty-three, a dispensation was obtained from the Holy See, and he was ordained priest December 18, 1790, at the last public ordination in Paris before the revolution. He was shortly appointed curate to his native parish and vicar-general of the diocese. And now broke out fierce and bloody that frightful revolution that surpassed in atrocities all that history has recorded. The persecution of the clergy and the faithful marked every step of its progress, for the disciples of Voltaire and Diderot sought far less the overthrow of the ancient monarchy than the destruction of the ancient religion of France. An impious oath was proposed to the bishops and priests, which, if they would not take, they were cast into prison, and the prison was the high road to death. J. de Cheverus having refused to take the oath, and being threatened with assassination, acceded to the request of his flock, retired from the city, and was concealed for a time among his friends. In the summer of 1792, he was seized and confined in the convent of the Cordeliers, with the Bishop of Dol, and several other clergymen. In this place they were confined for a fortnight, momentarily expecting to hear the doors grate upon their hinges and to see the murderer with his dagger at their breast. The place was destitute of furniture or provisions, and their distress was great until partially relieved by a few courageous friends to humanity and religion. Delivered from prison, J. de Cheverus repaired to Paris, and was concealed in that city on the second and third of September, during the memorable days of the massacre of the clergy. Four days after this bloody scene he left Paris, disguised in a military dress, having a passport bearing the name of his brother, whom, though much younger, he greatly resembled, and followed to England that noble band of exiled confessors who held their faith dearer than all things earthly. He now applied himself with great assiduity to the study of the English language, and made such progress that at the end of three months he was able to give lessons in French and mathematics at a boarding-school, where he became a teacher in 1793. Finding in the neighborhood a few Catholic families, who had no pastor nor place of worship, he applied to Right Rev. Dr. Douglass, bishop of the London district, and obtained permission to officiate for them. A house was procured, and part of it converted into a chapel, while the other part he appropriated for his own use as a dwelling-house; and from this arrangement he was enabled to invite a few clergymen to reside with him. J. de Cheverus had always cherished strong hopes of soon returning to France; but the hour of return was not at hand. In 1795 he was invited by Dr. Matignon, with whom he had been slightly acquainted in Paris, to join him in Boston. Having informed his ordinary, the Bishop of Mans, of his intention of crossing the Atlantic, he received an affectionate letter from the aged prelate, then an exile as well as himself, praising his zeal, yet urging him to wait and hope for better days; but nothing would alter his determination, and he arrived in Boston, October 3d, 1796."

Immediately after his arrival at Boston, Rev. J. de Cheverus wrote to Bishop Carroll, and was appointed to the Indian mission. He accepted it cheerfully. "Send me where you think I am most needed," he wrote, "without making yourself anxious about the means of supporting me. I am willing to work with my hands, if need be, and I believe I have strength enough to do it." He reached Pleasant Point on the 30th of July, 1797, and immediately took up his abode in the little house erected for him. "My house," he writes gayly, "(and with pride I say it, for it is a long time since I was in a house of my own), *my* house is about ten feet square and eight feet high, and the church as large again, but not a great deal higher. In both no other material than bark and a few logs of wood and sticks set up crossways to support the bark; no windows, of course — the only opening is the door. This makes the church dark, and I can hardly read at the altar. The only piece of furniture in the house is a large table made of rough boards. The altar-piece is made of two pieces of broadcloth — the one of scarlet and the other of dark blue."

Such was the state of this mission, and such the residence of the future Cardinal.

The Indians had received him with great joy, and with volleys of musketry. He addressed them on his arrival, and the next day offered up a solemn Mass for the dead, the Indians to his surprise chanting the Latin responses quite accurately. "What courage and patience," he exclaims, "in the first missionaries!"

Guided by the letters of Mr. Ciquard, whose experience had rendered his advice most precious, J. de Cheverus laid down rules for his flock, and set to work to repair the evil done by long privation of pastors. In the following year he ascended the St. Croix with some of the Indians, and reached Old Town, on the Penobscot, in June, 1798.

Here, beside the ruins of their old church, he found a new one of bark, with the cross of the former above the door, and the bell hung to a post hard by, still regularly sounding the Angelus. The vestments and church plate had been all carried to Canada, and the only ornaments of the church were a crucifix and a couple of statues.

At this place he remained some time confessing, teaching, baptizing, and endeavoring above all to restore their piety and love of religion.

Mr. Allen, who had been interpreter of these Indians, was still their firm friend, and obtained of the General Court of Massachusetts, in 1797 or 1798, a grant of two hundred dollars a year to a missionary, who would reside alternately at Penobscot and Passamaquody.

Having thus placed these missions in a fair way of prosperity, Rev. J. de Cheverus proceeded to Damarascotta Bridge or Newcastle. Here seven Catholic families from Ireland had settled, and invited the missionary to visit them. He said Mass and preached in a barn of the Hon. Matthew Cottrill, encouraged the people to persevere in their religion and raise a church as soon as possible, promising his best endeavors to get them a resident clergyman. They were not remiss; the next year a store was bought and fitted up as a chapel.

Returning to Boston, he devoted himself to his

labors there, and was rejoiced the next year to welcome the Rev. James Romagne, a townsman of his own, appointed by Bishop Carroll to the Indian missions.

Of this clergyman we can only say that his long apostolate among these tribes endeared him alike to all, to Catholic and Protestant, white and red man. He restored piety and religion, corrected abuses, encouraged industry, and trained all to God during the eighteen years he remained among them. Worn down at last by frequent infirmities, he left his mission and returned to France in 1818. Arrived at his native country, and his health having been so far restored as to resume spiritual duties, he was appointed curé of Sacé, which office he held till his death, November 19, 1836.

Rev. Dr. Matignon, a name ever dear to religion and learning, was truly a great man, content with doing good; but at this time he required the best assistance, and it was fortunate for the cause that such a coadjutor as Rev. J. de Cheverus should have been found. Their tasks, their pursuits, their dispositions were kindred, and they became inseparable. Their many virtues and social qualities were the admiration even of their adversaries, and a zealous Protestant clergyman, anxious to save from the superstitions of Popery men so amiable and so good, called on them, to strive to convince them of their errors. After an interval of some length, he returned to his friends, who were waiting to hear the success of his mission, exclaiming, "These men are so learned there is no doing anything with them in argument; so pure and evangelical in their lives there is no reproaching them; and I fear it will give us much trouble to check their influence." Thus did they by degrees win the hearts and gain the affections of all; prejudice was disarmed; many began to inquire into the truth, and the flock was constantly increasing in numbers.

A comparative view of the state of the Church during the first ten years of its existence in Boston, viz., from the year 1790 to the year 1800, will enable us to form an accurate judgment of the progress of Catholicity at this early period.

Years.	Baptisms.	Marriages.	Deaths.
1790,	30	1	4
1791,	23	3	4
1792,	15	4	2
1793,	28	12	11
1794,	42	5	18
1795,	40	5	9
1796,	47	11	6
1797,	60	11	10
1798,	59	26	34
1799,	77	18	8

In this table, which estimates the baptisms and marriages performed, and deaths that occurred, were in Boston only, no notice being taken of the baptisms, marriages, or deaths in remote or even in adjacent places. As new churches arose, new registers were kept in each Church. Rev. J. de Cheverus was in the habit of visiting annually those Catholics who were scattered in the various towns of Massachusetts, and indeed even some of the neighboring States, in which they were constantly increasing, such as Salem, Newburyport, Portsmouth, Damariscotta, Bristol, Waldboro', Plymouth, et cetera. He gave also, as we have seen, particular attention to Penobscot and Passamaquoddy, those Indian settlements, entirely Catholic, which derive their name from the tribes that had founded them. In all these, and in many other places which he visited annually or oftener, he never failed to preach, baptize, and administer the other sacraments, to the great delight of his hearers, both Catholics and Protestants, to the great increase of the faith and the edification and improvement of all.

Erection of the first Catholic Church in Boston.

Hitherto the Catholics had always assembled for divine worship in the small house on School Street. But the lease they had taken had now nearly expired; it was all-important, therefore, for them to seek some other place. As their numbers were now greatly augmented, they preferred to purchase at once a lot of land, and proceed to erect, with as little delay as possible, a church which should be at once decent and capacious. With this resolution and determination to accomplish the great object so near and dear to their hearts, they assembled on Sunday, the 31st of March, 1799, at their usual place of worship, and appointed, to carry their object into effect, a committee composed of the following gentlemen: —

The Hon. Don Juan Stoughton, Consul of His Catholic Majesty; John Magner, Patrick Campbell, Michael Burns, Owen Callaghan, John Duggan, Edmund Connor.

On the following Sunday, April 7, in conformity with a report of the same committee, it was unanimously resolved to open a subscription for the purchase of a lot of land; Rev. Drs. Matignon and Cheverus being treasurers. On the same day the books were opened for subscriptions, with a preamble, to the effect that the subscribers bound themselves to pay one half of the promised sum immediately, and the rest in six months. Within a very few days two hundred and twelve persons had signed the promise, of whom, two subscribed, each, $250; one, $333; one, $200; eight, $100; one, $60; seven, $50; two, $40; one, 35; two, $30; two, $26; two, $25; nineteen, $20; one, $15; fifty-one, $10; and others from $8 down to $1. The whole amount was $3,202, — a large sum for so poor a community.

This was the excellent beginning, which evinced the great zeal and exemplary piety of these first members of the Church, and their determined resolution to accomplish the great object that was so near and dear to their hearts. The very poorest among them came forward with a generosity truly characteristic of the best ages of Christianity, and laid at the feet of their pastors all they possessed in the world, and pledged themselves moreover to contribute the half of their earnings, in monthly payments, till the church should be completed.

In the mean time, another subscription was opened, and many among the Protestant community generously contributed to the new church. At the head of these donors was the name of the venerable John Adams, at that time President of the United States. Dr. Matignon solicited also the aid of his Catholic friends at the South, and his appeal was kindly responded to.

The amount of sums collected was as follows: —

From members of the Congregation,	$10,771 69
Other Catholics,	1,948 83
Protestants,	3,433 00

The plan of the church was generously furnished by James Bulfinch, Esq., who kindly offered at the same time to superintend gratis the execution of it, for which he received the thanks of the congregation, together with an elegant silver urn, valued at about two hundred dollars, which was unanimously voted him by the congregation.

The church measured eighty feet in length and sixty feet in width. It was of the Ionic order, and fronted on Franklin Square. It had two spacious galleries, and another for the organ choir. The basement story was nine feet in the clear, of equal length and breadth with the church. The basement was of stone and the superstructure of brick. The entire cost of the building was twenty thousand dollars.

It was dedicated by Most Rev. Bishop Carroll, September 29, 1803, with great solemnity, and called the Church of the Holy Cross. An altar-piece, representing the Crucifixion, painted by Mr. Sargent, was placed over the high altar. Thus by the prudence, zeal, and indefatigable exertions of Dr. Matignon, and his worthy colleague, Dr. de Cheverus, with the coöperation of the congregation of the Holy Cross, was this great undertaking happily achieved.

CONSECRATION

OF

RIGHT REVEREND JOHN DE CHEVERUS,

First Bishop of Boston, November 1, 1810.

In the year 1808 Boston was erected into an Episcopal See by Pius VII.; but in consequence of the troubled state of affairs in Europe at that period, the Bulls did not reach America until 1810. By those it soon appeared that Rev. John de Cheverus was appointed, by His Holiness, First Bishop. This appointment had been effected at the solicitation of Rev. Dr. Matignon, with the concurrence and approbation of Most Rev. Dr. Carroll. Shortly after the arrival of the credentials from Rome, Dr. De Cheverus was consecrated Bishop by the Most Rev. Dr. Carroll, in the church of St. Peter's, Baltimore, on the feast of All-Saints, November 1, 1810. The ceremony was performed with great pomp and solemnity, amidst an immense concourse of people, who had assembled from all parts to witness the imposing scene.

From the address, published at the request of the Right Rev. Bishops, after alluding to the sublime dignity and sacred responsibility connected with the

INSTALLATION

RIGHT REV. CHEVERUS, BISHOP OF BOSTON, ETC.

From "Annals of Boston," November 1, 1810.

In the year 1808 Boston was erected into an Episcopal see by Pius VII; but in consequence of the troubled state of Europe at that period, the Bulls did not arrive until the spring of 1810. It then appeared that Rev. J. L. A. L. Cheverus was named by His Holiness Bishop, and Rev. F. A. Matignon had been appointed his Theologian. So on the arrival of the necessary Bulls from Rome, Dr. Cheverus was consecrated Bishop by the Most Rev. Dr. Carroll, in the church of St. Peter's, Baltimore, on the 1st day of November, 1810. The ceremony was performed with great pomp in the presence of an immense crowd of spectators, both

RG^T REV. BISHOP CHEVERUS.

office of Bishops, as successors of the Apostles, the Orator, Rev. Dr. Harold of Philadelphia, speaks in language so appropriate to priests and pastors in general, as well as to Prelates, that we take the liberty to transcribe his concluding remarks.

"To this place of pastoral eminence, of distinguished honor, and most awful responsibility, you, very reverend Father, have been selected by your superiors, and separated by the Spirit of God, for the highest work of the ministry. To your guidance is committed a portion of that flock which Christ purchased on Calvary; and never was the commission given at a period more eventful, and in circumstances more truly interesting. By your testimony to the faith of the Catholic Church, they are henceforward to abide; from you, they are to receive the food of wholesome doctrine, the saving evidence of a blameless example. The duty you are called to is arduous, but the remuneration you are promised is splendid; your path is strewed with difficulties, your office is beset with perils, but at the finishing of your course, the Prince of Pastors has pledged His eternal truth, that He will reward your faithful services with a diadem of unfading glory.

"When we consider the inestimable worth of the human soul, the glorious purpose for which it was called into existence, the nameless variety of causes which threaten to defeat that end, we cannot feel surprised at the exalted qualifications required in him to whom the guardianship of that soul is committed. We cannot affect astonishment when we learn that the good shepherd is one who despises every danger, who braves every difficulty, who suppresses every feeling, who stands prepared to devote life itself for the safety of his flock.

"The virtues that, in common men, might fairly challenge our applause and justify our hopes, move far below the perfection required in a Bishop — his worth must be commensurate with his dignity — his life must be heavenly as his office — his heart must answer this solemn appeal which Christ three times repeated to the first of His Apostles, 'Simon, son of John, lovest thou Me more than these?' And as he values the imperishable crown which awaits him, he will give evidence of that superior love required by Christ, not in vain, empty, inoperative professions of attachment, but in real, living, indubitable proofs of love; in imparting safety and support to that cherished flock, which our adored Redeemer prized above His life. A Bishop must not only feel in his heart that love which is strong as death, but he must aspire to that abundant charity, which alone can smooth the rough road of pastoral care, and lighten the oppressive burden of pastoral solicitude. He must seek, with indefatigable perseverance, the salvation of souls, but science must enlighten and discretion must guide the impulse of his zeal.

"When I speak of the science of a Bishop, I do not mean the chilling noxious vapor of mere human learning, which engenders pride, and points the way to ruin, — his must be the science of salvation, the knowledge of God, created, improved, and made perfect by the Gospel. When I call for discretion as a quality necessary to his office, I do not mean the timid, time-serving thing which the world knows by that name, that worthless prudence which bends the venerable form of Religion to promote the wretched speculations of selfishness; his must be that discretion which originates in the fear of the Lord, and renders all passing things justly subservient to man's more lasting and more glorious destination.

"Placed on an eminence, 'held up as a spectacle to the world, to angels, and to men,' the conduct of a Bishop can never be a matter of indifference; his deportment is measured; his every word is marked; the eye of a world, that never pardons, is fixed upon him; to him no middle course is granted; the opinion of mankind coincides, in this instance, with the spirit of the Gospel; if he does not build up, he destroys; if his life breathe not the odor of edification, if his actions do not carry glory to the Father who is in heaven, he dishonors his place, he betrays his trust, he breaks his allegiance to the Prince of Pastors, Christ Jesus our Lord. To the Episcopal office it peculiarly belongs to minister to the spiritual wants of mankind the word of eternal life, and point out to their people the narrow path that leads to blessedness; hence they are styled in the Gospel, 'the light of the world;' but if that light be obscured by passion, or hidden under the mantle of indolence and sloth, what hand will conduct the unhappy flock to safety? What power can lure them from the wide and perilous road of reprobation and misery? The flock may perish, but the faithless shepherd shall perish with them; the blood by which they were redeemed may be made void, but let it be remembered, 'that blood cries louder than the blood of Abel.'

"It is, therefore, of indispensable necessity that a Bishop impart to his flock the word of eternal life. But it is yet more important that he support the authority of his instruction by a blameless sanctity of manners, and an unimpeachable integrity of life. The fire of heavenly charity must glow in his words, and be visible in his actions; for, if the world can contrast the life of a Bishop with his doctrine, from that moment he has lost the power to save. His discourses may sparkle with eloquence and abound with erudition, but they will fall from his lips cold, fruitless, and lifeless. They may amuse the imagination, they cannot reform the heart. Instead of encouraging the growth of virtue, and co-operating with Heaven to save the immortal soul, he kills every feeling of good, he confirms the doubts of the unbelieving, and hardens the obduracy of the impenitent. Instead of evincing a shepherd's tenderness, in rescuing his hapless flock from danger, his example encourages their disastrous wanderings, and strengthens the chain of moral death by which they are bound.

"Heaven will shield the Church of America from such a misfortune as this. Her Bishops will labor to deserve the encomium which the martyr Cyprian bestowed on Pope Cornelius: 'Whilst you advance to glory,' said that illustrious man, 'you attract companions to your victory, and induce your people to confess their faith by seeing you prepared to confess for all.'

"Very reverend Fathers! You have not to resort to antiquity for an example of Episcopal virtue. That bounteous God, whose manifold blessings overspread this land, whose boundless mercies claim our warmest gratitude, still preserves, for your advantage, a living encouragement to such virtue, and a fair model for your imitation. You will seek both in your venerable and most reverend Prelate — you will find both in the father of the American Church, and under God the author of its prosperity. In him you will find that meekness which is the best fruit of the Holy Ghost, that humility which, for Christ's sake, makes him the servant of all; that richly polished character which none but great minds can receive, which nothing but virtue can impart. Fathers! You are called to a great work; a treasure of countless value is deposited in your hands; even the eternal hope of your people. Your place henceforward is between them and their offended Maker. You are to avert His vengeance, to implore His pardon. You must call down mercy and reconciliation from heaven. The first of your prayers will be for the everlasting salvation of mankind, let your second and last invoke blessings on this dear country. May this land, which Providence has prepared for the day of the world's distress, — this last refuge for the broken spirit of man, — never feel the arm of grinding oppression; may the foul fiend of intolerance never cast her dark and baleful shade upon it; may liberty and religion hold it up to the admiration of mankind to the last day of the world. Grant this, Thou God of mercy, through Thy dear Son, and our adored Saviour, Christ Jesus. Amen."

The new dignity conferred upon Dr. De Cheverus made no alteration, either in his simple mode of life or in his former occupations. Immediately after his consecration, he returned to Boston, where he continued to occupy the same humble dwelling in the rear of the church, and to share, with his esteemed friend, his frugal fare, as well as the minutest duties of the ministry.

His first care was to visit his diocese, for the purpose of administering the holy sacrament of Confirmation, which had not been conferred since the visit of Archbishop Carroll in 1803. In the course of his first visitation he confirmed three hundred and forty-eight persons, of whom one hundred and twenty-two belonged to the Indian tribe in Maine. The following year he repeated his visit, and this he continued to do year after year, everywhere announcing, in his peculiar happy manner, the glad tidings of salvation to his widely-separated flocks, and gathering in at every visit a new and increased harvest of souls.

A few small churches now began successively to spring up in different places, for the accommodation of the Catholics newly formed into congregations. Salem, New Castle, Whitefield, New Bedford, South Boston, and Claremont saw the cross arise in their midst, and many faithful disciples of the crucified Redeemer flocked around it.

Rev. Dr. Matignon, after having edified the church of Boston during twenty-six years, died on the 19th of September, 1818, deeply regretted by the whole diocese. For some time before his death, his health had been greatly impaired by the constant discharge of the duties of the ministry ; yet, such was the ardor of his zeal, he would by no means spare himself on account of its decline, or omit any portion of those which devolved on him to perform, especially during the absence of his Right Rev. friend, in the frequent visitations of the diocese. He died as he had lived, a faithful servant of God, an exemplary pastor, a sincere friend, and a true pattern of a good Christian. His remains lie in the Catholic cemetery at South Boston. The following is the epitaph inscribed, in gilt letters, on a white marble slab affixed to the wall, on the epistle side of the altar : —

Here lie the remains of
FRANCIS ANTHONY MATIGNON, D. D.,
and for twenty-six years
Pastor of the Church of the
HOLY CROSS
in this town.
Ob. September 19,
1818.
Æt. 65.

"Beloved of God and men, whose memory is in benediction." — Eccl. xlv. 1.

"The law of truth was in his mouth, and iniquity was not found in his lips: he walked with me in peace and equity, and turned many away from iniquity; for the lips of the priest shall keep knowledge, and they shall seek the law at his mouth; because he is the Angel of the Lord of Hosts."—Mal. ii. 6, 7.

Far from the sepulchre of his fathers repose the ashes of the good and great Dr. Matignon; but his grave is not as among strangers, for it was, and will be watered by the tears of an affectionate flock, and his memory is cherished by all who value learning, honor genius, or love devotion. The Bishop and congregation, in tears, have erected this monument of their veneration and gratitude.

R. I. P.

The following stands on the record of his interment, in the handwriting of Bishop De Cheverus:—

"Sept. 21st. . . . Francis Anthony Matignon, D. D., and for twenty-six years Pastor of this congregation — Holy Cross. On Saturday the 19th he died as he lived — a saint. . . . Æt. 65."

The following table will show the increase of Catholics in Boston during the first twenty years of this century:—

A. D.	Baptisms.	Marriages.	Deaths.
1800	54	9	7
1805	94	20	32
1810	151	15	18
1815	160	26	25
1820	112	44	17

After the death of Dr. Matignon, owing to the small number of priests, Bishop De Cheverus was compelled incessantly to discharge the ordinary functions of the missionary priest, in addition to his own arduous duties. Obliged to travel unaccompanied through the different missions, he had to sustain alone the entire burden of the ministry in every town and village through which he passed, preaching, baptizing, and confessing. It became evident to his friends that his health was sinking under these great exertions.

In 1822, the Baron De Neuville, who had been residing in this country as minister from the Court of St. Cloud, returned to France, and represented the state of the Bishop's health to the king, Louis XVIII. The talents of the prelate, and his attachment to the royal family of France, were well known, and the fact of his health rapidly declining, induced Louis XVIII. to nominate him, by an ordinance dated January 15, 1823, to the Bishopric of Montauban. In April following his appointment, he received a letter from the minister of the interior, informing him of this ordinance, and requesting him to return to France.

The Prince De Croy, Grand Almoner of France, likewise, by the first and second letter, pressed him to return, and many other letters from his own family and from the most distinguished persons of the realm were equally urgent.

For these and other reasons, and more particularly as the physicians had declared that his health could not endure another winter in the severe climate of Boston, the Bishop thought he saw the will of Providence, and his choice was made; but it cost him many pangs. To leave Boston was like rending his heart in twain; it was a partial death. And, as if he regarded the departure as the day of his death, he wished, before it arrived, according to his own expression, "to execute his will." He gave to the diocese the church, the Episcopal residence, and the Ursuline Convent. He left to the bishops who should succeed him his library, which consisted of standard works, and which he parted with most reluctantly. Finally, he distributed all the rest of his possessions among his ecclesiastics, his friends, and the poor; and as he had come to Boston a poor man, he chose to depart poor, with no other wealth than the same trunk which, twenty-seven years before, he had brought with him.

He embarked at New York on the 1st of October, 1823, accompanied by a French ecclesiastic, M. Morainville, who had for a long time exercised the priestly functions in the United States, and whose impaired health forced also to return to Europe.

After a miraculous escape from shipwreck, he arrived in France, and shortly after repaired to his Diocese of Montauban, which he governed only a few years, when, on the death of the venerable Monseigneur D'Aviau Du Bois De Sanzi, Archbishop of Bordeaux, he was translated to that Archiepiscopal See, which he governed, respected, beloved, and revered by all, until the 20th of July, 1836, when he left this world for a better one. Boston, Montauban, and Bordeaux wept over his death, and his name is still in benediction.

RGT. REV. BISHOP FENWICK.

CONSECRATION

RIGHT REV. BENEDICT J. FENWICK.

After the departure of Bishop Cheverus, the Very Reverend William Taylor, his vicar-general, succeeded to the administration of the diocese during the vacancy, and governed it till the year 1825, when his Holiness, Pope Leo the Twelfth, was pleased to appoint a new Bishop to the See of Boston. This was the Reverend Benedict Joseph Fenwick, who was born on the 3d of September, 1782, in St. Mary's, Charles county, in Maryland. Many of his ancestors had been amongst the most respected Catholics that originally came over from England to settle in the colonies of Maryland and southern Pennsylvania.

He was consecrated at Baltimore by the Most Rev. Archbishop Marechal, in the cathedral of St. Mary's, assisted by the Right Rev. Dr. England, Bishop of Charleston, and the Right Rev. Henry Conwell, Bishop of Philadelphia, on the Festival of All Saints, November 1, 1825, just fifteen years after the consecration of his predecessor. Learned, pious, and

CONSECRATION

OF

RIGHT REV. BENEDICT J. FENWICK,

Second Bishop of Boston, November 1, 1825.

After the departure of Bishop Cheverus, the Very Reverend William Taylor, his vicar-general, succeeded to the administration of the diocese during the vacancy, and governed it till the year 1825, when his Holiness, Pope Leo the Twelfth, was pleased to appoint a new Bishop to the See of Boston. This was the Reverend Benedict Joseph Fenwick, who was born on the 3d of September, 1782, at his father's plantation, on Beaver-dam Manor, in St. Mary's county, Maryland, and was lineally descended from one of the two hundred families that originally came over from England under the charter of Lord Baltimore, and settled in that State.

He was consecrated at Baltimore by the Most Rev. Archbishop Marechal, in the cathedral of St. Mary's, assisted by the Right Rev. Dr. England, Bishop of Charleston, and the Right Rev. Henry Conwell, Bishop of Philadelphia, on the Festival of All-Saints, November 1, 1825, just fifteen years after the consecration of his predecessor. Upon his arrival at Boston, he entered the Cathedral of the Holy Cross, amidst a large concourse of people who had come to witness his inauguration, and was there received by the Very Rev. William Taylor, who welcomed him at his entrance, and exposed to him, in a brief manner, the state of the diocese, and especially of the congregation of Boston. He concluded his discourse by giving in his resignation, and making known his determination to leave America, and return to Europe. This he did shortly after. Sailing for France, he fixed himself at Bordeaux, where he was made honorary canon by his friend and benefactor, Archbishop De Cheverus. When the Cardinal Archbishop, who had been raised to the peerage, went to Paris, to take his seat in the house, Rev. Mr. Taylor accompanied him. He was there taken sick, and died in the Irish College, in August, 1828.

After the departure of Rev. Fr. Taylor, Bishop Fenwick had many serious difficulties to encounter. He found at his disposal only one clergyman in Boston, Rev. Patrick Byrne; one at some hundred miles distant, Rev. Denis Ryan, pastor of the congregations at Whitefield and Damariscotta, Me.; and one at Claremont, N. H., Rev. V. H. Barber. He was far, however, from desponding; he had put his whole confidence in God, who is the strength of the weak, and who could out of the very stones raise up children to Levi as well as to Abraham. He had not taken the honor to himself, but through Leo, the Vicar of Jesus Christ, was called of God, as Aaron was; and he knew that he who had called him could impart to him sufficient strength and grace to accomplish his end, and could also furnish him, in due time, with all the money requisite for its full accomplishment.

The Ursuline Convent.

His first care was to visit the educational establishment of those good sisters, the Ursulines, who, during the past five years, had devoted themselves untiringly to the spiritual welfare of the female portion of his flock. He found their situation exceedingly uncomfortable. Cooped up within four narrow walls, the want of pure air had reduced them all to a sickly and infirm state, and two of the most efficient members had already died. After viewing the premises, and seeing the impracticability of improving them to any advantage, he resolved at once to remove these good ladies to some situation better adapted to the establishment of an Ursuline Community, and which would afford ample space for the erection of buildings calculated to embrace the whole scope contemplated by their institute, as well as for a garden and for spacious and airy walks. He accordingly selected what he deemed a good location in the town of Charlestown, about two miles and a half from the centre of Boston, whither the Ursulines removed on the 17th of July, 1826.

This new, ornate, and valuable educational establishment, erected at so much labor and cost by the good Bishop, is thus described by one who was a witness to its rise and progress, and who lived, alas! to weep over its destruction by misguided fanatics.*

"The building is situated on the summit of the mount now called Mount Benedict, and, although considerably elevated above the country immediately surrounding it, the ascent to it is so gradual on the side of Boston that it is scarcely perceptible. The prospect from it on every side, for beauty and extent, is unrivalled in any country. In front, you see Boston, with its beautiful State House and dome towering over all other buildings, and its capacious harbor, with the varied scenery about it; of vessels perpetually entering and departing from it; of islands covered with rich verdure, and others surmounted with fortifications. Between, lies Charlestown, with the United States Navy Yard, Bunker and Breed's Hills, on the latter of which stands the obelisk to mark the spot where Warren fell. A little to the left may be seen, from the same position, the towns of Chelsea and of Malden, connected with Charlestown by two bridges over the Mystic River, and the beautiful hills rising in that direction with a gentle slope; and again, a little to the right, you have, still from the same position, a clear and perfect view of the city of Roxbury, of the town of Brookline, and of the beautiful azure hills which skirt the horizon at a distance, in the direction of Dorchester, and, still nearer

---

* For the destruction of this beautiful Educational Establishment by a Mob, see Review of the Incidents, and Record of the principal Actors. P. Donahoe, 1870.

to you, of East Cambridge, with Charles River, and the bridges connecting it with Boston.

"Again, if you look from the rear of the building, your eye will range over Cambridge, Medford, and Malden, with the verdant fields and highly cultivated country lying between them, adorned with innumerable country seats and cottages, gardens, orchards, rich meadows, and all the variety of both town and country, with the Middlesex Canal winding around the different hills, and leaving the Convent lands on its way to mingle its waters with those of Charles River. On this side, the view is again intercepted only by the distant hills, which rise higher and higher as they recede, until they are so blended with the pale blue of the distant clouds as scarcely to be distinguished from them. Nothing can equal the beauty of the setting sun in this quarter.

"The whole of this interesting spot is laid out with an eye to the object to which it is appropriated. A large garden, tastefully arranged, occupies the rear of the building, while extensive gravel walks, shaded with select forest trees, consisting of the elm, the horse-chestnut, and the sycamore, afford a large and spacious play-ground in front. The parts adjacent to the canal, already mentioned, are appropriated to meadow, or are cultivated for culinary purposes. The south side, which is of steep descent, is distributed into a number of artificial falls, where a vineyard of the choicest grapes is planted '*en Espalier*,' affording, at the same time, most delightful walks. In short, every advantage has been taken, under the direction of the Bishop, of the situation, naturally beautiful, to make it one of the most lovely and agreeable spots in the vicinity of Boston."

Enlargement of the Cathedral.

The next important work, on the part of the Bishop, was the enlargement of the Church in Boston, for the accommodation of the congregation, now greatly increased, and which, though not originally designed for the purpose, had become the Cathedral of the Diocese.

The gable end of the original church was removed, and an addition of seventy-two feet in width, and nearly forty in length, was erected, which, united with the former, made the edifice one hundred and twenty feet in length, by sixty in its narrowest, and seventy-two in its widest part. This arrangement was the more loudly called for, as, besides its other advantages, it afforded ample space in the basement story for large and convenient school-rooms. The work was commenced in the summer of 1827, and completed the year following, and the schools, which had been long a desideratum, were immediately commenced and superintended by the candidates for the ecclesiastical state.

It was at these schools that many received their early religious education, and of their number those who, subsequently, became the most zealous defenders of the faith, and of those who, in after years, pursuing higher studies, devoted their lives to serve the Sanctuary.

In penning these Sketches of the early establishment of the Church in New England, — as there are now five, where, a quarter of a century ago, there was but one Diocese, — we give, for the convenience of future historians, under the head of each, such facts as may be in our possession.

Right Rev. Bishop Fenwick, upon his return, after his visitation of the Eastern portion of the Diocese in 1827, as will be seen under the head of PORTLAND DIOCESE, still had but one priest in the city to assist him, Rev. P. Byrne, with whom he alternated in the duties of preaching every Sunday and Holy Day, performing the baptisms, celebrating the marriages, attending constantly at the confessional, visiting the sick, and attending at interments; yet, independently of these laborious duties, he had also taken a class of young theologians, whom he instructed daily in the science of divinity, hoping that, at a future day, they would be able to take part in the duties of the ministry, and become useful and active laborers in the Lord's vineyard. And in this hope he was not disappointed. These students were to him, to use his own expression, like another self. He lavished on them every care; his house was their house, his table their table, his time entirely at their disposal, and they lived with him as at their father's house, receiving lessons in theology from his own lips, and profiting by his experience; and his proficiency in all the ecclesiastical sciences, and his knowledge of the human heart, and his experience, were second to no man's.

The First Ordination by Bishop Fenwick in Boston.

The Ember Days of December, 1827, saw two of these young Ecclesiastics, who had learned from the wise experience of their spiritual father, and been taught the ecclesiastical sciences in his house, promoted to the holy office of the priesthood, — Rev. Messrs. Fitton and Wiley.

In the mean while the members of the Church increasing throughout New England, and the humble circumstances and limited means of many precluding the possibility of their journeying miles distant to receive the aids of religion, it became necessary for the good Bishop, whose pastoral care extended to all, to select one of his little band of priests to attend the distant calls. The appointment fell to the lot of the author of these sketches, whom we shall henceforth designate as the Missionary.

His first tour was to the Passamaquoddy tribe of Indians, Maine, where he was taught the importance of that divine admonition of being unsolicitous about "food and raiment;" an admonition which, till then young and inexperienced, he had read in Scripture, but which he soon understood practically. He then learned that a priest of the church should be completely detached from the things of this world; that his duties are purely of a spiritual character; that gold and silver, fine clothing and dainty living, are altogether foreign to his calling. He ever after blessed what he called the happy days of his first mission, where he learned the sufficiency of this world's daily comforts in a plentiful meal of fish.

On this mission, he exercised the twofold office of priest and pedagogue. The object for which he had been specially commissioned was, to fortify the Indians, and particularly the youthful portion, in the Catholic faith, and frustrate the designs of a certain Puritan or Congregational minister, who, to the nominal character of school teacher and preacher of the "Society for Propagating the Gospel among the Indians of North America," united the office of colporteur, distributing his Protestant Bibles, and using other no less potent means — for gold and silver are powerful auxiliaries, at times, for pliant and rapid conversions — to pervert the faith of the youthful Indians.

In this attempt, however, he was foiled in time by the foresight of the great and good Bishop Fenwick, who loved all his children so well, and who sent the Catholic missionary once more among them. The devoted Indian youth soon rallied around the standard of the cross floating over their school-house, while the pious canticles of faith were again heard as they paddled their canoe on the bosom of the bay, or roamed the forest in pursuit of game. There were at the time, at Pleasant Point, as the village is called, between three and four hundred souls, of whom about sixty attended school.

For other information of the duties of the missionary among the Indians, see PORTLAND DIOCESE.

ST. MARY'S CHURCH, CHARLESTOWN.

For the greater convenience of those who, as mechanics and laborers, were employed at the Navy Yard, Charlestown, and at the glass works, East Cambridge, as well as for their families, and that their children particularly might have the benefit of more frequent instruction, the Bishop, having selected the site, blessed the foundation of the present St. Mary's Church, October 3. 1828. The building, which was subsequently enlarged, during the administration of Very Rev. P. F. Lyndon, was originally eighty by forty-five feet, and the congregation were attended, small as were their number at the time, by the clergy from the Cathedral till the month of July, 1830, when Rev. Patrick Byrne, the only priest found at the arrival of the Bishop in Boston, was appointed pastor, and held this responsible station till June, 1843, when the faithful at New Bedford, soliciting the Bishop for a priest to reside amongst them, he selected Father Byrne, who had also the Island of Nantucket, which he attended till his death, December 4, 1844. Agreeably with his wishes, while living, his remains were interred at St. Augustine's Cemetery, South Boston.

Reverend Fathers Byrne and Ryan had been among the first priests ordained by Right Rev. Bishop De Cheverus for the Boston diocese, and long and faithfully did these two good priests, originally from Kilkenney, Ireland, labor during the infancy of the Church in New England, Father Byrne, in Boston, and Father Denis Ryan, at Whitefield, and the neighboring missions of Maine.

The remains of Father Byrne, accompanied by Rev. Fr. Murphy of Fall River and Rev. Fr. O'Beirne of Taunton, together with numbers of his late parishioners, were brought to the Cathedral, where, on the morning of the 6th of December, several private masses having been said, Rev. George Goodwin, his successor at Charlestown, offered the Solemn Requiem in presence of a large number of the clergy, the Bishop himself pronouncing the funeral oration. The corpse was then borne to its last resting-place on earth, and interred near the Sacristy of the little church of St. Augustine, where he, when living, had, in years gone by, performed the last rites of religion over many of those for whose spiritual welfare and eternal interest he had faithfully labored.

His funeral was attended by a large number of those who once formed his charge at the Cathedral, Charlestown, and New Bedford, and the clergy, Rev. Messrs. Hardy, Lyndon, Haskins, and Crudden, of the Cathedral; Rev. Messrs. Flood and O'Reilly, of

St. Mary's, Endicott Street; Rev. Mr. T. Lynch, of St. Patrick's, Northampton Street; Rev. Mr. Fitzsimmons, of St. Augustine's, South Boston; Rev. Mr. McMahon, of St. John's, the Free Church; Rev. N. O'Brien, of St. Nicholas's, East Boston; Rev. G. Goodwin, celebrant of the Mass; Rev. P. O'Beirne, of Quincy; Rev. Ed. Murphy, of Fall River, and Rev. John O'Beirne, of Taunton.

Rev. George J. Goodwin, successor of Rev. P. Byrne, at Charlestown, was born of Protestant parents, and became a convert to the Church in his sixteenth year, and from that hour determined to consecrate himself to God, and live for the spiritual welfare of others.

Having completed his classical and philosophical studies, and begun the study of divinity at Montreal, he went to Paris, where, under the direction of those eminent masters of piety and ecclesiastical science, the children of the sainted Olier, he distinguished himself by his talents, while by the purity and amenity of his manners, the ingenuousness and warmth of his heart, he became universally esteemed and beloved. Having completed his course, he was ordained at Paris, and shortly after returned to Boston. In a few months he was appointed pastor of St. Mary's, in Charlestown, in which charge he continued till his death, September 13, 1847. He was remarkable for his zeal, his discretion, and his eminent success in reclaiming the victims of error, and winning the unbelieving and indifferent to the love and practice of our holy religion. He was eminently pious, unremitting, and fervent in his tender devotion to Our Blessed Lady, from the moment of his conversion to his happy and edifying death.

Church of St. Augustine's, South Boston.

This, in 1819, was originally erected for a mortuary chapel, and was used as such at interments which were made, by passing over what is now called Dover Bridge, the only carriage way then leading from the city proper to South Boston. The number of Catholics spreading over this suburban portion of the city, and the distance being so far from the Cathedral on Franklin Street, the Bishop had the little chapel, in 1833, enlarged for their accommodation, and the cemetery, in 1841, equally enlarged by the additional purchase of the lots adjoining.

The pastors were Rev. Thos. Lynch, from 1833 to 1836; Rev. John Mahony, from 1836 till his death, 1839; Rev. Michael Lynch, from 1839 to 1840; Rev. Terence Fitzsimmons, from 1840 till his appointment to SS. Peter and Paul's new church, in 1844.

St. Mary's Church, Endicott St., Boston.

Notwithstanding the extensive enlargement of the Cathedral in 1827, such had been the numerical increase of the congregation in less than ten years subsequently, that the Bishop deemed it advisable to erect a second church in the easterly part of the city. After several ineffectual attempts to procure sufficient land and a favorable location, he at length, in 1834, secured four lots, of twenty by eighty-five feet each, on what was called Pond, now Endicott Street, and such was his anxiety to accommodate the many, unable to find room at the Cathedral, that, superintending the erection of the building himself, amid his many other official duties, he had the basement so far completed as to have the Holy Sacrifice of the Mass offered therein at Christmas the year following; from which time the same was continued weekly till the entire completion of the edifice, at Pentecost, May 22, 1836, when the church was dedicated to God, and placed under the special auspice of the Ever Blessed Virgin Mary.

Up to this time the congregation had been attended by some one of the clergy from the Cathedral. After its dedication, Rev. William Wiley attended the congregation to April, 1837. He was succeeded by Rev. Messrs. P. O'Beirne, Michael Healy, Thomas J. O'Flaherty, John B. Fitzpatrick, and Patrick Flood, till 1847, when it was placed in charge of Rev. Father McElroy, S. J.

ECCLESIASTICAL STATISTICS.

THE PUPILS AT SUNDAY SCHOOL IN 1829. — At an examination of the pupils attending the Sunday school in 1829, there were at the Cathedral three hundred and eighty, at St. Mary's, Charlestown, seventy, and at East Cambridge, fifty; thus making an average attendance of about five hundred.

The following table shows the census of the Catholics of the Diocese ten years after the arrival of Right Rev. Bishop Fenwick, i. e., in 1835: —

	Catholics.	Priests.	Churches.
Massachusetts,	28,975	14	8, and 3 building.
Maine,	3,150	6	6 " 2 "
New Hampshire,	387	2	2
Vermont,	5,620	2	1
Rhode Island,	1,230	1	3
Connecticut,	720	2	2
Total,	40,082	27	22, and 5 unfinished.

Table of the census of the Diocese in 1845, twenty years after the arrival of Bishop Fenwick, omitting the States of Connecticut and Rhode Island, erected into a new Diocese in 1844: —

	Catholics.	Priests.	Churches.	Chapels and Stations.
Massachusetts,	52,990	21	22	11
Maine,	5,845	5	10	7
New Hampshire,	1,450	2	2	9
Vermont,	5,911	2	3	5

St. Vincent's Orphan Asylum, Boston.

In the year 1832, Sister Ann Alexis, Sister Blandina, and Sister Loyola, young, zealous, and devoted members of the Sisters of Charity, arrived in Boston, and under the patronage of Right Rev. Bishop Fenwick, opened a free school for girls in Hamilton Street. With the introduction of these ladies to the city dates the origin of the above charitable Institution. The Catholic population of Boston were then few in numbers, and comparatively poor, and the project of even purchasing a dwelling-house for an Orphan Asylum was a great undertaking.

The first effort made to raise a fund for the purpose was on the 2d of October, 1833, being the festival of the Guardian Angels. A Fair for the benefit of the orphans was opened at Concert Hall, and the proceeds, amounting to about two thousand dollars, were placed at interest, with the intention to add to them, from time to time, such funds as might be received, anticipating, with God's blessing, that the sum might be so increased as to realize the ardent wishes of the pious originators of the design.

A second Fair, for the same object, was opened at Horticultural Hall, on School Street, the 2d of September, 1839, which also yielded about two thousand dollars; and from a third Fair, in Amory Hall, on the 20th of October, 1841, the proceeds amounted to about three thousand dollars.

The proceeds of these three Fairs were increased

by several small legacies, including one thousand dollars from John Mullanphy, of St. Louis, which summed up the amount to nine thousand dollars. Encouraged with this amount, a building on the corner of High and Pearl streets was purchased, November 16, 1841, for eleven thousand dollars, the Right Rev. Bishop paying for the building in full, having borrowed the balance of the money on his own responsibility.

It will be thus seen that it required nine years, from the time of the arrival of the Sisters in Boston, to raise funds sufficient to purchase a building and establish an Orphan Asylum, while there are those still living who remember that the result of the Fairs at the time were looked upon as almost marvellous, particularly that at Amory Hall.

During those nine years, however, the Sisters of Charity were not idle. The schools under their charge flourished and prospered. Many of the most respectable matrons, now in the city, look back upon the years they attended these schools as the happiest of their lives. In their temporary home, the good Sisters also frequently sheltered many a poor, friendless, and destitute child. The good work they had already accomplished became manifest, and they were not only respected and loved by Catholics, but by the citizens generally of all denominations.

In the early days of the Sisters in Boston, outward respect was deeply marked and manifested. The Cathedral on Franklin Street was then attended by the Catholics generally throughout the city, and the sidewalks in front were well filled on Sundays about half an hour before services commenced. The Sisters always walked in procession with their little orphans, and Sunday School children following, headed generally by the very respectable person of Mr. Ward, then an aged and well known Catholic citizen. As soon as the procession of little ones reached Franklin Street, Mr. Ward always made the fact known to the assembled Catholics, by saying, "Gentlemen, the Sisters are coming." In a moment every head was uncovered, and the Sisters, with their band of children, entered the church amid the blessings of the assembled multitude.

Early in 1845 the building occupied by the Sisters was found insufficient for the purpose, and the Pray estate, so called, a fine commodious and well-built house on Purchase Street, was purchased for the sum of eighteen thousand dollars.

In the mean time the fourth Fair realized only seven hundred and fifty dollars, in consequence of bad weather during its continuance; but for the success of the fifth, for which Faneuil Hall was secured in the fall of 1850, extraordinary exertions were made. The result of this Fair was fully up to expectation, the handsome sum of three thousand five hundred dollars having been realized. All the debts were now paid on the building occupied by the Sisters, and the balance left from the proceeds of this Fair was made the nucleus for a New Asylum, their present residence having become full to overflowing, and altogether inadequate. The want of the New Asylum soon became so manifest, that in November, 1855, about forty-five thousand feet of land was purchased on the corner of Shawmut Avenue and Camden Street, for the sum of twenty-one thousand dollars. Upon this site the building was commenced in the spring of 1857, and occupied in 1858. Its cost, completed, including land, was eighty-one thousand dollars, and so far as its internal arrangements are concerned, is considered a model of its kind. Distinguished Catholic clergymen and others have pronounced it one of the best buildings of the kind in the country, comparing very favorably with similar buildings abroad. It is a noble monument of Catholic charity, estimated, at this day, at one hundred and seventy-five thousand dollars.

During the forty years that the Sisters of Charity have been in Boston, Sister Ann Alexis has stood at the head of the great work, care of the poor and the orphan, for which the Institution of the Sisters is known the world over. No labor has been too great or arduous for her to undertake. Work, work, work, early and late, for the protection of the orphan and the glory of God, has been her occupation from the first day she arrived in the city to the present time.

Sister Blandina, one of the three Sisters who first came to Boston in 1832, is still at her post, ministering to the poor and the orphan with a vigor unabated, and a countenance almost as youthful as remembered long years ago. Sister Loyola has passed to that "bourn from whence no traveller returns." She is now, we trust, in the enjoyment of that inheritance which alone a Sister of Charity hopes for or lives for — an eternal crown.

In connection with this brief history of St. Vincent's Orphan Asylum, we may add its incorporation by an act of the Legislature of Massachusetts on the 23d of March, 1843. The gentlemen named in the act of incorporation were Thomas Murphy, Lawrence Nichols, Wm. J. McDonnell, Roger Flynn, and Henry B. C. Greene. The Directors since have been Edwin A. Palmer, appointed in 1845, Geo. F. Emery, in 1849, John Boman, in 1850, Hugh O'Brien, in 1851, Francis McLaughlin, in 1866, and Hugh Carey, in 1869.

When the present Asylum was commenced, there was only about ten thousand dollars in the treasury; but after the work was commenced, it went on without interruption until its completion, notwithstanding it was during the severe panic of 1857, — a year of commercial failures and disasters. The largest contributor to the present building was Andrew Carney, Esq., who gave about twelve thousand dollars; but one of the most energetic in pushing on the work was the late Daniel Crowley, Esq., who paid the architects' fees, and was otherwise a liberal contributor. Some gentlemen, also interested in the Asylum, but whose names we refrain to make public, as they are yet living, pledged at one time their available personal property, rather than the work should be discontinued.

Since the Asylum was opened, between two and three hundred orphans have been yearly accommodated; and among our Protestant fellow-citizens, the late John E. Lodge, Esq., may be mentioned as the most liberal benefactor, making frequent donations of clothing, food, and money. Messrs. Picard and Iasigi have also been quite liberal in their donations, Mr. Picard also presenting the splendid painting of the Immaculate Conception, by Murillo, now over the Altar in the Chapel, estimated to be worth twenty thousand dollars, — the sum, in fact, offered for it by J. E. Lodge, Esq. The main reliance, however, of the orphans has been the generous support of the Catholics, and with the blessing of God, since the Asylum was first organized, there has always been money enough in the treasury to pay all floating debts, and to provide the necessaries of life for the Sisters and their orphans — now a very large family.

There is at present a small debt on the Asylum of about five thousand dollars, the result of an additional building called for, the erection of which cost about twelve thousand five hundred dollars, while the property, as already stated, is estimated to be worth at least one hundred and seventy-five thousand dollars, — a noble monument of charity!

St. Patrick's Church, Northampton St., Boston.

The faithful of the easterly portion of the city having been provided with church accommodations, there was a similar want felt for those residing at the

South End, and the adjoining town of Roxbury. The Bishop, solicitous for the spiritual welfare of all, was again in pursuit of a favorable location, and one that might be the most central. He at length, April 24, 1835, decided upon the lot on Northampton Street, measuring ninety by sixty feet, which he purchased at a valuation which was then considered fair, which now would be regarded as singularly favorable to the purchaser, — twenty-five cents the square foot.

Excavations for the foundation of a church sixty-five by forty-five feet, were commenced in October of the same year, and the building completed December 11, 1836, when it was dedicated to God, under the patronage of St. Patrick. Rev. Thomas Lynch was appointed pastor, — a sacred trust, which he held most faithfully, and sustained assiduously till the hour of his death, March 27, 1870.

St. John's Church, East Cambridge.

The crowded state of the church at Charlestown, and the increasing numbers of the faithful at East Cambridge, — without mentioning children, whose numbers were sufficient to fill the church, — prompted the faithful of East Cambridge to invite the Bishop to look at a lot which they deemed eligible, and upon which, with his approbation, they were decided to build a church for themselves. The site being ap-

RG᷊ REV. BISHOP FITZPATRICK.

THE CHURCH IN THE DIOCESE. 143

...ed of, the lot was purchased, January 29, 1842.
...the opening spring the foundation was laid; in
... it was blessed, and in autumn of the same
... October ..., the building was so far advanced as
... of the Holy Sacrifice being offered in the
...

The entire church, of blue limestone, from the
...ville quarry, was at last completed, and being
finished, was blessed September 4, 1843, and
... Rev. John B. Fitzpatrick, who
... first Mass, and who was appointed its
...

DIOCESAN SYNOD.

The year 1842 was one of great rejoicing to the
...p and Clergy of the Boston Diocese. It was
... assembling of all the clergy for an eight
... Retreat, conducted by Rev. Father
... the conclusion of which, An-
... of the Diocese was held
... the Divine assistance being in-
... all was serene ..., prayer said by the Re-
... Rev. Bishop celebrated
... of the ... which the clergy
... received ...

Rev. ... A. ... G. being Promoter,
... Procurator, and Rev.
... Fitzpatrick ... the Clergy at the feet
Bishop, ... the formula as prescribed in

proved of, the lot was purchased, January 29, 1842. With the opening spring the foundation was laid; in April, it was blessed; and in autumn of the same year, October 9, the building was so far advanced as to admit of the holy Sacrifice being offered in the basement.

The entire church, of blue slate-stone, from the Somerville quarry, was soon completed, and being neatly finished, was blessed, September 3, 1843, and placed in charge of Rev. John B. Fitzpatrick, who had said the first Mass, and who was appointed its first pastor.

Diocesan Synod.

The year 1842 was one of great rejoicing to the Bishop and Clergy of the Boston Diocese. It was the first assembling of all the clergy for an eight days' Spiritual Retreat, conducted by Rev. Father McElroy, S. J., at the conclusion of which, August 21, the First Synod of the Diocese was held.

At this Synod, the Divine assistance being implored, all was carried out as prescribed by the Roman Pontifical. The Right Rev. Bishop celebrated the Mass of the Holy Ghost, at which the clergy assisting received Holy Communion.

Very Rev. William Tyler, V. G., being Promoter, Rev. Jeremiah O'Callaghan, Procurator, and Rev. John B. Fitzpatrick, Secretary, the Clergy at the feet of the Bishop, fulfilled the formula, as prescribed in the Pontifical. The Sessions were then opened, and all was conducted to the end in the greatest peace and harmony.

The names of those present were, —

Right Rev. J. B. Fenwick.

Very Rev. William Tyler,   Rev. Adolph Williamson,
Rev. Richard Hardy,   Rev. Patrick Byrne,
Rev. James Fitton,   Rev. Jas. T. McDermott,
Rev. John O'Beirne,   Rev. Michael Lynch,
Rev. William Ivers,   Rev. John Brady,
Rev. William Wiley,   Rev. P. O'Beirne,
Rev. Edward Murphy,   Rev. Fr. Roloff,
Rev. John B. Daly,   Rev. John Corry,
Rev. Patrick Flood,   Rev. James O'Reilly,
Rev. Thomas O'Sullivan,   Rev. John D. Brady,
Rev. John Strain,   Rev. Jer'h. O'Callaghan,
Rev. John B. Fitzpatrick, Rev. Patrick Canavan,
Rev. Thomas Lynch,   Rev. John B. McMahon,
Rev. Ter'ce Fitzsimmons,   Rev. T. J. O'Flaherty,
Rev. Denis Ryan,   Rev. James Conway.

St. John's Free Church, Moon St., Boston.

Notwithstanding the church accommodations that had been provided within the last few years, there were still those who had not provided themselves with seats, or were indifferent about being seated in any particular church, or felt too poor to subscribe towards the support of any. That none might have excuse for absenting themselves from Mass, or for not duly observing the Lord's day, the Bishop, in the fervor of his zeal and generosity of his heart, projected the erection of what should be known as the FREE CHURCH. In furtherance of this benevolent design, he authorized Rev. John B. McMahon, November 20, 1842, to receive the offerings of those who were able and felt disposed to aid this pious enterprise.

The Bishop learning, January 17, 1843, that the substantial brick building on Moon Street, measuring sixty by forty-two feet, which had originally been erected for a store-house, could be easily fitted up and serve this admirable purpose, and that the same could be purchased for eight thousand dollars, authorized Rev. Fr. McMahon to secure it. This building was subsequently very neatly fitted up, and with its altar, organ, choir-gallery and settee-framed seats, was opened to all, free of expense, and Reverend Father McMahon appointed pastor.

SS. PETER'S AND PAUL'S CHURCH, SOUTH BOSTON.

The connection of South Boston with the city proper by the free bridge from Federal Street, the introduction of extensive and heavy mechanical works, and the adding its thousand acres for private residences, and homes of ready access to the industrious of every class, soon rendered St. Augustine's little church in the cemetery too limited for the many who would attend Mass on Sundays, and partake of the other aids of religion. Another and more spacious church was thus called for, and in December, 1843, a desirable lot having been secured on Broad Street, the foundation of a spacious stone Gothic structure was immediately commenced, and the building so far advanced that the basement story was prepared for the purpose of divine service as early as February, 1844, and all completed in 1845, when Rev. Terence Fitzsimmons, formerly of St. Augustine's, was appointed its pastor.

Trinity Church, Suffolk Street, Boston.

For the accommodation of the faithful from Germany, among whom were those who were not familiar with the English language, but dearly attached to holy religion, and who sought its consolations in a strange land, and having no priest from whom they might hear the holy Gospel explained in mother tongue, the Bishop invited Rev. Father Raffeiner, pastor of the German congregation in New York, to visit Boston from time to time, to preach, and administer the sacraments in the Cathedral, for their special benefit.

Their numbers increasing in the city, at East Boston, Roxbury, and adjacent suburban districts, a church lot on Suffolk Street was secured in July, 1841, upon which the corner-stone of a substantial edifice, ninety by sixty feet, was laid with due ceremony June 28, 1842, and the structure so far completed as to admit of the services of religion in the basement, March 3, 1844. While the interior of the main building was being finished, the congregation were attended by Rev. Messrs. Roloff and Plathé, successively. The Church completed, it was solemnly dedicated by Right Rev. J. B. Fitzpatrick, October 25, 1846, and Rev. Alexander Martin, O. S. F., was appointed its pastor.

SS. Vincent's Church, Purchase St., Boston.

The earnest call for church accommodations on the part of the Catholics residing in the vicinity of Fort Hill, induced Right Rev. Bishop Fitzpatrick, the worthy successor of Bishop Fenwick, to secure, for the sum of thirty thousand dollars, the large granite meeting-house of the " Purchase Street Unitarian Society."

Having been fitted up, it was opened for divine service, May 14, 1848, under the title of St. Vincent's. After a *benedictio loci* by the Bishop, High Mass was sung by Rev. N. O'Brien, and the choir, composed exclusively of boys and girls, sang Demonti's Mass in C, with great correctness and taste. After the Gospel, the Bishop preached on the necessity of belief in *mysteries* in a divine religion. The congregation that crowded every nook and corner of the spacious edifice would have been sufficient to fill another church of the same dimensions.

Church of East Boston.

The history of East Boston, as forming an important part of the city proper, may be said to have begun with the formation of the East Boston Company. This company was incorporated by the legislature of Massachusetts on the 25th of March, 1833, and the beginning and growth of the improvements upon the island was, for the first few years, but the history of the operations of the company, as it was the mover in, and was identified with, the commercial and manufacturing enterprises which give to East Boston its character and importance.

The land, comprising six hundred and sixty acres, was originally put into a common stock, and divided into thirteen hundred and twenty shares, each share representing half an acre. When lands were sold, the proceeds were to be passed to the credit of the company, constituting the fund from which its expenses were paid and its dividends were made. It was soon thought best, however, to increase the number of shares, and, by a vote of the stockholders, changes were made from time to time, and at length permanently fixed at twenty thousand.

One of the first and most important subjects demanding the attention and action of the company was the location of streets. The narrow and crooked streets of Boston were a continual and sufficient warning to the proprietors to lay out wide and straight streets on the island before houses and stores were built, for in this way only could regularity and convenience be secured; and we cannot do otherwise than acknowledge, in our day, the wisdom and foresight of the projectors of the beautiful avenues that now traverse every portion of the Island ward.

In the settlement of East Boston, many adopted citizens, and their immediate descendants, held a conspicuous place. They were among the first who, with strong arms and willing hearts, came to level the hills, fill up the low lands, drain the marshes, erect docks, and map the island with its present wide and spacious streets and pleasant squares. The names of Crowley, McManus, Cummisky, and others, were among the first of the permanent householders, among the first to build, and the first with whom contracts were entered into for the general improvement.

With the rapid growth of this delightful portion of the city, destined to become the great depot of our commerce, many others, professing the creed of the Catholic Church, with those already mentioned, here sought employment, either as mechanics, tradesmen, or laborers, or, crossing over from the more densely populated parts of Boston, came to purchase lots, or erect private dwellings for themselves.

The first child, now living, who was born on the

island, was Thomas J. Lavery, son of Matthew and Jane Lavery. He was born on the 17th of November, 1833, in a house on Saratoga Street, which was then occupied by three families, Mr. Lavery, Mary Trotten, and Mr. McNulty.

In consequence of the increasing numbers of the faithful, and the inconvenience of leaving their families to attend divine service in the city proper, it was proposed by Mr. Daniel Crowley and others to erect, with the approbation of the Bishop, a place of worship for themselves. While deliberating upon the most desirable site for this object, a legally notified meeting of the "Maverick Congregational Society" came together on the 24th of January, 1844, at which a vote was passed to sell their meeting-house and land for the sum of five thousand dollars; that a committee of three be raised to carry this into effect; and that the treasurer, Mr. W. R. Lovejoy, be authorized to sign a deed of conveyance to such person as the committee should designate. The Catholics, availing themselves of this favorable opportunity, came forward, the first of February, six days after this suggestion, as willing purchasers of the property, and thus secured for themselves and children a place to assemble for public worship.

The house having undergone some alterations, and an Altar having been erected, it was dedicated to God, under the patronage of St. Nicholas. The first clergyman appointed to the charge of the congregation was Rev. N. J. A. O'Brien, which office he discharged till his recall to the Cathedral in March,

1847. He was succeeded by Rev. Charles McCallion, who, for the better accommodation of the increasing numbers, and with the sanction of the successor to Right Rev. Bishop Fenwick, Bishop Fitzpatrick, enlarged the church some forty feet, and administered to the wants of the congregation till November, 1851. He was succeeded by Rev. William Wiley, who held the responsible situation, fulfilling every duty with zeal and piety, till removed by death, April 19, 1855.

To afford to the still increasing number of Catholics more ample church room, the necessity of which may be deduced from the fact, that while in 1844 the number baptized was fifty-eight, the baptisms for 1854, just ten years afterwards, were three hundred and thirty-eight. Father Wiley, a few months previous to his death, projected, with the approbation of the Bishop, the erection of the substantial and imposing stone edifice, located on the corner of Maverick and London Streets, on a line with the frame church on the corner of Maverick and Havre Streets, an intermediate space of thirty-five feet being left between the two upon which the parochial residence stands.

Encouraged by the anticipated zealous co-operation of the congregation, he laid the foundation and completed the basement walls of this noble structure, which is sixty by one hundred and thirty-two feet in the interior, and for the most part above ground and well lighted. Having contracted for materials, and made other arrangements to further the work, he could do no more. In the fifty-second year of his age, and the twenty-eighth of his priesthood, he was prostrated on the bed of suffering, from which he never rose.

The day of the funeral obsequies of Rev. Fr. Wiley, Rev. F. X. Branagan was sent to attend the immediate spiritual necessities of the congregation, while Rev. J. Fitton, who had just completed the magnificent church at Newport, R. I., was solicited to accept the pastorship of East Boston. Like many incidents that appear striking, when viewed in the distance, the latter reverend gentleman little thought he had decided upon work for himself when he encouraged Father Wiley to build a stone, rather than as contemplated, a brick church; but such was the result. As soon as arrangements could be made by Right Rev. B. O'Reilly, Bishop of the Hartford diocese, he came to carry on the work of his departed bosom friend, Rev. Father Wiley.

We will here give a brief description of the church of "Most Holy Redeemer." The plan of the church is Gothic, of the thirteenth century style, one hundred and ten by sixty-two feet in the interior, with a chancel twenty-eight by twenty-three feet, and sacristies on either side. The main walls are covered with a span roof, with ornamental slating. The interior is divided into finely proportioned nave and aisles, and of sufficient height for beauty of effect, voice, ventilation, and all other conveniences. At the southwest corner of the church there is a very substantial, as well as ornate, tower and spire of nearly two hundred feet, which forms a conspicuous beacon for the guidance of travellers for miles around. In this is placed a sweet-toned bell of upwards of two thousand pounds. The walls of the building are massive, and of solid masonry, supported by buttresses, and built in the very best manner. The cabinet work and entire of wood finish is all of seasoned chestnut, shellacked and varnished, which makes a very durable and rich finish without the expense of paint. The high altar and tabernacle, with its elaborate carving, emblems and ornaments, and the chapel altars of Mary Immaculate, together with that of St. Patrick, and their rich tracery, are beautiful specimens of art, as they are of devotion.

A very conspicuous feature in this edifice is the style of the windows, which, being lancet, so called, with emblematic designs in the heads, are filled as usual with stained glass and borders, while the lead sash is inserted in skeleton frames, that rise and fall with ordinary weights and pulleys, whereby abundant ventilation is given in summer, and the cold is shut out in winter.

Every foot of this church is occupied on Sundays and Holy Days by a large congregation, while the former church is equally filled with a congregation of children, gathered together for catechetical and other religious instruction on Sundays, and on week days, to the number of seven hundred girls, who are educated by the Sisters of Notre Dame, besides being used for the devotional exercises of the single and married Ladies' Sodalities, and for Library purposes.

The organ of the church of " Most Holy Redeemer "

is an instrument of rare sweetness, purity, and of unequalled magnificence of tone. Externally it is twenty-six feet high, twenty-nine feet wide, and ten and a half feet deep, and of a style corresponding with the architecture of the church. It is of a very novel construction, being built so as to show the nave window of the church between its principal parts. The key-board is extended from the front of the instrument, and is seen projecting from the front of the gallery, after the style of the choir organs in European cathedrals, — the organist facing the altar.

The basement chapel of this church, with its folding doors, is divided into different compartments while used for catechetical instruction, which at mass and vespers are thrown open, affording a view of the altar to fourteen hundred children and their teachers.

While speaking of the church of East Boston, though in point of time going beyond our intention in these sketches, we will add, that since the erection of the church of Most Holy Redeemer, such has been the progress of religion that a second church, " Star of the Sea," a frame building of forty-seven by ninety-one feet, erected on the fourth section in 1868, and capable of seating eight hundred, is already filled; and a third church, the " Assumption of our Lady," on the first section, commenced August 29, 1869, and in the basement of which mass was first offered on the festival of the Nativity of our Lord, the same year, is already crowded with a congregation of thirteen hundred souls, and where the female children, to the number of three hundred, are daily taught by the Sisters of Notre Dame; and on the third section, so called, a lot is secured for the fourth church, which will soon be needed for that growing portion of the Island, which church, as already contemplated, is to be under the special patronage of St. Joseph.

The Church at Salem.

Salem, the first town next to Plymouth settled in New England, enjoyed formerly great commercial prosperity while in active trade with the East Indies and China. This, her reputation as a great trading mart, introduced citizens from abroad, and among them a few Catholic families.

From the most reliable information gained, we learn that the holy Sacrifice of the mass, first offered in Salem, was by Rev. Father Thayer, in the Court House, which was loaned him by the citizens, both anxious to see a Catholic priest, and know what the mass really was. This must have been near to the close of the last century. In after years, among other stations attended by Right Rev. Bishop De Cheverus, Salem was visited monthly, and mass celebrated in a house occupied by a Mr. Connolly, on Herbert Street, at which time there were about twenty-five families, — three of French, and the rest of Irish nationality.

At the close of the war of 1812, a Mr. Newport, liberated from Dartmouth prison, England, returned to his home at Salem, and in the fervor of his zeal commenced, in 1815, collecting from house to house, among the little congregation of Catholics, funds for the erection of a small church for their mutual accommodation. This church, humble in its dimensions, was built about 1817, and though interiorly unfinished, was used for the purpose of divine worship till a much later period. When mass was therein offered, in 1821, by Rev. P. McQuade, of Boston, and attended by the writer, the lathing had not received the first coat of mortar. At the first visit of Bishop Fenwick, in 1826, it was plastered interiorly, but funds were as yet too limited to allow of the first coat of paint exteriorly. Rev. Fr. Mahony, who had been affiliated to the diocese in 1826, was appointed, in 1827, to look after the spiritual wants of the faithful here and at Lowell, — a duty which he discharged with the utmost fidelity, till the last place mentioned, becoming an extensive manufacturing district, and demanding the special services of a resident clergyman, Fr. Mahony was settled among them.

After his departure, Rev. William Wiley, who, since his ordination in 1827, had officiated at the Cathedral, was appointed, in the month of September, 1831, to attend the congregation at Salem, in connection with the rising church of Waltham.

Ever active and full of zeal, he soon completed and beautified the little church of Salem, and had it blessed by the Bishop the first of January, 1832. Rev. Father Conway, who succeeded Father Wiley, made an addition to the length of the church, and enlarged the interior by the introduction of galleries.

The congregation was subsequently attended by Rev. Messrs. John D. Brady, Strain, and O'Flaherty: the last Rev. Father departed this life March 29, 1846; since which time other churches, schools, asylums, and religious societies have risen up, the interesting account of which we leave to the future historian, confining ourselves merely, as intended, to the first churches erected.

Church at Lowell.

Rev. Father Mahony, to whom, in 1827, had been assigned the spiritual charge of the Catholics at Salem, visited Lowell, October 8, of the same year: returning to Boston, he reported to the Bishop that there were twenty-one families and thirty-one unmarried men already settled there. These were visited by the Bishop in person, October 28, 1828, when he offered the holy Sacrifice of the mass in a temporary building, which had been erected for the twofold purpose, for mass on Sundays and Holy Days, and for a day school, where the children were taught catechism, and the ordinary English branches, by a schoolmaster, whose time and talents had been previously devoted to the same employ in Ireland.

The water power having been introduced, and the erection of factories commenced, and the numbers of the faithful having increased to about four hundred souls, the church of St. Patrick, a frame building, seventy by forty feet, was projected in the month of July, 1830; and such was the harmony and united zeal in the enterprise, that in twelve months from the date at which it was commenced, it was dedicated, at which cheering event, July 3, 1831, thirty-nine were admitted to the sacrament of Confirmation.

During the above spiritual and temporal advancement of Catholicity in Lowell, Rev. Father Mahony was always at his post, superintending the wants of all, whether parents or children, till February, 1836, when he was transferred to the charge of the important and growing congregation of St. Augustine's, South Boston.

Rev. James McDermott was appointed successor to Father Mahony, and continued the good work that he had commenced, and the congregation continuing to increase, Rev. James Conway, in December, 1839, was appointed as an assistant. In less than two years, through the united exertions of these brother clergymen, the accommodations at St. Patrick's were found inadequate, and a second church needed; for this a lot was secured in August, 1841, upon which Rev. Father Conway built a brick church, St. Peter's, ninety by sixty feet, which, being finished, was dedicated to the honor and glory of God, October 16, 1842, and Rev. Father Conway, who superintended the work from the foundation to its completion, was appointed its first pastor.

Church at New Bedford.

The few sons of faith who formerly, from one circumstance or another, had found employment and a home miles distant from altar or priest, while in health and prosperity could retire to the woods, or some lonely spot, and spend Sundays in prayer, and unite, as best they might in spirit, with those more peculiarly blessed with religious instruction and the holy Sacrifice of mass; but when the hour of sickness or death approached, they felt most keenly their privation, and the loneliness of their condition in a strange land. Their only redress then was, to wait the returning messenger who had gone with all haste, or remain patiently for an answer to their request, forwarded by post, telling their anxiety for the aids of religion before leaving this world. Telegraphs there were none, rail cars and other improved and expeditious methods of modern conveyance, none; the mail stage, if the distance was far, running day and night at the rate of six or seven miles an hour, was the fastest and most reliable mode of travelling.

Amongst the first of such distant calls received by our young missionary, after his ordination, was one to New Bedford. The call was urgent; a poor old man, it was said, was near his end; the call came late, the stage coach had left; the only way, therefore, was a private conveyance; with this all haste was made that evening and night, but on arriving, at four o'clock in the morning, our missionary found that the soul of the poor old man had departed! He had died, it was said, with contrition in his heart, and with his last words lamenting, "O, if I but had the rites of my Church." We merely allude to such events to encourage the grateful acknowledgments of those who now enjoy, too often heedlessly, their many spiritual privileges.

The earliest information we have of any permanent settlement made by Catholics at New Bedford was in 1820, when, attended occasionally by Rev. Father Larasy, they erected a small frame building, small in reality, as we remember it, located among rocks, and enclosed with a high board fence, and, as it appeared to us, the last desirable spot in the town. Father Larasy, who was a priest of the order of St. Augustin, having left Boston for Philadelphia, the few Catholics residing at New Bedford were attended, in 1828, and had mass offered for their spiritual benefit once in every two months, by Rev. R. D. Woodley. The congregation having increased to the number of two hundred and forty, were attended, from 1842 to January 1844, by Rev. James O'Reilly. Continuing to increase in numbers, and promising to build a larger and more convenient house for divine worship, and to support a resident pastor, Rev. P. Byrne, formerly of St. Mary's, Charlestown, was sent to them, and was authorized by the Bishop to attend at the same time the few Catholic residents at Nantucket Island.

Church at Taunton.

As in reminiscence of early days at New Bedford, we have hinted at the propriety, while in life, of being prepared for death, and alluded to the living gratitude due for present spiritual advantages enjoyed over that of generations passed away, so before entering upon the dry details of the establishment of the Church at Taunton, — details similar to those of many other towns, — we have to record all we know of the first visit of a clergyman, which was to administer the last Sacraments to a dying Christian. Dry details, we say, for many, perhaps, may so account our labors; but we know not how to make these sketches otherwise, for to tell of the humble means collected from house to house wherewith to erect churches, of the disappointments experienced where much had been anticipated, of the oft-repeated story of priests "always looking for money," and the much to say on the part of those who generally did the least! to speak of the toil and drudgery, the debts contracted, the interest to meet, and creditors to satisfy, as has been the case in many instances for the smallest of the first churches erected, would only add to the aridity of our journal; we, therefore, content ourselves with giving simply the dates of their origin, the names of the clergy, and the commencement of former labors, that others may have a starting point for the interesting history they will record of the progress of Catholicity since.

At the first visit of the missionary to Taunton, besides attending the sick, there were other Sacraments administered. One of the few families of the place had been blessed with an heir to their estate, and their little one was baptized; in addition to which, there was mass and a marriage and nuptial benediction, which we mention, not only because the Church encourages the reception of this Sacrament at Holy Mass, but in illustration of the faith and piety of the early Catholic settlers of Taunton, who in this were actuated by the spirit of religion, and obedient to its laws, and left an example to their descendants.*

The first clergyman appointed to attend the Catho-

---

* In connection with the marriage alluded to, there was a wedding, which we remember distinctly, as it was the first we had ever attended; and it was, substantially, satisfactorily, and in every sense what our unsophisticated ancestors understood by a wedding, prior to the modern fashionable fly-away kind of weddings, with embossed card compliments of Mr. and Mrs. ——. It was what we conceived to be a good old-fashioned wedding, to which friends, relatives, and all well-wishers were invited. As far as we remember, there was a long table, and plates for all. There were meats, roast and boiled, fresh and salt, potatoes in heaps, and cabbage in abundance, with all else the season afforded; and not the least conspicuously accompanying this substantial meal, with tea for the ladies, was piled up a pyramid of that of which each might carry a slice to their little ones at home, called in these days ginger-bread, but then " sweet-bread."

This plain simplicity of a wedding of other days may provoke a smile, but nevertheless, though fashions may change, it was then considered satisfactory and highly commendable.

lics at Taunton, and say mass monthly, was Rev. R. D. Woodley. Hearing of their devotion and mutual edification, the Bishop visited them in the month of June, 1831, when, by invitation, he preached in the Town House, and administered Confirmation to thirty-one individuals; selecting at the same time a lot of land, upon which he encouraged the little congregation to build a church.

This church, a frame building of fifty-two by thirty-eight feet, at a cost of two thousand dollars, was built by the united efforts of the faithful, under the supervision of the successor of Father Woodley, Rev. John Corry, and was blessed by the Bishop at his second visit, October 28, 1833, at which time the adult members of the congregation were estimated at one hundred and fifty. Rev. Fr. Corry attended the Catholics here, and at Fall River and Newport, till his services were more particularly needed at Providence, R. I., when, in 1837, he was succeeded by Rev. William Wiley, who enlarged and beautified the little church, and the congregation were again visited and blessed by the Bishop, December 8, 1838, on which occasion he administered Confirmation to forty-two persons, who had been prepared for the reception of this Sacrament.

Church at Sandwich.

The faithful of this town, who, for the most part, were employed in the large manufactory of glass, by which more than one quarter of the population were supported, were visited the early part of 1830 by Rev. William Tyler, who, upon his return to Boston, reported the spiritual destitution and earnest wishes of the community. The Bishop, solicitous for the welfare of every portion of his vast diocese, visited Sandwich in person, in the month of June the same year, and said mass in the house of Mr. Doyle. Learning the number of the faithful, and solicitous especially for those who had families, he encouraged the erection of a small church, where they might assemble on Sundays, promising them the services of a clergyman, and the privilege of mass, and instruction, as often as possible, with the few he had at his command. The enterprise was entered into with spirit, and the little congregation, small as were their number, contributing generously of their daily earnings, had the satisfaction of seeing their little church, under patronage of St. Peter, blessed the following month of September; from which time they were attended by some one of the clergy in connection with other stations.

Church at Waltham.

This was a frame building, of fifty by thirty-five feet, erected in 1830, and although not finished, for want of funds, as the congregation were but few, and their means limited, still it was occupied for divine service on Sundays whenever a clergyman from the

Cathedral, or from some neighboring station, could be spared. Our missionary, whose stations at the time dotted the country from Boston to New York State line, gave this place a portion of his attention, and put the church in somewhat better condition for divine worship. In 1839, when the congregation were estimated at about three hundred souls, Rev. F. Fitzsimmons was authorized by the Bishop to attend their spiritual wants. The congregation increasing in numbers, he was succeeded by Rev. Michael Lynch, and upon his appointment to another district, Rev. Father Flood became their pastor. It was during his zealous care over the flock that the church, June 4, 1848, was burned to the ground. The firemen of the companies of the towns of West Newton, Newton Centre, and of Watertown, worked nobly to save the building, but in vain. The Selectmen of Waltham offered a large reward for the detection of the incendiary, and the same day proffered the Catholics the free use of the Town Hall for divine worship, as also most generously, and with commendable liberality, the Unitarian Society deputed their minister, Rev. Mr. Hill, and Dr. Mulliken, to offer Father Flood and his parishioners their house of worship for divine service.

Church at Watertown.

Rev. P. Flood, of whom mention is made in connection with the Church of Waltham, attended the few

Catholics, who, in 1846, were living at Watertown, Brighton, and the districts of Newton. Finding that Watertown embraced the largest number of the faithful, and that there was apparently a prospect of their increase, Rev. Fr. Flood, in conjunction with the few Catholic citizens of Watertown, petitioned the selectmen for the use of the Town Hall till their means would allow them to build a small house for public worship; this, their petition, through the chairman, Mr. H——, was positively refused. Far, however, from being discouraged at this disappointment on the part of those from whom they anticipated warmer encouragement for keeping the Lord's Day holy, they persevered in their efforts, and independent of those in high authority, for time being, succeeded in obtaining the use of what was known as the "Whig Reading-room," located on the Square. Here the little congregation continued to assemble for divine worship till they purchased the meeting-house belonging formerly to the Methodist Society, which, being remodelled, was the first Catholic church in Watertown.

The congregation continuing to increase, and demanding still larger accommodations, and co-operating with their zealous pastor, they secured for themselves the site of the present St. Patrick's church, the corner-stone of which was blessed by the Bishop, attended by Rev. Fr. Flood, the pastor, and Rev. P. O'Beirne, September 27, 1847, and in December following, the church being roofed, and though otherwise unfinished, served the congregation for divine service on Sundays; and by extraordinary and persevering efforts on the part of pastor and people, it was completed and dedicated to God by the month of June the year following, 1848.

Such, as in so many instances, we have to record, was the result of faith and perseverance of the few, and for the most part of limited means, who laid the foundations of our early Churches in New England.

Church at Fall River.

The first church at Fall River, a frame building, sixty by forty feet, was built in 1836, by the united effort of those who were among the first employed in preparing the foundations of those many heavy and substantial manufacturing establishments, which, since their erection, have given employment to thousands.

Previous to, and while the church was being erected, which was opened for divine service the 21st of August, 1837, Rev. John Corry said mass as often as circumstances permitted, and attended the spiritual wants of the faithful till November 22, when the congregation had a resident pastor in Rev. Richard Hardy, till April 6, 1840; he having been transferred to assist the Bishop at the Cathedral, the Rev. Edward Murphy was appointed pastor. For the accommodation of the increased number of the faithful, he immediately commenced the enlargement of the church; and such was the confidence in their pastor, and the good will of the congregation in seconding his efforts, that the work was forwarded with such rapidity as to see all completed by the 30th of August the same year, blessed and dedicated to God, under the title of St. John Baptist.

This enlarged church itself becoming in a very few years scarce sufficient for the convenience of the children of the congregation, whose spiritual welfare the pastor always looked upon as the first of his obligations, he commenced the present magnificent stone edifice, which he has been spared to see completed,— one of the largest, ornate, most substantial and beautiful among all the Gothic churches of the diocese.

Church at Saxonville.

The faithful at this village were attended by our missionary as early as 1834, when mass was offered in one of the largest rooms of a private house near to what then was Mr. Knights's carpet factory. In the course of time, the little congregation having been augmented by additional operatives at the woollen factory, the holy Sacrifice, by permission of the authorities, was offered in the school-house. With funds contributed on the part of the congregation, the site for a church and cemetery was bought in 1842. The missionary, at the solicitation of his Bishop, having been assigned to the charge of Rhode Island, was succeeded at Worcester by Rev. Adolphus Williamson, whose health becoming impaired, was assisted by Rev. Mathew Gibson, who for a while officiated at Saxonville.

In the Catholic Observer, of July, 1848, we find that " the church at Saxonville, under the title of St. George, was dedicated to God on the Feast of the Most Holy Trinity. The ceremony of the blessing was performed by the Right Rev. Bishop of the Diocese. Rev. Messrs. Williams and O'Brien, of the Cathedral, assisting as Deacons of honor. The mass was sung by Rev. J. Boyce, of Worcester. After the Gospel, Very Rev. Dr. Ryder preached in his most eloquent strain. At the end of the mass, the Bishop also addressed the congregation, lauding them for what they had already done, and exhorting them to persevere in their efforts for the advancement of religion and in their love for the house of God. Rev. George T. Riordan, pastor of Saxonville, has labored with great energy and great success in the noble work of finishing St. George's church, which is a credit alike to his good taste and his zeal."

Church at Quincy.

An acre of land having been secured in the month of November, 1841, the first church in this town, — a neat little edifice, — was erected through the united exertions and pious good will of those employed at the quarry, and dedicated to God under the title of St.

Mary's, September 18, 1842, at which time the faithful were attended by Rev. T. Fitzsimmons, of South Boston.

Churches at Chelsea and Lynn.

When in 1844 the Catholic residents of East Boston fitted up their church for the purpose of divine worship, the first public building erected on the island, which they had bought of the " Maverick Congregational Society," it was intended, as it afforded ample accommodation, for the benefit of the Catholics of Chelsea, as well as for themselves. The congregation, however, of Chelsea, solicitous, after a while, for more convenient accommodations, especially for their children, Right Rev. Bishop Fitzpatrick commissioned Rev. Fr. John O'Brien to look after their spiritual wants in connection with those living at Lynn, Newburyport, and other eastern sections of the State. Rev. Fr. O'Brien having eventually selected Newburyport as the head-quarters of his mission, Rev. Charles Smyth was appointed his successor at Chelsea and Lynn, who in 1849 purchased two small houses, the most convenient to be had at the time, one at Lynn and another at Chelsea, which being fitted up served the purpose for divine worship till the present spacious and handsome brick churches were erected, under the supervision of Rev. P. Strain, the present pastor of Lynn, Rev. James McGlew, having been appointed his successor at Chelsea.

Church at Milford.

The following communication appeared in the Observer of August 21, 1847. "On Sunday, the 8th instant, after mass, a meeting, presided over by the Rev. Mr. Gibson, was held at the house of Mr. Dominic McDavitt, for the purpose of taking into consideration the most effectual means of erecting a church to meet the spiritual wants of the rising congregation of this place. A subscription list was opened, and although the greater part of the congregation was not present or apprised of it, the sum of three hundred and fifty dollars was collected on the occasion, and the following gentlemen were appointed a committee to collect funds and superintend the building, viz., Messrs. Hugh McGown, Edward McGovern, and Dominic McDavitt."

In the month of April, the year following, Rev. Fr. Boyce, successor of Fr. Gibson, at Worcester, received permission from the Bishop to commence the church, the foundation for which being prepared, the corner-stone was laid the 29th of the following month of July, on which occasion, in the absence of any more convenient place, the holy Sacrifice of the mass was offered in the engine-house, and the Bishop, at the invitation of the citizens, preached in the afternoon in the Universalist meeting-house. The year following, November 4, 1849, the church was blessed, on which occasion Rev. Fr. Mathew preached on "the holiness of the house of God, and the reverence and respect due to it;" and, in the afternoon of the same day, administered the temperance pledge to a large number of the congregation, who were thus anxious to encourage each other in the observance of their baptismal engagements.

Having thus far glanced at the establishment of some of the earliest Churches in Massachusetts, we discontinue our humble sketches, to record the demise of the great, the good, the sainted and untiring laborer in the vineyard of our Lord, Bishop Fenwick.

Obituary Notice.

The Right Reverend BISHOP FENWICK was born in St. Mary's County, Maryland, on the 3d of September, 1782, and died August 11, 1846.

In his last illness, which he bore with heroic fortitude, his faculties did not for a moment desert him. His death was most saintly, and as his dissolution approached, he uttered frequent pious ejaculations, such as these: "Most loving Jesus, have mercy on me;" "Jesus, zealous lover of souls, have mercy on me."

On the evening of the day of his death, the remains of this holy Bishop, clothed in full episcopals, were conveyed to Holy Cross Cathedral, where his body lay in state that night and the following day. Immense crowds thronged the church, and a great number of people remained there all night, as if loath to part with their saintly father, who loved them so well, and whose tender love they so warmly reciprocated.

Amongst the crowd that flocked to Holy Cross were many Protestants, who, by their respectful and subdued demeanor, testified to the high esteem in which this great and good man was held by all classes of citizens.

The city authorities, with a degree of respectful consideration that cannot be too highly commended, ordered, upon hearing of Bishop Fenwick's illness, that in the streets leading to his house all traffic should be discontinued, and likewise that the bells of public buildings in his neighborhood should not be rung. By the simple force of his blameless life, his manly integrity, and his exalted piety and learning, had he won " golden opinions from all kinds of people," even from those who were from principle, interest, or prejudice most strongly opposed to that Holy Church of which he was such a shining light.

On the evenings of Tuesday and Wednesday following his death, the office of the dead was chanted by the clergy of his diocese. A solemn requiem mass was celebrated on Thursday, at eight o'clock, after which his remains were removed to Worcester, to be interred in a spot chosen by himself, and which was close to the College of Holy Cross.

From numerous notices of the death of this venerable prelate in the Protestant press of the country, we select the following, which may be regarded as being perfectly impartial, considering the source from which they are taken.

"His learning was profound, and his piety unaffected, while in social intercourse nothing of scholastic reserve or misplaced austerity tinged the amenity of his manners and the cordiality of his bearing. Hence he was alike respected and beloved. His loss comes home to the hearts of thousands, who have yet the consolation of feeling, that as he lived a learned, wise, and good man, so his death was worthy of his life." — *Times.*

"He retained his senses to the last, and died without pain. He had many friends, even out of his own denomination, and will be held in long and kindly remembrance for the good he has done in the community." — *Advertiser.*

"Bishop Fenwick was a learned scholar, as most of his order are. He was a calm, far-seeing, and zealous prelate; a good Christian, a good citizen, a good man." — *Courier.*

A correspondent to the *Pilot* newspaper of the 29th of August, 1846, thus speaks of Bishop Fenwick's funeral obsequies: —

"At least fifty thousand people came to behold, for the last time, the Pontiff of the Church of God, and though many were strangers to our faith, and sympathized not with our belief, yet a sacred awe pervaded every heart. . . . On Thursday morning, at eight o'clock, began the Holy Sacrifice. Right Reverend Bishop Fitzpatrick officiated, with Rev. Dr. Manahan and Rev. Mr. Lyndon as deacon and sub-deacon. . . . Notice had been given by telegraph to the Most Rev. Archbishop and the Right Rev. Bishops of New York and Philadelphia, and to Georgetown College, of Bishop Fenwick's decease. Owing, however, to the derangement of the wires, Dr. Hughes was the only one who received the communication in time to come to the funeral. . . . The whole of the mass was sung in plain chant. After the solemn *Introit* Requiem, and the plaintive cry for mercy, *Kyrie Eleison*, the Right Rev. Celebrant, in a voice scarcely audible through his sobs of grief, implored the judgment of mercy and of love for the soul of the departed Pontiff, and all responded, ' Amen.'

"After the Gospel, strengthened by the blessing of the new Bishop of the diocese, the Rev. N. O'Brien, of East Boston, ascended the pulpit. After reading a few verses from the sixth chapter of St. John, he spoke to that sea of people of their bereavement and their hopes, of the labors of their deceased prelate, and the success with which God, in his goodness, had crowned them, and concluded by imploring him from his tomb once more to bless his children."

After the three absolutions were pronounced, the procession formed and set out for the Worcester depot. It consisted of Exorcist, Thurifers, Crossbearer, the clergy walking two and two, the Right Reverend Doctor Hughes, Bishop of New York, and the Right Reverend Celebrant, followed by the hearse, beside which walked the Sisters of Charity and the orphans. The different Catholic societies were well represented.

Amidst all the grief and anguish, it was indeed a consoling and a glorious sight to see the Cross, the emblem of man's salvation, borne in procession through the streets, and to hear the sublime chant of the *Miserere* go up to Heaven, and one could almost hope that the prayer for mercy might be fruitful in a rich spiritual harvest, in that city where its notes were probably by many for the first time heard.

On the route of the procession the stores were closed, and business seemed to be entirely suspended. An immense multitude lined the streets, and manifested, by every exterior sign of respect and sorrow, the greatest reverence and love for him who had so long labored amongst them.

On arriving at Worcester, the body was received by Fr. Gibson, the Collegians, the religious societies, and a great concourse of people.

"The procession," says the writer from whom we have quoted above, "again formed, and with the renewed chants of the Church, ascended Mount Saint James. As it entered the college grounds, the litany of the Blessed Virgin was intoned, and sung by the whole people. '*Regina Cleri,*' Queen of the Priesthood, was thrice repeated as it reached the grave, which was then blessed, and dust was committed to dust, ashes to ashes, and the spirit was praying, we trust, for the orphans who remained."

The following extracts are from Bishop Hughes's eulogy on Bishop Fenwick, delivered at the "Month's mind," in Holy Cross Cathedral, on the 11th September, 1846.

"He has departed; but not until he had surrounded himself with a numerous body of pious and devoted clergy, whose warm affection for him is his brightest monument. He was their father, but also their equal. To them he was an elder brother, their counsellor, their example. And I may appeal to all of them to say if there was ever one instance when, in sorrow and affliction, they had recourse to the kind, enlightened, and discreet tenderness of their Bishop, without being met, on his part, in the spirit of Christian holiness and brotherly love.

"His sickness was another labor. It was painful and distressing. It was announced to him beforehand that he could not survive; and he, the man who for forty years had known no glory but that of his Master, and given himself to no work but that of God; that man, notwithstanding his humility, — if that humility would permit, — could look back through all his course in life, and say, with the Apostle, 'I have fought the good fight, I have kept the faith.'

"In a word, from the moment when first he consecrated himself to God, to the latest breath in his life, we find in him but one continuous act, — the making himself a victim in the cause of the Lord.

"Such was the life of Bishop Fenwick. And if, as I have said, a pure, and high, and holy motive, combined with constant labor and the endurance of all suffering, constitute greatness, then was he great indeed. Even in his humility he was great. His memory, as a Prince of the Church, is great. The influence of his example is great. And not only was he great in life, but he is, and will forever be great, because there is a continuity in the works of God, and goodness and greatness will last throughout eternity. We can little conceive the true measure of such greatness, unless we can lift ourselves above the low standard of life, and the grovelling propensities which beset us in the world, and seek to attain the high and pure atmosphere of heaven. . . .

"He sleeps beneath the monument he himself had raised, though he dreamed not it would be for him. Every day a shadow from its top is cast by the sun of heaven upon the bed of his slumber, and every day the pupils whom he taught, and whom he loved, breathe over his remains a prayer. When they kneel before their God, they offer a petition for the repose of his spirit, believing and knowing that he is praying for and watching over them, and all of us.

"His brows are now encircled by the crown of glory which Christ, the chief of Bishops, has prepared for those who with Him are to reign forever and ever. Let us, my beloved brethren, endeavor so to live that we may make our calling and election sure, that we may join with him who has gone before, in eternal praise before the throne of God."

Dr. Brownson, in his Review for October, 1846, as seen in the following extract, has given a very just sketch of this eminent prelate.

"Few who had the honor of personally knowing the late eminent Bishop of Boston but looked upon him as a great and good man, and upon themselves as highly privileged in being permitted to love and revere him. Especially was this the case with those who were in the habit of daily intercourse with him, who sat familiarly at his table, and shared his intimacy. To them he was a pleasant companion, a faithful and affectionate friend, a wise and prudent counsellor, a watchful and loving father. They have no words to say how much they loved and venerated him, or to express how deeply they feel their bereavement. They never met, and they have no hope of meeting, his equal in another; and their grief would be more than they could bear, did they not find consolation in reflecting that it has been theirs to know familiarly one who gave them, by his virtues, a higher conception of the capacities of our common nature, and of the power and riches of divine grace; that they have felt the influence, enjoyed the friendship, and received the paternal counsels and blessing of one whose labors and example were a precious gift from Heaven to the community in which he lived; and that he is removed from them only to enter upon the rewards of his fidelity and life of self-sacrifice, and to be able to serve more effectually the children he so tenderly loved, by his more intimate union with the common Father of us all.

"Of Bishop Fenwick as an intellectual man and a scholar, we are not well qualified to speak. He was averse to all display, and was always so modest and unassuming that you were perpetually in danger of underrating him. Yet one was always sure to find his natural ability and his learning equal to the occasion, whatever it might be. His mind was evidently of a practical, rather than of a speculative cast. He had no special fondness for metaphysical studies and scholastic subtilties, but he was always at home in any speculative question which came up, and familiar with all the nice and subtile distinctions it might involve. His memory was remarkably tenacious, and was rarely at fault. He seemed to have read everything, and to have retained all he read. He spoke several languages with ease and fluency, was an eminent classical scholar, and apparently familiar with the whole range of modern literature and science. No matter what the subject, however obscure or remote from his professional studies, on which you sought information, he could either give it, or direct you at once to the source whence you could obtain it. That he was a sound divine, well read in dogmatic and moral theology, we suppose there can be no question; but his favorite studies seemed to us to be history and geography, in both of which, whether general or particular, he excelled.

"Humility was, perhaps, the most striking trait in his character. It gave to his whole character that placid beauty, and that inexpressible charm, which made his society so delightful, and which so endeared him to our hearts. He rarely spoke of himself, and when he did, it was always evident that his mind was not preoccupied with himself. He spoke of the transactions in which he had taken part, nay, in which he had been the sole actor, as if he had had no connection with them. He held no prominent place in his own eyes. He was not merely indifferent to praise, but seemed to have risen to that sublime degree of humility which takes pleasure in being contemned. He was happy in opportunities to humble himself deeper before God. Through grace his spirit had become as sweet, as gentle, as docile as that of the little child, of whom our Saviour said, "Of such is the kingdom of heaven." He had long ceased to live for himself, and he was incapable of thinking how this or that would or would not affect his own reputation. He chose always the lowest seat, and was anxious only to draw out and encourage others. He made himself nothing for Christ's sake, and was free and strong for whatever there was for him to do. It was a lesson and a blessing to contemplate one so truly eminent for his abilities and acquirements, able to rank with the greatest men and most learned scholars of the age, making himself of no account, completely annihilating himself for the love of God and the good of souls, and emulous only of serving the lowest, and assisting those who were most in need of being assisted. It abashed one's pride, made him ashamed of arrogating anything to himself, and feel that nothing is truly estimable, save so far as consecrated to the greater glory of God.

"It is hardly necessary to speak of this good father's tender solicitude for the flock committed to his charge. Every member was dear to him, and he took a lively interest in each one's concerns, temporal as well as spiritual. They were all his children, and no father's heart ever warmed with more generous affection, or overflowed with more tender solicitude. He lived only to serve them, and he brought all his energies to bear in devising ways and means to benefit them, both here and hereafter. Their joy was his joy, their sorrow was his sorrow. Especially was he the father of the poor. He gave everything he had, even the very considerable estate he had inherited, and, if all were not amply provided for, it was only because his purse was not so large as his heart. He carried his kindness and paternal love even to those who did not always make a suitable return, and possessed, preeminently, the power of rendering good for evil. No ingratitude ever discouraged him, no unworthy recipients of his bounty ever induced him to abandon or reproach them. If, as rarely happened, some rude or violent member of his flock forgot what was due to their father, he felt no resentment, but melted in compassion for the offender. All who had any real or fancied grievances were permitted to tell their story in their own way, were listened to with patience, and dismissed with gentleness and the paternal blessing. Yet his remarkable patience and gentleness, so obvious to all who were in the way of observing his intercourse with all sorts of people, were the work of grace; for we are inclined to think he was, naturally, somewhat impatient and irascible. This trait in his character was, therefore, all the more beautiful, for it proved the victory of grace over nature. The victory was complete: if nature showed sometimes a disposition to rebel, she was instantly suppressed, and nothing was seen but the meekness, gentleness, and forbearance of divine grace.

"His consideration for the feelings of others was another beautiful trait in his character. He could not bear to give the least pain to another, and he studied to hide his excessive tenderness under an affectation of harshness and severity, which, however, only made it the more apparent. He delighted to have his children, especially his clergy, around him, and was never happier than when they shared freely his boundless hospitality. Nothing could be more delightful than to mark his kindness to them, and their love and veneration for him. Nothing was constrained, nothing was cold or distant. It was truly the reunion of the father and his children. No one was overlooked, no one was unwelcome; and we have often admired the unaffected, and apparently unconscious, consideration shown to the feelings of each one present. If one had been longer absent than usual, without any sufficient reason, or seemed to show that he doubted whether he was perfectly welcome or not, the conversation was always sure to take such a turn, and without any one's being able to perceive when or how, as to make him certain that his absence had been regretted, and that, if anything had occurred to wound his sensibility, it was unintended, and would be atoned for at any sacrifice. All this was done so naturally, so spontaneously, so unconsciously, so from the heart, that none but a very nice and practised observer could detect or suspect it. He ever studied to make others happy, and his joy was always to see himself surrounded by glad hearts and smiling faces. He had his trials, and trials of no ordinary severity;

he had met with many things, in the administration of his diocese, to grieve his paternal heart; but he never permitted his own afflictions to cloud his brow, or that of another. With him all was smooth and sunny, and you imagined that he was free from all solicitude, and that no care ever oppressed him. This trait in his character was strikingly displayed all through his long and painful illness.

"Of his truly edifying death we cannot speak in detail. It was what was to have been expected from his life. He retained his faculties and his recollection to the last moment. He knew the change that was taking place, but it did not take him by surprise. All his life had been but a preparation for it, yet he made all the acts and preparations the time and the occasion required. His last words were, '*In te, Domine, speravi; non confundar in æternam.*' As he repeated the words, half formed, the agony seized him; he stretched forth his hands as if for absolution and the last indulgence, which were given; some one thought they heard him respond, 'Amen;' the agony was over, the spirit was emancipated, and its joy was reflected on that countenance which had been so dear to us all.

"We have nothing more to add. His monument is in the grateful recollections of his people, whom he fed with the bread of life, and governed with equal affection and wisdom for over twenty years. Everywhere in his diocese we may read the proofs of his paternal solicitude, his wisdom and energy, his devotion to the people of his charge, and of his having lived and labored with no thought but for the greater glory of God and the advancement of the Church. He has stamped his character on his diocese, and his influence will continue to be felt till that day comes when the elements shall melt with fervent heat, and the heavens and the earth be dissolved."

Churches and Clergy in the Boston Diocese, 1846.

The zeal, fervor, labor, and perseverance of the illustrious Bishop Fenwick, cannot be more clearly seen than by the following statistics of the churches and clergy, twenty-one years from the day of his installation, when there were but three clergymen and seven small churches or chapels throughout the New England States.

Boston, Cathedral,	Right Rev. Bishop Fenwick and Coadjutor, Right Rev. Bishop Fitzpatrick, Rev. Messrs. P. F. Lyndon, Ambrose Manahan, D. D., and John J. Williams.
Boston, St. Mary's,	Rev. Messrs. P. Flood and James O'Reilly.
Boston, St. Patrick's,	Rev. Thomas Lynch.
Boston, SS. Peter and Paul,	Rev. Terence Fitzsimmons.
Boston, St. John Baptist,	Rev. George F. Haskins.
Boston, Holy Trinity,	Rev. Alexander Martin, O. S. F.

Boston, St. Nicholas,	Rev. Nicholas O'Brien.
So. Boston, St. Augustine,	Vacant.
East Cambridge, St. John's,	Rev. Manasses Dougherty.
Roxbury, St. Joseph's,	Rev. P. O'Beirne.
Charlestown, St. Mary's,	Rev. Messrs. George J. Goodwin and M. McGrath.
Quincy, St. Mary's,	Rev. Bernard Carraher.
Waltham and Mission,	Rev. James Strain.
Salem, St. Mary's,	Rev. James Conway.
Lowell, St. Patrick's,	Rev. James McDermott.
Lowell, St. Peter's,	Rev. Peter Crudden.
Fall River, St. John Baptist,	Rev. Edward Murphy.
Taunton, St. Mary's,	Rev. Robert Wilson, D. D.
New Bedford, Sandwich, } St. Peter's,	Rev. Thomas McNulty.
Chicopee, Northampton, Pittsfield, } St. Matthew's,	Rev. Messrs. John D. Brady and Bernard O'Cavanagh.
Springfield, Saxonville,	Rev. Timothy Reirdon.
Worcester, St. John Evangelist,	Rev. M. W. Gibson and M. McEvoy.
Dover, N. H., Newburyport, } St. Aloysius',	Rev. Patrick Canavan.
Burlington, Vt., St. Peter's,	Rev. Jeremiah O'Callaghan.
Middlebury, Vt., Castleton, Vt., Claremont, N. H., }	Rev. John B. Daley, O. S. F.
Portland, Me., St. Dominick's,	Rev. James McGuire.
Whitefield, Me., St. Denis,	Rev. Patrick Carraher.
New Castle, " Augusta, " } St. Patrick's,	" "
Bangor, " Old Town, " } St. Michael's,	Rev. Thomas O'Sullivan.
Benedicta and Houlton,	Rev. William Moran.
Eastport, Machias, Calais, Pleasant Point, }	Rev. John Boyce.

In the above enumeration, it will be observed, are omitted the churches and clergy of Connecticut and Rhode Island, those States that were formerly under the spiritual jurisdiction of Bishop Fenwick, and which, in 1844, were erected into a new Diocese, and placed under the government of Right Rev. Bishop Tyler.

Boston Diocese, 1872.

The following, from the Catholic Directory of 1872, shows the increase of Catholicity in what is now the Boston Diocese, Right Rev. John Joseph Williams, D. D.: —

Churches,	96
Churches building,	6
Chapels and Stations,	26
Priests,	157
Clerical Students,	75
College,	1
Female Academies,	3
Free Schools,	12
Hospitals,	3
Orphan Asylums,	6
Number of Orphans,	565
Catholic population, about	300,000.

DIOCESE OF HARTFORD.

Comprising the States of Connecticut and Rhode Island.

This Diocese was established in the year 1844. Right Rev. William Tyler, D. D., its first Bishop, was consecrated March 17, 1844.

The following is an estimate, made at that time, of the number of Catholics:—

	Members.	Priests.	Churches.
In Connecticut,	4,817	3	4
" Rhode Island,	5,180	3	4
Total,	9,997	6	8

The first Mass offered in Connecticut, as far as ascertained, was by the Reverend Chaplain of the French troops who came to aid America in the war of independence. This was on an extensive plain, at the left of the road to Wethersfield, about one mile south of the court-house, the place being pointed out, in 1830, by one who had been present on the occasion, and remembered all the circumstances.

The first public sermon, in English, at the invitation of Rev. Dr. Strong, a Congregationalist clergyman, was delivered by Rev. Dr. Matignon, of Boston, about the year 1813, who, in those days, when "travelling on the Sabbath" was by law prohibited, arrived at Hartford, on his way to New York, late of a Saturday evening; stage-coaches then being the only public inland conveyance between these two important cities, now, by the agency of steam, brought within a few hours of each other. For this courteous and friendly attention to a stranger, and he a Catholic priest, the reverend doctor was waited upon at an early hour, Monday morning, and gravely censured by the deacons for having allowed his pulpit to be so disgraced by a "popish priest." The reply was characteristic of the man, who knew somewhat of human nature: "Well, gentlemen," said he, "do your best, and do your worst; make the most of it; I have the ladies on my side!" Curiosity had been gratified, and the outspoken, liberal minister knew it.

The excavation for the canal at Windsor Locks, a few miles north of Hartford, may be looked upon as the first gathering, in any considerable numbers, of the sons of faith in the "land of steady habits." One of the hard-toiling, adopted citizens, a native of Ireland, employed at Windsor, fell sick, and was visited by Very Rev. Fr. Power, of New York, in the month of August, 1827. In October, of the same year, he made a second visit, and offered the holy Sacrifice of the Mass in a dilapidated building which stood near where the railroad bridge now crosses the river.

Learning, thus, of there being sons of the faith in

this distant part of the diocese, Bishop Fenwick, unable, at the time, to give them his personal attention, authorized Rev. R. D. Woodley, a young clergyman whom he had lately admitted into the diocese, to visit Connecticut, which he did in November, 1828. The year following, Rev. B. O'Cavanagh, having been ordained, was commissioned to look after the spiritual wants of the faithful.

The forming of what may be considered the first permanent congregation in the State was at Hartford, in the upper room of house number 204 Main Street, which room was used also as an office for the Catholic Press, one of the earliest weekly publications in defence of truth issued in New England. The family of Taylor, citizens of Hartford, were the prime movers in this enterprise. Mr. Francis Taylor, in his visit to Montreal, Canada, prompted by what he there heard and saw, — religion exemplified, the church doors always open, and the happy, cheerfully devout, passing in and out, at all times, — was led to examine the divine truths of Catholicity; the result of which was, by Heaven's grace, his conversion. Returning home, to impart to those he dearly loved the happiness which glowed in his own bosom, he encouraged them to read the books of devotion, and works of unanswerable arguments, and the plainest evidences of the true religion, which he had brought with him, and the happy result was, that his aged mother, sister, and three brothers, in course of time, followed his example. These, with the few Irish, French, and German Catholics then living in the neighborhood of the city, came together on Sundays for prayer, pious reading, and mutual edification.

Firm in faith, and relying on the divine promise to those who were united in His name, though small their number, they drew up a respectful petition to their Right Rev. Father in Boston, and proposed, with his permission, the erection of a small building for public worship. With that paternal love and solicitude which carried him to every portion of his vast diocese, wherever the voice of the least of his flock was heard, the good and ever-devoted Bishop visited Hartford, and offered the holy Sacrifice of the Mass in the room mentioned above, July 12, 1829. The Sunday following, the few little ones were brought together, and the first Sunday school instructions given; and here parents and children continued to assemble weekly till June 17, 1830, when, to their inexpressible joy and delight, they secured for themselves larger and more commodious accommodations. The Protestant Episcopalians, having projected the erection of a new and more substantial edifice for themselves, sold to the little congregation of Catholics their frame building, which was subsequently removed to a lot on Talcot Street. The following notice of the joyful event appeared in the Catholic Press at the time.

"On Thursday, the 17th inst., we witnessed, with mingled emotions of pleasure and delight, the dedication of the Catholic church in this city. This neat and handsome edifice formerly belonged, under the name of Christ Church, to our respected fellow-citizens of the Episcopal order. Having lately undergone considerable repairs, it was dedicated to the immediate service of One God in three Persons, under the title of 'The Church of the Holy and Undivided Trinity.' The Catholics of Hartford and its immediate vicinity may well rejoice in having a place now to offer up sacrifice and prayer, and to worship their Eternal Creator in spirit and truth, according to the dictates of their conscience. Who could have believed, two years ago, that in a section of country where our holy religion was scarcely known, there would be this day a 'chosen and sanctified place' to present the pure, clean, and holy oblation, which, according to the prophetic Malechias, was to be offered up from 'the rising of the sun to the going down thereof?' After the ceremony of dedication, the Catholic pastor commenced a solemn High Mass, which, making due allowance for unacquaintance with Catholic worship, the singers being mostly converts, was satisfactorily taken up and pleasingly executed by the newly-organized choir. After the Gospel, Rt. Rev. Dr. Fenwick ascended the pulpit, and very appropriately selected for his text the sixteenth verse of the seventh chapter of Paralipomenon, — 'I have chosen and sanctified this place, that my name may be there forever, and my eyes and my heart may remain there perpetually.' The Rt. Rev. Prelate entered into an historical detail of the mode whereby man should offer up acceptable sacrifice of praise to the eternal Author of truth.

He appealed to the sacred volume, and lucidly proved therefrom that this sacrifice could only be pleasing to the great Creator when performed according to the manner by Him prescribed and designated. He afterwards alluded, in couched and courteous language, to the unacquaintance of a large portion of our respected fellow-citizens with Catholic rites and ceremonies. He lamented the misrepresentation of Catholic tenets, and assured those present who were not Catholics, that an impartial investigation of our holy doctrines would lead to a very different conclusion from those generally drawn by the enemies of the Church. In conclusion, he pathetically observed that if what was given, though but a cup of cold water, to relieve the corporal necessities of a suffering fellow-creature, would not lose its reward, how great the reward of those who have it in their power to contribute to the spiritual necessities of thousands yet unborn! To us, the dedication of Trinity Church appeared truly sublime and strikingly significant. May such scenes increase and multiply."

The Catholic Press, from which the above extract is taken, was, after the fourth volume, transferred to the city of Philadelphia, and appeared under the name of the Catholic Herald. It was published weekly, in the room mentioned, 204 Main Street, which, as we have seen, served as chapel, office, and Sunday school, till transferred to the basement of the newly-dedicated church, which had been fitted up and made to serve the purpose of printing office.

Sunday and day school, as well as quarters for the teacher, printer, and a corner for the Missionary, who, by the by, when suffering from rheumatism in after years, raised his voice strenuously against church basements, which, among other base evils, he pronounced the smallest economy ever projected, especially for sleeping apartments.

From this basement office, while the Press was in being, were issued many useful works, such as books of devotion, pamphlets on religious subjects, and other publications called for at the time. Among those who became converts to the faith, this served as sanctum, where their writings were edited, to encourage others to partake of their spiritual consolation. Among these publications, was the " Connecticut Convert," by Joseph Brigden, who, from the day of his reception into the Church, during the many years he subsequently lived, — and his life, as school teacher and catechist, was ever active, — allowed no day to pass without spending at least an hour in presence of his Adorable Redeemer in the Blessed Sacrament of the Eucharist. And so of many others; — gratitude for the inestimable gift of faith was evinced by piety of life, and love for the spiritual welfare of their neighbor.

Through the infinite goodness and mercy of divine Providence, from the establishment of the Church in Connecticut till 1836, upwards of eighty adults — and many of them, with their families, men and women, from the various societies of Protestantism — had the happiness of being admitted to the sweet consolations of the One, True, Holy, Catholic and Apostolic Church.

PRUDENCE IN DELAY. — In receiving those who, from the varied ranks of Protestantism, sought admission into the Church, our Missionary always thought it best, where circumstances permitted, to subject them to a long delay. He felt the necessity of that true Catholic spirit that loves God *above all things*, and holds His precepts dearer than *anything earthly*, and is willing and determined to sacrifice everything rather than displease Him.

On the other hand, he was well aware of the difficulty of divesting one's self in a moment of the ideas and associations of early days. He knew how hard it is to begin a new career, and, breaking with all the past, enter life anew. Hence it was only after they had been fully instructed, not only in what is absolutely necessary to their salvation, but also in the practices of piety, and those other devotions of the Church which distinguish the thorough Catholic, that converts were admitted to the Sacraments of Baptism, the Holy Eucharist, and Confirmation.

Thus the grain of mustard-seed had found congenial soil in the very land of Puritanism, and spread most wonderfully in an incredibly short period of time. Among the citizens of Connecticut converted to the faith, are the names of probably a larger number of those who were formerly preachers and promoters of Protestantism, than in any other State of the Union. The Reverend Messrs. Barbers were of this State; so was Rev. Calvin White, of Waterbury, and others, whose names are omitted, as they are still living, and among the most devoted of the Catholic priesthood of the nation.

New Haven.

From Hartford, the Missionary extended his journeys to wherever a child of the faith was to be found. Consequently every county was traversed repeatedly, and stations established at Middletown, New Haven, Bridgeport, New London, Norwich, Stonington, Tariffville, Thompsonville, Waterbury, and Westerly, in Connecticut, and at Saxonville, Springfield, Amherst, Barre, Blackstone, Chicopee, Barrington, Northampton, Ware, Warren, Webster, Westfield, and Worcester, in Massachusetts, where, at present, there are large and most respectable congregations, and at several of these, two or more congregations, with their schools, academies, asylums, and other flourishing institutions. In a letter written by one of the earliest Catholic residents of New Haven, communicating to a friend his joy at the spread of Holy Church, the writer says, " When we heard that a church had been purchased at Hartford, and was about to have a priest, we were delighted. This appointment gave us an opportunity of having mass at New Haven about once in three months, and happy we then were for so great a privilege. Hearing, for the first time, that the priest was about to visit us, we were at a loss to know where we could find a place for offering the Holy Sacrifice. After many efforts to secure a respectable and suitable place, we were in the end necessitated to take up with an old barn, which we swept and fitted up the best we could. By the next visit of His Reverence, we rented a room from a German, he not knowing for what purpose we intended it. We next needed a few benches; but the joiner, hearing what we wanted them for, refused positively to make them, saying that 'they — his fellow-townsmen — were determined to put down that religion, at least in Connecticut, whether or no.' We succeeded, at length, in finding one who made us a few, not suspecting the place for which they were intended; but as soon as he found out, declared ' he would not have made them for fifty dollars apiece if he had known it in time.'

"Whenever we expected the priest, we all came together to receive him. One Saturday, in particular, it was the Eve of Christmas, and anticipating midnight mass, we were all at our accustomed place of meeting, awaiting his arrival; but he did not come. We were certain he would not disappoint us, whilst, at the same time, we could not account for his delay. At length we concluded to go and see if we might meet him. We did so, and met him on the road, about four miles outside of New Haven. The sleighing from Hartford had been good part of the way, and then failed, till nothing remained but bare ground, and his horse gave out — the distance from Hartford to this city is about thirty-four miles;

but the good priest, not wishing to disappoint us, determined to walk the rest of the way. When we met him, he had his valise, containing his vestments, &c., on his shoulders. The walking being rough and frozen, his shoes were nearly worn out, and when he arrived that night he was scarcely able to preach, though he did so at the end of mass; after which we secured a conveyance to leave him where he had left his horse, for he had to return and say another mass at Hartford the same day.

"There is another little incident that occurs to my mind in connection with the early establishment of our religion at this place. As our numbers began somewhat to increase, I called upon a certain gentleman who owned an old building that we thought might be fitted up for church purposes, but neither for love nor money would he listen to our proposition, declaring that he would not encourage Catholicity in any way. We felt disappointed, and my reply to him was, 'Sir, I hope that you and I may live to see Catholic churches in this city with spires as high as any of yours.' He doubted it; but, thank God, it has come to pass; and he has lived to see our splendid churches all well filled, and even crowded, every Sunday."

While these reminiscences of one of the pioneer Catholics of New Haven are so interesting, and he finds such deep sense of gratitude for being permitted to live to praise God for His infinite mercies, in the increase of Holy Church, there are others still living, equally grateful, who remember the tedious journeys, made often in the depth of winter, sixty and eighty miles, in pursuit of the priest, to attend their dying father, mother, or friend.

In consequence of the many stations to be visited, and distant calls to be attended, Bishop Fenwick admitted, in 1832, Rev. James McDermott to Holy Orders, and sent him to aid the missionary. The Rev. Mr. McDermott, after having been partially initiated at Hartford into the practical duties of mission life, was commissioned to attend New Haven, Bridgeport, Derby, Norwalk, and other stations in the western part of the State. Having attended these for a time, he at length found means, May 14, 1833, to purchase the lot on Davenport Avenue, where a frame building, sixty by thirty-five feet, exclusive of sacristy, was built.

The day assigned for its dedication was the festival of the Ascension, May 8, 1834. The Bishop said mass at an early hour, gave communion to four or five persons, and was told there were fifteen prepared for Confirmation. At ten o'clock, the hour appointed for dedication, the church was crowded to excess; the Bishop, accompanied by Rev. Mr. McDermott and the Missionary, having made a circuit around the church, as prescribed by the Ritual, and advanced in the interior towards the Altar, the choir-gallery gave way, and fell with all its incumbents upon the mass of people below. The scene of confusion that ensued can be better fancied than described. One lad fourteen years of age was killed instantly, and several others seriously wounded, of whom one died in the course of the day.

The cause of this disaster (and we particularly allude to the sorrowful event, that others may take warning from it) was ascribed to the carpenter, who had deviated from the original plan and specification, which called for two columns. He deeming these unnecessary, had attempted to support the gallery by trussing it,— a plan under certain circumstances good enough in itself, provided the space is not too wide, the main timber large enough, and not cut half away.

The debris of the gallery having been removed, and the blood-stained floor scoured, the church was blessed the Sunday following. The number of Catholics then residing in New Haven and its immediate vicinity, were about two hundred souls. Two years subsequently, when the census was taken, there were at New Haven, of adults, three hundred; at the town of Derby, twenty-five, at Bridgeport, one hundred, at Norwalk, twenty-five, and at Waterbury, thirty.

Rev. Fr. McDermott having been transferred to Lowell, Mass., in June, 1837, his place was filled by Rev. Fr. Wiley, till the appointment of Rev. James Smyth, September 5, 1837, who, in connection with his charge over the congregation at New Haven, attended Bridgeport, Derby, and all other stations of his predecessor, till 1848, when he was succeeded by Rev. Philip O'Reilly, during whose residence the church at New Haven accidentally took fire, and was consumed.

To accommodate the faithful, previous to rebuilding a new church, the house originally occupied by the Congregational Society on Church Street was purchased by the Bishop, and Rev. Edward J. O'Brien appointed pastor. The increased numbers and wants of the Catholics demanding still other accommodations, the Church of St. Patrick, a substantial brownstone edifice of sixty by one hundred and twenty feet, was erected, and in 1852 placed under the immediate charge of Rev. Matthew Hart, during whose pastoral care, as we learn, the congregation has increased to five thousand souls, with a Sunday school of one thousand little ones, besides the parish of St. Francis, so called, of Fair Haven, composed of fifteen hundred souls, which was set off from St. Patrick's in 1867, and for whom a church has been built of sixty by one hundred feet.

Church at Norwich.

With the opening of the Worcester and Norwich Railroad, the missionary found the same opportunity of affording the consolations of religion to its toiling workmen and their families, without, however, the same arduous duties and frequent hurried calls that attended the opening of the Western Road, where the many rock sections, so called, and the essential use of blasting powder, rendered casualties more frequent. The services of religion on the Norwich road were generally held in shanties or in groves, and but few permanent stations were established. The town of Webster, through which it passed, had been previously attended from Hartford, as had been other places equally so on this route.

The city of Norwich and flourishing manufacturing village of Greenville, where a few Catholics had found employment, and settled with their families, suggested the propriety of selecting the site for a church the most convenient for all; hence the missionary secured a lot midway between both places, and had the foundation laid early in the year 1844, and the building so far completed as to offer on its altar the holy Sacrifice of the mass on the joyful festival of Christmas the same year. The number composing the congregation at the time were about two hundred and fifty; they have since increased, and are estimated at the present day to be, within the circuit of four miles, between five and six thousand, for whose additional accommodation, the present zealous and devoted pastor, Rev. Fr. Mullen, has secured a most desirable lot on one of the finest streets on the Plains, so called, upon which he contemplates the erection of a spacious and beautiful church edifice, worthy the place and the cause.

Church at Stonington.

From Norwich the missionary tour generally extended to Stonington, where the holy Sacrifice, as usual, was offered in the largest room of some private dwelling. The principal members of the Church then residing at Stonington were the families of McCarthy,

Sullivan, Gilmore, Carr, and Kirby, the last named gentleman, brother of Rev. Dr. Kirby, President of the Irish College in Rome, sustained his family by teaching a select number of young Protestant gentlemen the classics and higher branches of mathematics. Mass was often said in the private parlor of his house for his convert wife and family of little ones.

The present church at Stonington, St. Mary's, a building of sixty by forty feet, was erected in 1845, through the exertions of Rev. Fr. Duffy.

Church at Westerly.

This town was visited occasionally while the Providence and Stonington Railroad was under construction; subsequent to which, however, not a solitary Catholic family was known to have remained in the place, though at present they have a church and resident pastor, Rev. P. Sherry, and his assistant, Rev. J. Reynolds, who attend also Stonington and Mystic.

Westerly is well remembered from the fact of the first mass there offered having been under an aged oak, as well as from the first ride ever enjoyed on a hand-car, — a truck used by the workmen on the railroad, — being of a Sunday evening.

A family residing a few miles distant, strangers in the woods, had, not knowing the deleterious effects of certain roots and brush-wood, been preparing dinner in a good old-fashioned sized chimney-place, using as fuel wood found in the neighborhood, when, to their surprise, they were blinded, neither mother nor little ones able to see one another! "The sick call" was rather amusing than alarming. They had inhaled the fumes of dogwood!

Church at New London.

Leaving Stonington, New London was the next station. The faithful here, though few, had received occasional visits from the Missionary, both while at Hartford, as early as 1831, and after his removal to Worcester. To be hooted, and occasionally stoned, by urchins who had imbibed the prejudice of their parents, was not an uncommon occurrence in former days. But deep-rooted as was the prejudice of the majority of the people, there were not a few found better informed at New London, who were inclined to liberality and tolerance, and who allowed the use of the Court House for occasional preaching.

The members of the Church, after a while, becoming too numerous to find accommodations as usual in any private house, it was decided to erect a small church; for which purpose, a vacant lot, located between two very respectable frame buildings, on Jay Street, was purchased in January, 1843. Although it was anticipated at the time that this edifice would prove too limited for increasing numbers, yet it was considered that the fact of the proprietors of the houses right and left being good Protestant fellow-citizens, would be the best insurance against casualties that otherwise might happen. The foundation of this little church was soon laid, and the building so far completed as to be ready for divine service in the month of April.

Ten years subsequently this cradle church becoming entirely too small for the increasing numbers of the faithful, another and more commodious building was erected on Truman Street; and even this, in time, being found inadequate, another lot was purchased in 1869, on Huntington Street, where is erected a magnificent Gothic church, surpassing, both in size and beauty, any other edifice in the city. Thus the few Catholics, who in 1831 were so happy at being present at the holy Sacrifice of the mass, as the Missionary could be occasionally with them, and found ample accommodations in the room of a private dwelling, have augmented to three thousand, while the children of sufficient age to attend catechism number five hundred.

Church at Middletown.

This town and Chatham, now Portland, on the east side of the Connecticut River, were, as early as 1830, stations, attended by the Missionary from Hartford, when mass was said, and the Sacraments administered in private houses. The extensive work at the brown stone quarries of Portland gave employment to several laborers, the majority of whom, with their families, were members of the Church, who, after their week's toil, had occasionally the privilege of mass on Sundays, or before their day's work on other occasions.

Residing on both the east and west side of the river, when their numbers had increased to two hundred souls, an acre of land, to serve the purpose of a church and cemetery, was secured at Middletown, November 18, 1841, and on this a brick edifice, measuring sixty-five by forty feet, was erected in 1843.

Church at Bridgeport.

The earliest date we have of mass being o ered in the room of a private house in this town was 1830, when the Missionary had, as far as remembered, a congregation of married and single, together with children, about seventeen souls. Tradition, however, says, that previous to this date a dying Christian had been attended, and received the aids of religion by some one of the good Catholic clergy from New York State; which is not improbable, since we have learned that as early as 1827, Very Rev. Fr. Power was on a similar mission of love to Windsor, near to the heart of the State.

As already mentioned, this portion of the State formerly attended by our Missionary, whose *parish*, as he was wont to call it, extended from Boston to New York, was, in 1832, placed in charge of Rev. Fr.

McDermott, which he visited from time to time, till, being transferred to Lowell in 1837, he was succeeded by Rev. James Smyth, who, in 1841, when the congregation numbered two hundred and fifty, selected an eligible site for a church, which was subsequently built of brick, measuring sixty by forty feet, with a choir gallery and convenient sacristy, which he had dedicated under the title of St. James the Apostle, July 24, 1843. Rev. Michael Lynch was appointed in charge of this congregation, in connection with the missions of Derby and Norwalk, November following.

Of the growth and spread of Catholicity, and the splendid churches since erected in the thriving and pleasant towns of Bridgeport, Derby, Birmingham, Waterbury, Norwalk, Danbury, Norfolk, Wenstead, and Stamford, in Connecticut, where there are now churches and devoted pastors, we will not speak, as we leave these to the future historian of the diocese, it being our aim to confine ourselves merely to early events; events which, though at this day may appear small, were viewed as grand efforts by the pioneers of Catholicity of other days.

Church at Newport, Rhode Island.

The first Catholic church erected in the State of Rhode Island was at Newport. "The discovery of America," writes J. G. Shea, LL. D., in his interesting history of the Catholic Missions among the Indians of the United States, "like every other event in the history of the world, had, in the designs of God, the great object of the salvation of mankind. In that event, more clearly, perhaps, than is often given to us here below, we can see and adore that Providence which thus gave to millions long sundered from the rest of men by pathless ocean, the light of the gospel and the proffered boon of redemption."

The legend of St. Brendan's western voyage, which was widely diffused in the middle ages, versions of which abound in Irish, Dutch, German, Italian, Spanish, Portuguese, and in all parts of the Continent, is most interesting, to say the least; and with the indefatigable labor and researches of such scholars as Professor Rafu, of Copenhagen, more convincing evidences of anti-Columbian voyages to America may be discovered than are as yet generally acknowledged.

"Kerry was the native home of St. Brendan, who lived in the fifth century; and as he stood," writes M. F. Cusack, the authoress of Ireland's History Illustrated, "on its bold and beautiful shores, his naturally contemplative mind was led to inquire what boundaries chained that vast ocean, whose grand waters rolled in mighty waves beneath his feet. His thoughtful piety suggested that where there might be a country there might be life, — human life and human souls dying day by day, and hour by hour, and knowing of no other existence than that which at best is full of sadness and decay.

"Traditions of a far away land had long existed

on the western coast of ancient Erinn. The brave Tuatha dé Dananns were singularly expert in naval affairs, and their descendants were by no means unwilling to impart information to the saint.

"He at length decided to set out on the important expedition. St. Brendan's Hill still bears his name; and from the bay, at the foot of this lofty eminence, he sailed for the 'far west.' Directing his course towards the south-west with a few faithful companions in a well-provisioned bark, he came, after some rough and dangerous navigation, to calm seas, where, without aid of oar or sail, he was borne along for many weeks. It is probable that he had entered the great Gulf Stream, which brought his vessel ashore somewhere on the Virginian coasts. He landed with his companions, and penetrated into the interior, until he came to a large river flowing from east to west, supposed to be that now known as the Ohio. Here, according to the legend, he was accosted by a man of venerable bearing, who told him that he had gone far enough; that further discoveries were reserved for other men, who would, in due time, come and Christianize that pleasant land.

"After an absence of seven years, the saint returned once more to Ireland, and lived, not only to tell of the marvels he had seen, but even to found a college of three thousand monks at Clonfert."

Whatever credence may be attached to the foregoing, it is certain that the Irish and Norwegians, in the ninth century, were a naval and commercial people, and their fleets scoured the Atlantic and North Seas.

Of the voyages of that period, the historians of Iceland preserve us details, which the almost entire destruction of Irish manuscripts has buried in oblivion. "According to these," writes the author of the Discovery and Exploration of the Mississippi, J. G. Shea, already quoted, "the Irish first discovered Iceland, and established Christianity there, then planted a colony on the southern coast of North America, at a part called, in Iceland annals, Hvitramannaland, that is, Whiteman's land, or Irland it mikla, Greater Ireland. This colony subsisted as late as the year 1000, and we know that the colonists were not insensible to the great work of evangelizing the heathen, from the fact that a pagan Icelander, Aré Marsôn, who was driven there in 983, was baptized in the colony.

"Soon after the settlement of Greenland by Eric the Red, his son Leif visited Norway, and was induced by St. Olaus, then king of that country, to embrace the true faith. Returning to Greenland in 1000, Leif bore with him priests to convert the colonists, and in a short time most of the Northmen in America embraced Christianity. Churches and convents arose in different parts, rivalling those of Iceland in piety and learning.

"Before this Biarni, son of Heriulf, sailing from Iceland to Greenland, was driven on the American coast, and in the very year of the introduction of Christianity into Greenland he sailed again to explore the countries which he had seen, and naming Labrador, Helluland, Nova Scotia, Markland, proceeded to

Narragansett Bay, where, from one of his company finding wild grapes, he called the country Vinland.

"Thorwald, Thorstein, and subsequently Thorfinn, of Irish origin, visited this place, and a settlement was gradually formed. As yet all were not Christians; some still adored Thor and Woden, and missionaries left Greenland to establish religion in Vinland. Of these missionaries, the most celebrated was Eric, who arrived in Greenland, and after laboring a few years proceeded to Vinland. Spending some years here, he returned to Iceland in 1120, and sailed to Europe to induce the establishment of a bishopric, and a proper organization of the Church. Deeming Eric the most suitable person, the Scandinavian bishops selected him to found the first American See, and the missionary was consecrated at Lund, in Denmark, by Archbishop Adzer, in 1121.

"After his consecration, Eric returned to America, but still attached to his mission, led a body of clergy and colonists to Vinland: here he found so ample a field for his labor, that he resigned his bishopric and never returned to Greenland.

"Of the future career of this zealous and self-denying missionary we know no more, the researches of northern antiquarians not having as yet drawn from the dust of centuries any further details.

"He was not, however, the only missionary; for we find that about this time John, an Irish or Saxon monk, sailed from Iceland to that country, but was there slain by the heathens whom he had endeavored to convert.

"As to the position of Vinland, there can be little doubt; a careful study of the narratives of the early voyagers, narratives stamped with the imprint of truth, leaves no doubt that they turned Cape Cod, and entered the waters of Narragansett Bay. To corroborate this, a ruin exists at Newport, evidently of Runic or Scandinavian origin. It was found at the settlement of the country, and is clearly no Indian work, while its resemblance to acknowledged Scandinavian works in Greenland and Iceland, places the question beyond a doubt." So far the researches of the historian, J. G. Shea, Esq.

"The ancient *tholus* in Newport, the erection of which," say the Royal Society of Antiquarians, "appears to be coeval with the time of Bishop Eric, belonged to a Scandinavian church or monastery, where, in alternation with Latin masses, the old Danish tongue was heard seven hundred years ago."

A cloud hangs over the fate of the colonists of Vinland and Greenland, who sank at last under war or pestilence.

Apart from what has been said of the discoveries of the Irish and Norwegians in Iceland, Greenland, Vinland, and other parts of America, the next acquaintance we have, coming down to a more recent date, of the presence of the Catholic clergy, and of the holy Sacrifice of the mass being offered at Newport, was during the war for American independence, when France, with her thousand troops, her ships and frigates, military stores, wealth, and other substantial sinews of war, came to our aid when battling for Freedom's cause. At that time the State House, a building still maintaining its excellent proportions and worthy of note, was used as a hospital, and as a chapel, where the consolations of religion were administered to the sick, the wounded, and dying soldier. In the south room is pointed out the spot where the altar was erected, and holy Sacrifice offered by the chaplains who accompanied Count D'Estaing and his gallant band to the American shore in 1778. One who still lived in 1840, and delighted to recount former events, remembered well the interment of the lamented Chevalier De Ternay, was in the room where he departed, followed his remains to the grave, and looked upon the priests who performed the funeral service.

From the pages of the first Baptismal Register of the Cathedral of Holy Cross in Boston, there are the names of two admitted to the Sacrament of Baptism at Newport by Rev. John Thayer, one in 1791, and the second in 1798, and one by Bishop Carroll, who, upon his return to Baltimore, after having been at the dedication of the church at Boston, in September, 1803, put into Newport, in consequence, probably, of a heavy storm, and baptized a little one born about that time; from which we are at liberty to conjecture that there were a few Catholics residing at Newport after the departure of the French fleet.

From the same Register we learn that occasional visits were made by Rev. Drs. Matignon and Cheverus to the town of Bristol as early as 1811 and 1812, where the children of certain French-Americans were baptized, at which time, no doubt, the few Catholic residents had mass, and received the other consolations of their religion.

Coming down to a later date, what remains fresh in our memory is, that Rev. Patrick Byrne, of Boston, in the month of February, 1827, visited the Catholics employed at Fort Adams, and those laboring in the coal mines on the north part of the island, and reported, upon his return, that he had administered holy communion to over one hundred and fifty men. Encouraged by this report, Right Rev. Bishop Fenwick authorized Rev. Robert D. Woodley, whom he had appointed to the charge of Providence, Pawtucket, and Taunton, to attend Newport, which he did, and in the month of April, 1828, purchased a small building, which had been used previously for school purposes, on Barney Street. This he fitted up, had an altar erected in it, and small as it was, it had the honor of being the first Catholic Church blessed in Rhode Island.

In the month of October, the same year, the Bishop visited Newport in person, said mass, preached, and administered the Sacrament of Confirmation to eleven persons in the same little church, and encouraged the purchase of additional land for the convenience of the congregation at a future day.

The successor to Father Woodley, 1830, was Rev. John Corry, who in time finding that the faithful had so far increased as to warrant the undertaking, erected on Mount Vernon Street a frame building sufficient to accommodate between seven and eight hundred, which was blessed, and known as St. Joseph's, August 20, 1837, at which visit the Bishop confirmed others prepared for the Sacrament. The successors to Father Corry were, in 1837 and 1838, Rev. C. Lee, and in 1839 to 1842, Rev. Jas. O'Reilly, who was transferred to New Bedford, as, in the absence of employment for either mechanics or laborers, the congregation had become very small; and ten dollars per month, all that the clergyman acknowledged to have received, was hardly sufficient for his support and contingent expenses.

At the arrival of Right Rev. Dr. Tyler at Providence, in 1844, our missionary was permitted to look after the spiritual needs of the faithful at Woonsocket, Pawtucket, and Newport, till other laborers being admitted into the diocese, Newport was selected as his residence.

The Brown-stone Gothic Church at Newport.

The frame building erected on Mount Vernon Street was considered far from being safe. The builder, whoever he may have been, was evidently a stranger to church architecture, particularly on the seaboard, for though the materials used in its construction were of the best, the saw and chisel had left the building in a very shaky condition.

Mrs. Goodly Harper, and her devoted daughter, Miss Emily, of Baltimore, the worthy relatives of the first Bishop of America, and of Charles Carroll, of

Carrollton, who resided at Newport during the summer months, encouraged the erection of a more substantial edifice, and one that would be a credit to the religion they dearly loved. With their substantial aid, and the lot on Spring Street, which their donation of four thousand dollars secured, and subsequent annual assistance, together with the generous aid of the congregation, according to their means, the present truly grand church of "Our Lady of the Isle" was erected.

The subjoined, which was engraved on the plate and written on the parchment, deposited in the corner-stone, tells its history.

Engraven on the plate was: —

"TO THE GREATER HONOR AND GLORY OF ALMIGHTY GOD, and under the patronage of the Ever Blessed Virgin, conceived without sin, this corner-stone of the church, of the HOLY NAME OF MARY, was laid June xiv., A. D. MDCCCXLIX."

On the parchment was written: —

"TO THE HONOR AND GLORY OF GOD: This church was commenced August 7, 1848, in the two hundred and ninth year of the settlement of Newport, when the members of the Catholic Church numbered five hundred and eighty-six souls, out of the whole population of about nine thousand.

"The trenches having been dug by voluntary and cheerful hands, the first stone was laid August 15th, and the foundation walls were commenced the day following.

"This corner-stone was laid, June 14, 1849, under the pontificate of His Holiness Pius IX., an exile at Gaeta, with the approbation of Right Rev. William Tyler, Bishop of the Diocese of Hartford, which embraces the States of Connecticut and Rhode Island, in the seventy-fourth year of American Independence, during the administration of Zachary Taylor, President of the United States, Henry B. Anthony being Governor of the State of Rhode Island, and Rev. James Fitton, Pastor of the Catholic congregation at Newport. At an eventful period, when the Continent of Europe is being revolutionized by wars and the overthrow of thrones, when many, notwithstanding earth is but a pilgrimage in which men, in consequence of original sin, have been condemned to eat their bread in the sweat of their brow, are, after six thousand years that it has produced its thorns and thistles, attempting, they say, to ameliorate the condition of society, and under the name of Socialism, Fraternity, &c., about to render earthly home an Eden! Time will tell the result, and some future generation, who will read this, will, it is to be hoped, profit by the admonition."

As it was among the first of the churches planned by that prince of church architects, soon after his arrival in America, P. C. Keely, Esq., we will give a brief description of it, allowing due honor to the mechanics who did their part so faithfully. The exterior walls and interior carved columns, each a shaft of solid stone, and the tower, were built by Messrs. Meginn and Ponsonby; the stuccoing and beautiful interior ornamental finish was completed by P. Foley, and the slating by Messrs. Dugans, all true sons of the Church. The carpentering was by J. B. Weeden, the carving by Messrs. Smith and Crane, the stained glass by G. Morgan, and the polycrome painting by T. Coggeshall.

The edifice is of the second period of Gothic architecture. It has a clerestory, and comprises a well-defined chancel, a nave and aisles, a tower, porch, and sacristy. It is from out to out of walls, north and south, sixty feet; from east to west, one hundred feet; with a chancel of twenty-four by thirty feet. The aisle walls are twenty-four feet, the clerestory walls forty-eight feet, and from the floor to the ridge-moulding seventy feet. The chancel walls are thirty-three feet, and to the peak of roof is forty-eight feet. To the cornice of tower, where the spire springs, is about sixty-five feet.

It is built of sized brown-stone, with window and door jambs, table mouldings, sills, corbel tables, gable offsets, &c., neatly cut.

The front, which is to the west, is supported by massive buttresses, placed diagonally at the corners of the edifice, with deep bases, drip-stones, and offsets. The tower, which is at the north-west corner, is supported by still more massive buttresses, with bases of bold projection, and is lighted by six richly wrought windows in the first and second stories, while the upper, which is really ornate in its character, is pierced on every side by belfry windows, whose openings are filled with louver-boarding. High over the doorway is seen conspicuously the monogram of the Blessed Mother, and under whose fostering care the first stone of the building was laid. At the angles of the tower, upon which rests the spire, stand the four Evangelists, beautifully carved, who, as when first commissioned, appear to be announcing the glad tidings of salvation to the four quarters of the world. The spire, "pointing in silence heavenward," surmounted with its finial and cross, the emblem of man's salvation, present a graceful and characteristic feature in the outline of the edifice.

The nave and aisle walls are supported by buttresses divided into two or more stages, with offsets, and finished with corbel table. The east and west view are in fine perspective, in consequence of the buttress quoin being carried up the gable and corbelled to support the coping which at the gable ends is stopped by large bold gable offsets, which impart variety to the outline of the building.

The door of the west entrance, the tower and south porch doors, are set in deeply splayed jambs and graceful mouldings. The large west window, divided by mullions into three, the clerestory and aisles into two, and the grand chancel window into five compartments, are all filled, as are the circular and quaterfoils in the gables and east end of aisles, with stained glass of varied designs, and present the most beautiful contrast in massive flame-like tracery.

The south porch, with its high-pitched roof, is an ornamental as well as useful appendage to the church, as it is here, agreeably with the rubrics, that the religious ceremonies of Baptism, the office in Holy Week, &c., are commenced, and where the benatura, or holy-water font, is usually placed in the first compartment from the west end. The plan is square, the interior is lighted by small windows, the walls are of stone, while the roof shows the framework of the timbers, and the high-pointed gable, on which is engraven, on a prominent star, *Sancta Maria, ora pro nobis*, is surmounted by a floriated stone cross.

The Sacristy is built on the south side of the chancel, and is covered with a sloping roof, which falls just below the circular window at the east end of the aisle. It is lighted by small coupled lancet windows, widely splayed in the interior, and is connected by a side doorway through the wall of the chancel which opens to the rear of the Altar.

The church was dedicated under the patronage of the Holy Name of Mary, Our Lady of the Isle, 1853.

Church at Woonsocket, R. I.

In this flourishing manufacturing village, on Blackstone River, near the line of Massachusetts, Catholics sought employment as early as 1834, and were occasionally visited by our Missionary from Worcester. Their number of about thirty having increased in time to upwards of two hundred, a small church of forty by sixty feet was, in 1843, projected for their accommodation. In a few years after the departure of our Missionary to Newport, Rev. Charles O'Reilly, in consequence of the demand for church room, enlarged the little building to eighty by one hundred and twenty feet; since which time a new, spacious, and beautiful church edifice has been erected of seventy by one hundred and sixty-four feet.

The healthful increase of the congregation, from 1845 to 1865, may be estimated by the baptisms conferred, which averaging one hundred and fifty each year, gives an increase of two thousand from births alone. The zeal and devotedness of both pastor and people to-day cannot be more clearly illustrated than the fact that they have a Catholic day school of four hundred and fifty pupils.

Church at Providence and Pawtucket.

As early as 1813, the small colony of Catholics at Providence, who were attended by Rev. Dr. Matignon, and occasionally by Right Rev. Bishop Cheverus, from Boston, had mass in a small wooden building, then standing on the north side of Sheldon Street, about one hundred feet east of Benefit Street. This building, which had previously been used for school purposes, was, subsequent to its removal to another lot, blown down in "the great gale" of 1815. The names of the principal members, or those who then had families, as we learn from the children baptized, as found on the Baptismal Register of the Church at Boston, were: Francis McGill, Charles Delahunty, Luke Higgins, William Jordan, William Rumford, and John Condon.

In 1828, Rev. R. D. Woodley, who labored in the Boston diocese between two and three years, was commissioned by Right Rev. Bishop Fenwick to look after the immediate spiritual wants of the Catholics of Rhode Island and the neighboring State of Connecticut. From his report we learn that he administered, while on the mission, the Sacrament of Baptism, and of course performed his other ministerial duties in the following places. That at Providence, he baptized adults and children, eighty-two; at Pawtucket, eleven; Woonsocket, three; Newport, sixty-eight; Hartford, twenty-five; New Haven, two; and at New London, two.

Learning the spiritual destitution of the faithful dispersed over this portion of his diocese, the Bishop visited Providence, April 14, 1828, and offered the holy Sacrifice of the mass, and preached in Mechanic's Hall, and administered the Sacrament of Confirmation to five persons. The day following he waited upon David Wilkinson, Esq., of Pawtucket, and acknowledged his indebtedness for his Christian-like spirit and generous good feeling in presenting the Catholics a desirable lot whereon to build a church for their special accommodation. Upon this lot, which was one hundred and twenty-five feet square, the church was erected the year following, and the holy Sacrifice of the mass was first offered in it by Rev. Fr. Woodley.

Providence having thus received occasional clerical visits, as circumstances permitted, Rev. John Corry, a few months previously ordained, succeeded Father Woodley, November 30, 1830, and in connection with this city, attended Taunton and Newport. The wants of the faithful in these two latter places demanding more particularly the special attention of Father Corry, Providence and Pawtucket were attended during 1833 and 1834 by Rev. Father Conelly, and in 1835 by Rev. Fathers Lee and McNamee.

Church of SS. Peter and Paul.

A site for the church in Providence, on High Street, measuring fifty by two hundred and ten feet, was secured February 15, 1832, for fifteen hundred dollars; but the edifice, for want of funds, was not commenced till three years later; the faithful, in the meanwhile, through the kindly spirit and generous good feeling of their fellow-citizens, were allowed the privilege of the Town Hall for Sunday services. It was here in 1836, when the Bishop came to see and encourage the erection of the church, the foundation of which had been already laid by Rev. Fr. Lee, measuring eighty by forty-four feet, that he offered the holy Sacrifice, and preached to a delighted congregation, composed of all the Catholics who then resided in the city, and for miles around, who were assembled on that occasion, and were estimated as numbering near a thousand souls.

Many were the difficulties that arose, from one cause or another, from the time the foundation was laid till the church was completed, and principally for the want of funds; the mechanics threatening from time to time to lay an attachment on the building, to secure their wages; on all which occasions, the Bishop, poor as he himself was, had to come to the rescue. Rev. Fr. Lee having been relieved the latter part of May, 1837, Rev. Fr. Corry took charge of the congregation in the month of August and encouraged the completion of the church, so far, that the holy Sacrifice of the mass, to the delight of the congregation, was therein offered the second Sunday of Advent the same year; and the year following, November 4, 1838, it was dedicated to God under the title of SS. Peter and Paul, though it was then not entirely finished, there being not even a sacristy or vestry, so that the Bishop had to be vested in the porch. This, however, he considered of small inconvenience compared to a much greater, a debt yet standing of five thousand dollars.

Among the generous donors to this first Catholic church in Providence, Messrs. Philip Allen & Son presented a fine-toned Spanish bell, weighing about one thousand pounds. In 1841 a sweet-toned organ was placed in the church, and as far as we learn, the whole expense of the lot, church, organ, and church furniture, amounted to about twelve thousand dollars.

The following notice appeared in the public press of the day: "The church covers an area ninety-eight feet by forty-four. It is thirty-four feet high, having a fine basement story, in which are two good school-rooms. The walls of the house are built of slate-stone, covered with cement. It is a castellated Gothic structure, with a tower of fine proportions and finish."

The census taken in December, 1839, gave the adult population as ten hundred and eighty-seven. Children of four years of age and under, two hundred and seventeen; between four and ten years, two hundred and seventy-three; between ten and seventeen years, one hundred and nineteen. Total Catholic population, sixteen hundred and ninety-six.

The following table shows the baptisms and marriages performed during the first ten years, from the opening of the church of SS. Peter and Paul: —

Years.	Baptisms.	Marriages.
1837 to 1838	164	41
1838 to 1839	163	55
1839 to 1840	204	50
1840 to 1841	190	43
1841 to 1842	198	60
1842 to 1843	174	52
1843 to 1844	240	53
1844 to 1845	281	78
1845 to 1846	312	82
1846 to 1847	333	81

While the Baptismal and Marriage Registers of this

one church alone show the healthful increase of Catholicity for the first ten years from the establishment of the church in this city, the Registers of other churches, since erected, are equally satisfactory, as we learn that the baptisms administered in Providence during the year 1870 amount to thirteen hundred and thirty-eight, and the marriages to two hundred and ninety-nine ; and that during the same year, 1870, the baptisms administered in all the churches of the State amount to two thousand seven hundred and twenty-three, and the marriages to six hundred and twenty-one.

Church of St. Patrick.

In consequence of the spread of Catholicity in the city, and the Church of SS. Peter and Paul being insufficient for their accommodation, the Catholics at the North End, so called, invited the Bishop to visit them, and view the site which they thought desirable for another church, for themselves and families. With this invitation the Bishop complied, and the eligible location on Smith's Hill having been approved of, Rev. Mr. Fenelly, the pastor at Pawtucket, was authorized to superintend the undertaking, April 19, 1841. The excavation was forthwith commenced, and the foundation walls were blessed by the Bishop, agreeably with the Ceremonial, the 13th of July following.

Rev. Fr. Fenelly receiving permission, August the 24th, to visit Europe, Rev. Denis Ryan, who for near a quarter of a century had labored in the State of Maine, had temporary charge of the enterprise till the appointment of Rev. William Wiley as pastor of the congregation, January 11, 1842.

The church completed, and its altar and decorations finished under the immediate supervision of Father Wiley, whose taste, love and zeal for everything pertaining to the greater honor and glory of God and appropriateness in His holy sanctuary, it was difficult for any one to surpass. The day selected for its dedication was the first Sunday of the following month of July. Pontifical Mass was celebrated by Right Rev. Bishop Fenwick, assisted by Rev. Fr. Donohue, of Philadelphia, as Deacon, and Rev. Fr. Fitzpatrick, of Boston, as Sub-Deacon. Right Rev. Bishop Hughes, of New York, preached on the occasion, while the music was by the choir of the Cathedral, Boston. There were likewise present in the sanctuary, besides the pastor, Rev. W. Wiley, Rev. Fr. Corry, of SS. Peter and Paul, and Rev. Ed. Murphy, of Fall River.

This edifice, the style of which is Gothic, and the material blue slate stone, was dedicated to God under the title of St. Patrick, and was at the time — for it has since been enlarged by the addition of side galleries — seventy-five feet in length by fifty-five in breadth, exclusive of tower, which was twelve feet square, and sixty-two feet high, in which was hung a sweet-toned bell of two thousand pounds, the offering, in part, of P. Allen, Esq., a generous Protestant gentleman, who, of his own free will, contributed three hundred dollars towards it. The church, independent of the choir gallery, was fitted up to accommodate eight hundred sittings, and with its vestments, sacred vessels, and all requisites for divine service, cost eighteen thousand two hundred and seventy dollars.

The Bishop visited Providence again October 23, and administered the Sacrament of Confirmation in this church to one hundred and twenty-eight persons; at SS. Peter and Paul, to two hundred and thirty; and in the afternoon of the same day, at Pawtucket, to one hundred and five.

The number of Catholics in Providence, eight years subsequently, who availed themselves of the spiritual advantages of the Jubilee, that is, in 1850, was about eight thousand. Over five thousand approached the Altar at the Cathedral Church of SS. Peter and Paul, and two thousand six hundred at St. Patrick's. There were then, in both churches, religious Confraternities, schools, and temperance societies.

Having thus sketched the early establishment and rapid progress of the churches in Providence, we will retrace our steps a few years, that we may — as if living and sharing in the work of the day — look upon the extension of the first church of eighty by forty-four feet, to its present roomy dimensions.

Rev. Fr. Corry, who in 1841, in consequence of ill health, petitioned the Bishop to be relieved of his charge over the congregation, was, in October, 1843, succeeded by our Missionary. The church at the time had been placed under an interdict, the result of lay interference with affairs beyond their control; electing, irrespective of authority, and assuming responsibilities, without so much as the formula of invitation! In a word, there was a self-constituted committee of thirteen, who, after the departure of Fr. Corry, had taken possession of the keys, books, and church property in general, and who, unconscious of the danger, had inaugurated what was known at the day as Trusteeism.

Mass having been said, the congregation were addressed on the propriety of obedience to authority; on the sad consequence of lay interference with clerical affairs that did not concern them; that the cause of strife and contention that had been, and which probably would be till the end of time, was the result of man's neglecting his own, to attend to his neighbor's business.

At the close of the familiar address, which all seemed to understand, the question was put whether the congregation were prepared to receive the Missionary, who, in obedience to authority, stood before them; and if so, whether it was their wishes that the keys, the account-books, and all else belonging to the Church, should be produced and placed in the sanctuary before them; and if so, to manifest their pleasure by rising. The appeal was sufficient. The self-elected committee saw the propriety of obedience. All was restored, and a blessing imparted, for each to retire quietly, and take their dinner in peace and comfort.

Encouraging the education of youth, and establishing schools, as had been done at Boston, Hartford, and Worcester, was one of the first movements the Missionary made. This was done wherever sufficient numbers could be assembled for the purpose, not only for acquiring knowledge, whereby they might become more useful and better citizens, but for the practical and every day acquaintance with their religion, its duties and obligations, the knowledge of salvation, and the end of their creation, which he always contended could not be sufficiently taught in a few short hours, and with little ones distracting each other, on any one day of the week, however well disposed, zealous, or industrious any Sunday school teacher might possibly be.

Catholic schools for boys and girls having been thus advocated, in no former place where the same had been introduced were parents to be found more willing to second these efforts than in Providence. This has been ever found one of the first grand secrets for establishing and maintaining mutual good will between pastor and people. Catholic parents love their children, and are generally aware of their responsibility. Whoever, therefore, would labor with profit for the salvation of souls, let little ones, particularly, be esteemed and cared for. In heaven, it is said, we know our own; and if parents so toil for the support of their children in this life, one of the greatest inducements, as faith teaches, must be to have them so educated in the science of sanctity that hereafter there may be no separation.

Church of Our Lady of Mt. Carmel, Crompton.

Apart from Pawtucket, the largest number of the faithful living in any town contiguous to the city, and who were considered as belonging to the charge of the pastor of SS. Peter and Paul, were at Crompton.

This place having been attended monthly, and the hard-working and industrious operatives in the factory, among whom were those having families of little ones, being anxious to have a place where they might assemble on Sundays, and willing to contribute according to their means, an acre of land was secured, September 23, 1844. A small church, a frame building, was immediately erected, and, as the location selected was on the hillside of the village, overlooking the country for miles distant, was styled the "Church of Our Lady of Mount Carmel."

The congregation of Crompton and its neighborhood was confided to the special care of Rev. James Gibson, who attended it occasionally, as his duties at other stations permitted, till August, 1851, when, assuming its sole charge, he added seven and three quarters acres to the original purchase, thus making eight acres and three quarters of land, all enclosed within a substantial stone wall. Besides which, for the better accommodation of the congregation, he has added twenty by fifty-eight feet to the church, making it one hundred and eight by fifty feet, independent of Sanctuary and Sacristy, twenty by twenty-one, and a tower, twelve by twelve square and forty-five feet high, with a sweet-toned bell, of over fourteen hundred pounds' weight.

He has also built a pastoral residence of thirty by twenty-eight feet, tastefully and conveniently arranged, and a school-house eighteen by forty feet, wherein to gather and superintend the little ones of his spiritual charge.

Untiring in his efforts for the convenience and good of all, he has latterly secured, on what is known as Birch Hill, a very fine building, over thirty-one by forty-five feet, erected originally for the purpose of a select high school, which he has converted into a neat little church, with its porch, of eight by ten, and its sacristy, twelve by fifteen feet.

Enlargement of the Church of SS. Peter and Paul.

Right Rev. Bishop Tyler, soon after his consecration in March, coming to take charge of his diocese, which embraced the States of Rhode Island and Connecticut, selected, as it appeared to him best, at the time, the city of Providence, as the most convenient point for his residence. As our Missionary, upon his arrival, finding that, from some cause or other, windows had been originally put in but on one side of the church, thus leaving a smothered, fainting, suffocating crowd to the sweltering heat of summer, had soon called upon masons and carpenters to remedy the evil, so good Bishop Tyler, having selected the same church for his Cathedral, and finding it so very limited, intimated to the congregation the propriety of enlarging it. To this they cheerfully assented, and, after the example of Bishop Fenwick, who, upon his arrival at Boston, found the church of Holy Cross too small for the accommodation of the faithful, and having land that he could use for the purpose, by removing the house occupied by his Right Reverend predecessor, added forty feet to the length by seventy feet in width, at the Sanctuary end, so Bishop Tyler, similarly circumstanced, enlarged his church, giving it the form of a T, and making it more than double its original dimensions, and thus affording ample room for the congregation, previous to the demand for other churches that have since been erected.

Another passing illustration of small beginnings. The Missionary, at his coming to Providence, had no place outside of the church sanctuary for chair or table; nor had Bishop Tyler, upon his arrival, anything better for his accommodation than a small, one-story, wooden building, with its kitchen, dormitory, and room for all work. This, though large enough for the Missionary, who built it for himself, and whose work lay principally in the church basement, was rather diminutive for an Episcopal residence; but, notwithstanding, it had to serve the purpose till larger accommodations could be secured.

During his brief pontificate, from his consecration in 1844 till his death in 1849, Right Rev. Bishop

Tyler was indefatigable in the discharge of the many arduous duties which fell to his lot as first Bishop of so extensive a diocese, provided in the beginning, as it was, with but six priests to assist him, — two in Providence, one at Pawtucket, one at Hartford, one at New Haven, and one at Bridgeport.

Death of the First Bishop of Hartford.

Right Rev. William Tyler, first Bishop of Hartford, died the 18th of June, 1849, at his Episcopal residence in Providence, in the forty-fifth year of his age.

Bishop Tyler was born of Protestant parents, in the town of Derby, Vt., but had the happiness of being brought, by divine grace, to the knowledge and profession of the true faith at the early age of sixteen. His father and mother, and all the other members of his family, were received into the bosom of the Church about the same time. From the moment of his conversion to the true faith, Bishop Tyler was distinguished by his modest virtues, and by the eminent sanctity of his life.

He pursued his course of classical studies at Claremont, N. H., under the direction of his reverend cousin, Father V. H. Barber, who had been also converted from Protestantism, and was formerly a minister, with a comfortable maintenance. He was now a priest; but, unwilling to tax the little congregation he had gathered around him, who, for the most part, had once been Protestants like himself, he earned a partial support by teaching the classics and higher branches of education.

Whilst Bishop Tyler was yet a student in the academy of Claremont, his rare virtues and the solid qualities of his mind and judgment attracted the attention of Bishop Fenwick, and, as he exhibited satisfactory signs of a vocation to the ecclesiastical state, he was taken by this eminent prelate into his own house in Boston, and under his immediate guidance commenced and completed his course of theological studies.

In the year 1828 he was elevated to the priesthood. From that moment forward it may be said with truth that " he had been delivered, through the grace of God, unto the work which he accomplished." His life as a priest was a model for ecclesiastics. Not an hour was given to idleness, vain amusements, or visits. He was well ordered in the distribution of his time, and every portion of it well spent. Zeal for the glory of God and the salvation of souls, true humility, total indifference to popular favor or applause, and a perfect spirit of poverty, were his peculiar virtues, and his whole life was spent in the practise of them. His aversion to honors and distinction of every kind was so great, that he could hardly be induced to accept the episcopacy to which he was appointed. Nothing but his great deference for the will of Bishop Fenwick, whom he revered as a father, and a formal decision of Father Dzierazinski, under whose direction he made a spiritual retreat at the time, could have extorted his consent.

He was consecrated by Bishop Fenwick, in the Cathedral at Baltimore, on the 17th of March, 1844. His career as Bishop, like his priesthood, was humble and unassuming, but laborious and fruitful. His natural constitution was not strong, and for two years before his death his medical adviser endeavored to dissuade him from taking part in the active labors of the ministry; but he persevered to the end, taking always upon himself the larger portion of the work in the confessional and the pulpit, and sparing the young clergymen who were his assistants. He ever continued to attend the sick until within the last year of his life.

He was thus proceeding in the discharge of his Episcopal duties with unremitting assiduity, and with a success proportioned to his zeal, when it pleased the Lord of the Vineyard to call him from his labors, and invite him to sweet repose. Although enfeebled, and almost exhausted in strength, he attended, with great edification to his colleagues, the council held at Baltimore in 1849, and applied for a Coadjutor.

On his way homeward, he contracted the disease — rheumatic fever — which terminated his life. The morning after his arrival at Providence, which was Pentecost Sunday, he endeavored once more to offer up the august sacrifice of the altar; but when he arrived in the sanctuary, he found his strength of body unequal to the pious desire of his heart, and being unable to celebrate Mass, he assisted at the holy mysteries, seated in a chair near the altar. Immediately afterwards he was obliged to seek repose on the bed, from which he was to rise no more. He was attended in his last hours by his friend, the Right Rev. Bishop of Boston, Bishop Fitzpatrick, from whom he received the last sacraments of the Church.

During the last two days of his life the disease settled upon the brain of the pious sufferer, and deprived him of his reason. In the moments of delirium, his only care and his only complaint was, that he should be prevented from working for the souls intrusted to his charge, and he frequently implored permission to return to the labors of his office, from which he imagined that he was withdrawn.

But the Divine Master was satisfied with the labors already performed. Twenty years, of which every day and every hour had been devoted to the great and only work of the Bishop and the Priest — the sanctification of souls — gave sufficient evidence of the purity of his faith, the fervor of his love. For him the heat and burden of the day were over. He died June 18th, and was buried on the 20th of the same month, 1849, in the basement of SS. Peter and Paul's Church, which he had selected as his Cathedral. Bishop Fitzpatrick, of Boston, officiated pontifically, attended by a large concourse of the clergy of his own and the neighboring dioceses.

With this brief obituary notice of the sainted Bishop Tyler, we pass to the third Diocese established in New England, that of Burlington, leaving to others the pleasing labor of recounting the rapid spread of Catholicity throughout the Hartford Diocese, which, commencing, in 1844, with its six priests, eight churches, and nine thousand nine hundred and ninety-seven souls, now numbers its one hundred churches, besides sixty-four chapels and stations; its ninety-five priests, and seventy clerical students; its ten male and female academies; its forty-four parochial free schools; its orphan asylums; and its two hundred thousand Catholic population, — all within a quarter of a century!

While these Sketches are passing through the press, Providence, we learn, has been erected into a Diocese.

DIOCESE OF BURLINGTON,

Comprising the State of Vermont.

This Diocese was established in 1853. Right Rev. L. DE GOESBRIAND, D. D., its first Bishop, was consecrated October 30, 1853.

Jacques Cartier, a French navigator, who had been intrusted, as we have already seen, by Francis the First, with the command of an expedition to explore the western hemisphere, was, probably, the first European whose eye ever rested on the mountains of Vermont. On the second day of October, 1535, he arrived with a few volunteers at an Indian settlement called Hochelaga, which was afterwards called Mount Royal, whence the present name Montreal. Donnacona, an Algonkin Chief, conducted him to the summit of Mount Royal, which towered above the settlement, and showed him, " in that bright October sun," the country for many miles south and east, and told him of great rivers and inland seas, and of smaller rivers and lakes penetrating a beautiful territory belonging to the warlike Iroquois. These Indians had settlements in the interior of the State now called Vermont, but whose earlier name was Iroquoisia.

Many years afterward, Samuel de Champlain, accompanied by several friendly Hurons, proceeded to the locality described by Cartier, and on the Fourth day of July, 1609, entered the lake which, to this day, is known by his name.

For more than a century Lake Champlain was claimed by the French. French names were given to its rivers and islands, which they still retain. French seigniories covering the borders of the lake, and occupying eligible spots on both shores, were actually mapped out, granted, and named after their respective French proprietors.*

The Isle La Motte, in the County of Grand Isle, has the honor of being the first point within the limits of Vermont where a civilized establishment and occupancy were commenced. In 1664, M. De Tracy, then Governor of La Nouvelle France, or Canada, entered upon the work of erecting a line of fortifications from the mouth of the Richelieu (Sorel) River into Lake Champlain. The first year he constructed three forts upon the river; and the next spring — 1665 — he ordered Capt. De La Motte to proceed up Lake Champlain, and erect another fortress upon an island, which he had designated. It was completed that same year, and named after the mother of the Blessed Virgin, Fort St. Ann. The name of the island upon which the fort was erected took the name of the builder, and has been known ever since as the Isle La Motte.

* G. F. Houghton, Esq. Vermont Gazetteer. Franklin Co., vol. ii. p. 89.

This fortress, the remains of which are still to be seen, was not only built, but occupied, doubtless, for a long period of years by the French as a garrison; and the island itself was occupied by them for near a century.

We have not at hand the names of those Reverend Fathers, who, as chaplains, officiated at those garrisons of other days, or spent their lives among the aborigines of the forest. They, however, toiled not for worldly renown; they served not a Master subject to death; they have gone to their rest. It is gratifying. notwithstanding, to remark, that the holy Sacrifice of mass they offered is still perpetuated; that the Isle La Motte has, at this day, her consecrated altar and devout worshippers of French and Irish ancestry, and descendants of those who fought and bled for the liberty, peace, and plenty we enjoy.

Missions throughout the State.

From the Baptismal Register of the Church in Boston, we learn that in 1815 Rev. Dr. Matignon visited Burlington, and that all who were apprised of his visit assembled from the neighboring districts, being mostly French Canadians, to whom he administered the consolations of religion, and baptized thirteen of their children, from the age of twelve months and upwards.

Subsequent to this visit of Rev. Dr. Matignon,

Burlington, and the northern towns of Vermont, received occasional visits from Very Rev. Father Mignault, the beloved patriarch of Chambly, Canada, who, for years previous to his death, generously fulfilled the office of Vicar General to the Bishop of Boston. The good priest of Plattsburgh also, by permission of the Bishop of New York, was ever ready to attend sick calls on the Vermont side of Lake Champlain.

In the spring of 1821, at the earnest solicitation of Messrs. White and Nichols, of Vergennes, converts to the faith, and a few other devout souls, Right Rev. Dr. De Cheverus commissioned Rev. Paul McQuade to attend the Catholic residents of this part of the State. Having selected Vergennes as the centre of his mission, he visited Burlington, Middlebury, and other neighboring towns, and returned to Boston in the fall of the same year. A private room in the house of Mr. White, on the border of Otter Creek, twelve by fourteen feet, was then amply sufficient for altar, priest, and congregation.

The next account we have of any clerical visit throughout the State was in 1829. The end accomplished, for which the Missionary had been sent to the Passamaquoddy tribe of Indians in Maine, that is, next to the immediate object had in view, which was affording spiritual advice and encouragement to those devoted Christians of the forest, the reading a valedictory to a certain Puritan minister, who, uninvited, had taken up his residence in the neighborhood, and, in the character of school teacher, was attempting proselytism among the Indian youth; this end accomplished, his next commission was to look after the spiritual wants of the faithful spread over the State of Vermont. Several months were spent on this tour, administering the sacraments, hearing confessions, and wherever favorable opportunity presented, and one or more Catholic families could be found, offering the holy Sacrifice of mass, and preaching, not only to those of the household of faith, but those who were not thus peculiarly blessed, at one time in the village school-house, at another in the Town House, and occasionally, where liberality permitted, in the meeting-house, and not unfrequently where a Catholic had never been seen, much less a living Catholic priest!

The method pursued on such occasions, and that which seldom failed to secure attention and favorable hearing, was to invite the minister, elder, or deacon, if either was present, or if absent, some one of the audience, to select a portion of the Scripture that might be deemed advisable to hear expounded in a Catholic sense, or any other doctrinal subject that might be thought instructive or interesting. The kindliest feeling and attention was generally evinced, and stranger as the Missionary was, would be invited by some one of the audience to lunch with him before the evening discourse. On such occasions, a slice of pie and cheese and a mug of cider, and sociable conversation, made up the repast, for there was guileless honesty in those days, and the criminality of a mug of cider had not amounted to a penal offence. Exceptions there were, it is true, but the " Green Mountain Boys" ever seemed, from some cause or other, more open-hearted, courteous and obliging, more like the descendants of patriarchal society, than citizens of certain other States.

As far as learned, there were then residing at Pittsford about sixty Catholics, at Middlebury, thirty-seven, at Castleton, thirty, Poultney, twenty-one, at Wallingford, fourteen, at Tinmouth, fifteen, at Dorset, eleven, at Bennington, forty-eight, at Windsor and Shrewsbury, very few, as in the last place mentioned there was but one baptism.

BURLINGTON.

Learning the spiritual destitution of the faithful thus dispersed over the State, Bishop Fenwick, in the absence of so much as a priest to accompany him, made, in 1830, a tour of the northern part of the State; on which occasion he offered the holy Sacrifice of the mass at the private residence of Mr. Nichols, of Vergennes, where, having instructed, he administered the Sacrament of Confirmation to six persons. Continuing his journey, he said mass and preached at Burlington, both in French and English, in the hall of Mr. Howard's Hotel, where he likewise confirmed those whom he instructed, six in number; at which visit, finding several English-speaking as well as French Canadian Catholics, he encouraged the erection of a church.

Rev. Jeremiah O'Callaghan, a venerable clergyman, formerly of the city of Cork, Ireland, having been affiliated to the diocese, was appointed, soon after the Bishop's tour, to attend the spiritual wants of the faithful dispersed throughout the State, and to erect the much needed church at Burlington; this he in time accomplished, on land, a portion of five acres, which had been presented the Catholics for their sole use by one of Burlington's noble-hearted citizens, though not a member of the Church at the time, Colonel Hyde, but for which generous deed he subsequently received the gift of holy faith, — so true the remark, that love for God and charity towards our neighbor receives its hundred-fold reward.

The church erected was a neat little structure, with its tower and cross, measuring fifty by thirty-six feet, which was blessed by the Bishop, assisted by Very Rev. Fr. Mignault, of Chambly, and the pastor, September 9, 1832. The choir on the occasion, composed of French Canadians, performed their part passably well, all things considered, while the Bishop administered the Sacrament of Confirmation to twenty-seven persons. On the same day there were twenty-five children baptized, who were mostly of Canadian parentage, and belonged to the city or adjacent towns.

While Rev. Fr. O'Callaghan was visiting other parts of the State, the English-speaking portion of the congregation of Burlington were attended by Rev. John Brady and such other clergymen as the Bishop had at command, while Rev. Fr. Petithomme officiated for the French Canadians from May 21, 1834, till his appointment to the Indian mission of Maine, October 12, 1835.

The above little church was, from some cause or other, never satisfactorily explained, consumed by fire in the month of May, 1838. Soon, however, a new, more ornate, and spacious brick edifice was erected in another part of the city, which, under the title of St. Peter's, was dedicated to God, October 3, 1841. At its dedication, Bishop Fenwick was assisted by the venerable Bishop Janson, of Nancy, France, who was at the time giving missions, or spiritual retreats, in Canada, and who, in the benevolence of his great and generous heart, came, accompanied by Rev. M. L'Abbé and Rev. M. St. Germain, of St. Lawrence, to prepare the Canadian portion of the congregation for the reception of the sacraments on the joyful occasion.

Rev. Fr. O'Callaghan having had the entire charge of the rising congregations throughout the State till 1834, he was relieved in part by the appointment of Rev. J. A. Walsh to its southern portion, where he labored till 1835. He was succeeded, in 1837, by Rev. John B. Daley, who, in 1839, superintended the erection of the neat brick church, measuring sixty by forty feet, in Middlebury, which, with other stations, he attended till the consecration of Right Rev. Dr. Goesbriand.

St. Albans.

Leaving Burlington, Bishop Fenwick, accompanied by Rev. George Goodwin, repaired to St. Albans, and, at a temporary altar improvised for the occasion in the Town House, offered the holy Sacrifice of mass, and preached in French and English, as the audience, as at Burlington, were of different nationalities.

In the second volume of Vermont Gazetteer by Miss Hemenway, page 338, et seq., there is the following very interesting paper by Mrs. B. H. Smalley, which, though in its dates and details extend beyond what is contemplated in our early sketches of the Church, is so very interesting that we copy the article entire: —

When Rev. J. O'Callaghan came as Missionary to Vermont, and established his residence at Burlington, he found a few families of Irish and Canadian Catholics in St. Albans and vicinity, to whom he ministered at stated intervals until Rev. William Ivers undertook the charge some time in 1841. At this period the numbers of those professing the faith had increased to such an extent, through immigration from Ireland and Canada, that the congregation assembling at St. Albans, and gathered partly from the neighboring towns, amounted to one thousand; while there were several other congregations, more or less numerous, in different parts of Franklin County, for whose wants the most diligent ministrations of one Missionary were scarcely adequate. In 1842 an effort was made, under the suggestion of Fr. Ivers, to purchase land and build a church in some central location in or near the village of St. Albans, for the accommodation of the rapidly increasing congregation. The means of the people were found to be wholly inadequate, however, to the accomplishment of the undertaking, and it was abandoned. Not long after Rev. Fr. Ivers left, and the mission was again dependent upon the occasional visits of Rev. Fr. O'Callaghan, whose faithful services in Vermont have caused his memory to be held in veneration by every Catholic within her borders.

In July, 1846, Mr. William H. Hoyt and his family embraced the Catholic faith. He had been for some years the Protestant Episcopal clergyman of St. Albans, and was very much respected and beloved.

In June, 1847, Rev. George A. Hamilton came to St. Albans, and remained in charge of the Catholic congregation until January, 1850, when he was removed to Milford, Mass., and subsequently to Charlestown, where he has since erected, on the summit of Bunker Hill, one of the finest church edifices in New England. During the period of his residence at St. Albans his flock was largely increased by the immigration of many from other parts of the State and from foreign lands, and by the conversion of a number of Protestants to the Catholic faith, among whom may be mentioned the late G. G. Smith and his family; Hon. L. B. Hunt, with his wife, and, at a later period, his second wife, with her daughter; B. H. Smalley, Esq., a well-known lawyer of Franklin

County, with his sister, Miss Laura P. Smalley, and his whole family, as well as his mother-in-law, Mrs. Cynthia Penniman, widow of the late Dr. Jabez Penniman, of Colchester, and whose first husband was E. Marvin, son of Dr. Ebenezer Marvin, of Franklin.

In May, 1848, Rev. Henry Lennon, but just ordained to the priesthood, came to St. Albans, and remained a few months, assisting Father Hamilton. The climate of Vermont proving prejudicial to his health, he returned to Boston, and was soon after stationed at Newburyport, Mass., where his labors proved eminently successful. He was a young clergyman of extraordinary acquirements and eloquence.

In 1848, a lot of land, with a dwelling-house, barn, and orchard upon it, was procured for the Catholics of St. Albans, as a site for the church edifice which they had in contemplation to erect. The dwelling-house stood where the church is now located. It was removed to the present location of the priest's residence, and fitted up to serve as a temporary church while the new one was in the course of erection, and afterwards changed to a dwelling-house again; after which time it was occupied as the residence of the priest, until the present building was erected in its stead. The corner-stone of the proposed new church was laid in August, 1849, by Bishop McClosky, then of Albany, N. Y., now Archbishop of New York.

When, in January, 1850, Rev. Fr. Hamilton left Vermont, he was succeeded by Rev. T. Shahan, who had been admitted to the priesthood but a short time previously, and who left in August of the same year, Rev. E. McGowan taking his place at St. Albans.

Since the erection of Vermont into a See, Bishop De Goesbriand has seen the church edifice of St. Albans completed and dedicated to God, and placed under the auspices of Mary Immaculate.

The amiable writer to whom we are indebted for the above particulars of the establishment of the church at St. Albans, herself, by the grace of God, a convert to Catholicity, concludes her interesting report by observing that a large proportion of the congregation which assemble in this place is composed of young people, — descendants of Catholics from abroad, — who were born and brought up on the soil, and who will compare very favorably with any class descended from Americans for native intelligence, education, industry, morality, and piety, while in physical power and endurance they are greatly superior. The bitter prejudices, created and fostered by the rancorous partisans of the most *un*-American of all our parties, which styled itself, *par excellence*, *the* American party, have been proved to be cruelly unjust, and the experience of the country during the past war has abundantly demonstrated that the foreign Catholic population, and their descendants, so far from forming a dangerous element in our society, are, in fact, among its best and most reliable safeguards. Instructed by a clergy who abstain from all interference in political matters, except to admonish their people diligently of their duty to be subject to their rulers in all obedience; taught by the bitter experiences of oppression abroad the value of free and liberal institutions here, and unbiassed by the temptations of ambition, — which, unfortunately, lure too many of our fellow-citizens from the paths of rectitude and duty, in quest of office, — they are not to be outdone by any class in the practice of the social and domestic virtues, or in the exercise of true patriotism.

This persuasion, — the Catholic, — writes Thompson, in his turn, a candid Protestant author of Vermont, with the exception of a few native converts, owes its astonishing increase to the annual immigration that crosses the Atlantic from the mother country. When they first arrive, they are exposed to that prejudice and obloquy which invariably attend a stranger in a foreign land; but the good sense and discrimination of the Americans soon discover them to be a sober, industrious, and hard-laboring people, who, having passed through the ordeal of persecution at home, come prepared to appreciate and sustain the free laws and institutions of our republic. The greatest part of them have embarked upon the current of temperance, and are most faithful observers of the pledge. Many of them have purchased farms in different parts of the State, where they are doing well, are accumulating property, and making an important addition to the population and strength of the country.

Before leaving the pleasant and flourishing village of St. Albans, we must invite the reader, says the

Gazetteer, to look into its cemetery. There, not far from the entrance, stand three headstones in a line, large and white, with a garland and cross upon the marble, — the graves of three sisters, whose memories have been embalmed in that interesting volume of Mrs. Smalley, " The Young Converts, or the Three Sisters."

Debbie, Helen, and Anna Barlow were the daughters of Hon. Bradley Barlow, a man of wealth and influence in the county. Debbie reads a book that leads to the investigation of the grave claims of Catholic theology, becomes the earnest young convert, whom nothing can turn back, goes straight forward on; beautiful Helen follows her serene, persevering steps, and Anna follows Helen. The three are as sisters on the forehead of the morning. As the earliest sister-cluster of flowers of the Catholic faith in Vermont, these young lives have an interest, religious and historical, as one by one they transmute and pass away, as seen on the pages of the pleasing book referred to above.

A little farther on is the grave of the Smith sisters. Mr. G. G. Smith and wife, and five children, were received into the Catholic Church about 1848. They had previously buried their three eldest children while very young, and soon after they laid one of the remaining five here. Mr. Smith died next, leaving his wife, two sons, and two daughters, Frances and Sarah. Sarah first began to show symptoms of decline. The gentle Frances, says her biographer, as she had done all her sweet life, followed Sarah,

Sarah keeping about the same distance in advance; but as she entered every lane that leads down the dark valley, she looked back for Frances, and Frances desired to overtake Sarah. It seemed they could not be separated, and both so desired to go together to God. It is said they asked it, in their communions and their prayers, if such was pleasing to their heavenly Father. It was a sight that interested all around — two lovely village girls, who had grown up in their midst into young womanhood, fading, as a double rainbow in a summer sky. A few weeks before they died, a young lady friend, soon to be married, brought in her trousseau, to let these sisters see it. They had been her young friends and schoolmates. These dear sisters looked at the rich dress stuffs, the beautiful lace work, the lovely flowers. They pronounced everything pretty, very pretty, beautiful. It was sweet to see what an artless interest they took in it all. But when they had examined and innocently enjoyed all, said Frances, turning, with a bright smile, to Sarah, " But, Sada, we wouldn't exchange with her for the world; would we?" "O, no," said Sarah, the same bright look communicated to her face. It was thought Frances might yet live some days when Sarah was taken in her agony. Frances, who at once desired to be brought to her room, sat supported by her bedside, and encouraged her. Such was her love. She was jealous for her sister, lest she should, in the greatness of her sufferings, by but one moment's impatience dim the brightness of her sacrifice. It was a tender dying bed, upon which one sister lay in the last struggle, and by which another sat, that light in her eyes, and whiteness in her face — she was sure to go soon.

Sarah died about midnight. Frances was carried back to her room, and died at ten o'clock the next morning. It was talked, among the Catholics, that Sarah, upon first entering the spirit world, had besought this favor. They were buried in one grave, and one coffin. Robed in blue silk, they lay within each other's arms, in the double casket, the hair of Frances, rich and sun-hued, gathered back from her gleaming white forehead, scarcely more serene than in life. Sarah, who had had more changes and beauty, nestled with her face towards her sister, now very still and white. It was, perhaps, the most interesting picture of death the village had ever witnessed — two young sisters, between the ages of nineteen and twenty-two. Both had, in dying, received the sacraments of their religion. The Bishop of the diocese, who was present at their funeral, spoke of these young women as having given all their talents always to the Church, — by their voices having assisted in the choir, and Frances as organist. They died in the summer of 1866.

MISSIONS CONNECTED WITH ST. ALBANS. — When Rev. Fr. Ivers had charge at St. Albans, there were, according to his report, at Berkshire and vicinity, about one hundred members of the Church; at Troy and neighborhood, about the same number; and at St. Johnsbury, Peacham, and Danville, about eighty.

Church at Middlebury.

Soon after the appointment of Rev. Fr. O'Callaghan to look after the spiritual interests of the faithful throughout the State, he visited Middlebury, and had divine service in some one of the most convenient houses of the infant congregation. These his visits were made as often as circumstances permitted, till the arrival of Rev. James Walsh, in 1834, at which time the State was divided into two distinct missions. John B. Daly, in 1837, having been appointed successor to Fr. Walsh, and the congregation at Middlebury having so far increased in numbers as to warrant the undertaking, erected, in 1839, a neat brick church edifice, measuring sixty by forty feet, in which he continued to officiate till, in 1853, the State was erected into an Episcopal See.

Church at Castleton.

Few were the churches in Vermont previous to the consecration of Right Rev. Bishop Goesbriand. At Castleton, a private dwelling of eighteen by thirty feet, with a small lot of land connected with it, had been secured as early as 1837, which served as a temporary chapel for the infant congregation at the time.

Rev. Father Daly, in the report of his missions,

states that at Brandon, Pittsford, Shrewsbury, Rutland, and Wallingford, there were about four hundred Catholics; and about an equal number scattered between Woodstock, Plymouth, Windsor, and Rockingham, and at Bennington one hundred and fifty.

Church at Swanton.

Apart from the traditional story of a church having been erected, over a century ago, at the former Indian village on the Highgate bank of the Missisquoi River, on land now improved by A. H. Brooks, where relics of a religious character have been from time to time turned up by the plough, some of which we have seen, and in connection with the probable site of the church, the foundations of which were formerly more distinct than at present, — a few stones of which we gather, as a pious memento, — the Sacrifice of Mass offered at a later period by Rev. Father McGillon, of Plattsburgh, was at the house of Mr. James McNally, in the village of Swanton.

Encouraged by this visit of a clergyman among them, the faithful, small as were their numbers, concluded to build a church, where they might assemble on Sundays for prayer and mutual edification, and in the fond hope that at some future day their Bishop would be enabled to provide them, at least occasionally, with the services of a clergyman. Messrs. James and Henry McNally, Charles O'Kane, Frederick Arnault, James Birney, and a few others, were the prime movers in this enterprise. Mr. James McNally gave land for the purpose, and a portion of the materials, while the rest contributed equally, according to their means, and in a few months, to their delight, a neat little brick edifice of thirty by forty feet was erected. Here, in 1836, Rev. Fr. O'Callaghan offered the holy Sacrifice of Mass, which he, as circumstances permitted, continued to do till the appointment of other clergymen. Here, Rev. Messrs. Le Claire, Waters, Ivers, and Hamilton officiated; and the last-mentioned Reverend Father, seeing the church eventually finished and beautified, dedicated it to God, and assigned to it the name of the Nativity of the Blessed Virgin.

This building, to the deep regret of the congregation, was, on the Eve of Christmas, 1858, accidentally burned down from an overheated stove, unattended, in the vestry. The pastor, however, Rev. J. L. Cam, who had charge of the congregation at the time, numbering five hundred souls, soon commenced another, the present beautifully-proportioned Gothic structure, which is also of brick, seventy-two by forty feet, which, since its completion, and contracts settled, has been consecrated, and, like the first little edifice, bears the title of the Nativity of the Blessed Virgin.

While small was thus the grain of mustard-seed scattered over the soil of Vermont but a few years ago, consoling must it be, as well as cheering to the heart of its first Bishop, and to every fond lover of Holy Church, to contemplate the spread of Catholicity, as seen in the subjoined brief summary of the present state of the Diocese, eighteen years from its establishment, in which there are, besides its splendid Gothic Cathedral at Burlington, near fifty churches, twenty-eight priests, and ten clerical students; its orphan asylum, and many little ones so maternally cared for; its academies, its select schools, its free schools, and its thirty-four thousand Catholic population!

While it is our province to sketch the early state of events, cheering will be the labor of the ecclesiastical historian who, fifty years hence, will be called upon to write the progress of Catholicity in the Diocese of Burlington, the State of Vermont.

DIOCESE OF PORTLAND,

Embracing the States of Maine and New Hampshire.

This Diocese was established in 1855. Right Rev. Dr. D. W. Bacon, its first Bishop, was consecrated the 22d of April, the same year.

Having already spoken of the early Missionaries and their apostolic labors among the aborigines of Maine, we will here introduce an account of the first visit made to this part of his diocese, by the successor of Bishop De Cheverus, Right Rev. Dr. Fenwick; and as amidst his manifold and arduous labors he found time to minute in his journal, day by day, from the time he came to Boston until the fourth day before his death, such incidents as he deemed worthy of note, and as the reader cannot be otherwise than interested in all that relates to the religious improvements of those children of the forest, who are so fast disappearing from among us, we will quote the Bishop's manuscript for July, 1827, nearly word for word.

"I had scarcely landed," says the Bishop, at his arrival at Eastport, " when I saw a number of Indians, of both sexes of the Passamaquoddy tribe, who had just left their canoes, and were going up to one of the stores to trade. A perfect stranger in the town, I accosted one of the Indians, and requested him to show me the way. He paid no attention to my request, and proceeded on. I then addressed myself to another, whom I perceived just crossing the street. He stopped for a while, looked steadfastly at me, then shook his head and left me. I soon recollected that I had seen at Boston, the year before, an Indian of the tribe, whose name was Saco-Bason — James Vincent. I made up to a group of Indians, and inquired whether he had come to town. One of them answered in broken English, and informed me he had, and would go and look for him. He returned soon after with Saco-Bason, who immediately recognized me. The news of my arrival soon spread through the town. I informed Saco-Bason that my intention was to repair to Pleasant Point, their village, without delay, and wished him to acquaint his brethren with it. He promised me to notify them, and stated that he would himself shortly return home, and in the afternoon come again with several canoes to conduct me to it. He then led me to the house of Mr. Jeremiah Kelly, a respectable Catholic of Eastport, where I found Rev. Mr. Ffrench, whom I had sent to this town the preceding year. After making some inquiry into the state of religion at Eastport and the adjoining country, I requested him to accompany me to Pleasant Point, whither it was my intention to proceed immediately, in order to assist me in preparing the Indians and their children for the Sacrament of Confirmation, and of the Holy Eucharist. In the afternoon, as it had been arranged, the Indians, who were to conduct me to their village, arrived, in four bark canoes, with the Lieutenant Governor at their head. They were dressed in full costume of their nation, and in the gayest apparel. On entering the parlor, each of them alternately advanced and kissed my hand respectfully, and after a short conversation invited me to their canoes. The afternoon was pleasant, and we set out. The distance from Eastport to Pleasant Point does not exceed six or seven miles. On reaching the wharf, I was invited to take my seat in the middle of a large and beautiful canoe, which was paddled by Saco-Bason in front and another Indian in the rear. Rev. Mr. Ffrench, with two Indians, occupied another canoe. Our baggage was conveyed in the two remaining ones, which followed behind. We had scarcely put off from shore, when each of the Indians struck fire and lighted his pipe; a matter, it would seem, quite indispensable with them, for so great is their attachment to the pipe, that they would sooner, on some occasions, as they acknowledged to me, go without their dinner. When we had reached a point of land from which their village could be seen, a salute was fired with their carabines, which was answered from the village by a discharge as well of carabines as of a six-pounder, which they had mounted for the purpose of economy. A flag, bearing a red cross, on a white ground, was also hoisted. This firing continued without intermission until the canoes reached the shore. On arriving, the whole population flocked to the landing, with the

Governor, a venerable old man, at their head, to welcome me. He addressed me in tolerable good French, which he must have learnt in Canada, and expressed the liveliest joy at seeing once more a Bishop before he died. He knelt down, and received my blessing, which I also gave to all the others who had equally placed themselves on their knees to receive it.

"From the landing we proceeded to the church, where, after offering up a prayer, I expressed to them my happiness at being among them for the purpose of affording them the benefits of their religion. I then caused all the children above eight years of age, as well as those among the adults, who had not yet been confirmed, to be paraded before me, and inquiry to be made how many among them were sufficiently instructed to be admitted to the Sacrament of Confirmation. I had already been apprised that Rev. Mr. Ffrench had made frequent visits during the last two months, and had during that time taken pains to instruct them. I accordingly directed him to assist me in hearing the confessions of all those whom he should deem sufficiently instructed, and in otherwise preparing them for confirmation, which I intended to confer the following day.

"Sunday, July 15th, I said mass in the Indian church at eight o'clock; all the Passamaquoddy's were present. At eleven o'clock a solemn procession was formed to the church, which was composed of the whole tribe. As soon as it began to move, preceded by the cross bearer, the Indians who followed in it intoned a hymn in their own language, which was sung with enthusiasm by all the others. When it had arrived at the church, Rev. Mr. Ffrench began the *Asperges*. Mass was afterwards sang according to the notes of M. Dumont in his *Missa-regia*, with a precision which would have done honor to many of the choirs of Europe.

"A number of Protestants from Eastport and the adjacent country were present, attracted by the arrival of the Bishop. They conducted themselves with great propriety in the church; indeed, the behavior of the Indians themselves in the house of God was well calculated to inspire respect, as they never looked either to the right or to the left while there, and during the whole time of the celebration of the divine mysteries they appeared absorbed in the contemplation of what passed before them at the altar. At the end of mass I delivered a discourse to the Protestants present, in which I expounded the principal mysteries of our holy religion, and pointed out its superior excellence over other religions. The leading points of my discourse I caused to be interpreted to the Indians who did not understand English. I afterwards addressed myself particularly to the young Indians and those adults who were about to be confirmed, and endeavored to impress upon them the dispositions essentially requisite to receive Confirmation worthily; and at length proceeded to administer this sacrament to all those who were sufficiently instructed and prepared to receive it; several of them had already been admitted to holy communion at the early mass in the morning. After the solemn benediction, which I gave them at the conclusion, we left the church in the same order in which we had come, and returned to the village. In the afternoon, at four o'clock, Vespers were sung, in which the Indians acquitted themselves fully as well as in the forenoon, thanks to the good Missionary, their former pastor, who had so well instructed them. After vespers they recited their ordinary prayers for the evening, and then retired quietly to their cabins.

"July 16th. I again said mass at eight o'clock, after which we repaired, in procession, to the burying-ground, where I performed the usual service on the graves of those who had departed this life since the last visit of a priest.

"July 17th. I said mass at seven o'clock; all the Indians assisted at it. I again gave confirmation to those who had hitherto not been able to prepare for it, and among others to the son of an Indian named Stanislaus. So great was the desire of this good Indian to have his son confirmed, although confined to his bed at home by a violent fever, he, with the aid of some of his friends, conveyed the bed, with the youth sixteen years lying thereon, to the church in the midst of the ceremony. His ardent zeal edified me; but I was fearful that such an exertion, with the exposure, might prove finally prejudicial to the youth. He had, however, received the last sacraments the morning before, and was well disposed. I confirmed him with the others, to the very great joy of his father. After breakfast, which consisted of the ordinary diet of the Indians, I took the census of the tribe, and found that the entire population amounted to four hundred and fifty souls. About fifteen or twenty individuals were said to be absent at the time.

"In the afternoon I visited again the Indians in their cabins, and spent a little longer time with them, especially with the old and infirm. I went also to see the sick youth whom I had confirmed in the morning, and whom I found extremely low, his fever having considerably increased. I conversed a short time with him, and found him in the happiest dispositions. As he had received all the sacraments, I had nothing more to do than exhort him to submit with patience to the will of God.

"July 18th. I said mass at six o'clock. The whole tribe attended as on Sunday. Those Indians who composed the choir sang during the whole time of the celebration a number of hymns in their tongue. I addressed them in a short discourse, through their interpreter, to remain faithful to their duties to God, their neighbors, and to themselves, and especially to remain constantly attached to their holy religion, and live in union and charity with one another. I informed them that it was my intention to leave them to-day, in order to go to their brethren, the Penobscots, for whom I felt the same solicitude, and requested them to offer up their prayers to God for the success of my voyage."

At Old Town, the residence of the Penobscot tribe, the Bishop said mass, preached, and confirmed those who had been prepared by Rev. Father Barber, S. J., who was then with them.

The Bishop, after his first visit to these devoted children of the forest, became most anxious to procure a Missionary who would reside among them, and as English was not needed, he appealed to the Association for the Propagation of the Faith.*

While awaiting an answer to his earnest petition, the author of these Sketches, having been ordained, was sent among them, and he would add one or two instances of his reminiscences in illustration of the religious habits, as well as of the faith and piety, of these devoted Christians.

As winter approaches, it is customary with the Indians, before entering the forest in pursuit of game, to provide themselves with calendars, or a species of almanac, which have been previously prepared, wherein the days of the week, the Sundays, and whatever festivals are likely to occur before their return in the spring, are noted. A pin-mark denotes the day and date of their departure from the village, and this being moved forward daily, they know, in the depth of the forest, each day of the week and month, and whatever festival of obligation may occur, as well as those who hear it announced from the sanctuary every Sunday. As Saturday, or the vigil of any festival of obligation approaches, they prepare their encampment, provide fuel, and make all other necessary arrangements preparatory for sanctifying the

* See his interesting letter, Annales, v. 447-480.

approaching great day, which our Lord and His Church command to be kept holy. To fell a tree or chop wood, to hunt or use the rifle, should a moose, bear, or deer pass their camp on such days, would be considered derogatory to their Christian duty, a burden on their conscience, and be recalled on the next occasion of confession. At a given signal, all who are of the party in the forest assemble for prayer, at which they sing in unison the Kyrie, Gloria, Credo, Sanctus, and Agnus, of the Missa-regia, hymns, and so forth. Upon their return home in the spring of the year, they all, with true Christian piety, approach the sacraments of Penance and the Eucharist, seeking forgiveness for any faults committed during their absence, and the divine assistance to persevere in their good resolutions.

Among other edifying traits that might be mentioned, illustrating the practical idea they have of sin in general, which they understand, as taught in their catechism, to be any violation or transgression of the law of God, in thought, word, or deed, we will mention one, simple, as perhaps it may be considered by some.

Two women, towards the close of the week, were doing up their family washing at a little brook which runs through the village. Something rather tart, incidentally said by one, roused so far the feelings of the other, that, on the spur of the moment, in retaliation, she gave her a dash of the towel just at hand! Reflection on the impropriety of what they had done, as not unfrequently happens, came afterwards. The next day being Sunday, and obligated to hear mass, apprehensive that others, and perhaps children, had seen or heard of their unchristian-like behavior, neither one nor the other would enter the church, — the house of God, — but, prompted alike by remorse of conscience, they prostrated themselves at the door, imploring the prayers of those who entered, that God would pardon any scandal or bad example given.

Parents thus solicitous for their own salvation, must needs be blessed in their children; and so, indeed, are those devoted Christians of the forest. Not only are children taught their *morning*, as well as evening prayers, but every other Christian duty, and evince their gratitude for all favors received from the Giver of all. Often is a little one seen coming out of the wigwam, with a crust of bread in his hand, but never is he seen to take the first morsel, nor to dip his tiny birch bowl into the spring, without having first made the sign of the cross, and asked God's blessing. Such, we have witnessed, is their Christian teaching, faith, and morals.

In his appeal to the "Association for the Propagation of the Faith," the efforts of the Bishop were crowned with success. Before his next visit, the Penobscots had a resident missionary, and showed how much good they had gained by his presence. A beautiful church, with its towering steeple, and a neat parsonage, had replaced Father Romagné's hut. The cabins of the Indians, in many instances, too, were replaced by neatly-painted cottages, and an air of comfort pervaded all the settlement. After administering Confirmation, the Bishop dedicated the church in honor of St. Ann, the patroness of the tribe.

Upon the arrival of the missionaries, Rev. Messrs. Edmund Demilier and Petithomme, finding but one Penobscot able to speak French, they commenced the study of the native language, Demilier at the villages, Petithomme in their winter camp. They continued their mission with great profit, and, early in 1834, the Bishop, in possession of a manuscript prayer-book of Fr. Romagné, had it printed, and thus facilitated the labors of the missionary school.

Rev. Fr. Petithomme, receiving subsequently another destination, Fr. Demilier was left alone. His study of the language was most successful. He was soon able to confess his penitents in Abnaki, and when the Bishop next visited the mission, he could not withhold the expression of his astonishment at the facility with which the Father preached in his newly-acquired language. Turning his knowledge to account, Father Demilier drew up a new prayer-book, and translated also the Quebec catechism.

Notwithstanding the insignificance of his mission in numbers, Fr. Demilier devoted himself to it without a murmur till his death, on the 23d of July, 1843, when his flock lost a kind and self-sacrificing pastor.

In connection with what has been said of the Abnaki, their conversion, faith, and piety, and the devotedness of those self-sacrificing missionaries who have lived or died among them, we will add a short account of the monument erected to that illustrious martyred priest, Father Rale.

Memorial of Rev. Father Rale.

Right Rev. Bishop Fenwick purchased the site of the ancient village where once stood the church of this illustrious martyred priest. The following communication, written about the time the monument was erected, August 23, 1833, will explain the event: —

"The ancient village of Naurantsonak, — now called Norridgewock, — that is, the place where the Indian village of this name formerly stood, is situated on the Kennebec River, five miles above the present village of Norridgewock. The site of the monument is on the edge of the town of Madison, a little above, and nearly opposite the place where Sandy River empties into the Kennebec, and immediately adjoining Norridgewock. This ancient Indian village was situated on a beautiful plain, surrounded by high hills, extending a quarter of a mile on the eastern bank of the river, and as far as the bend. The cabins of the Indians were constructed in parallel lines along the plain running north and south, leaving a common road on the bank of the river the whole length of the village, and having besides a street two hundred feet in width, running between the rows of cabins, in the same direction. The church was erected towards the southern extremity, with the principal entrance on the street, and the altar to the east. The residence of Father Rale adjoined the sacristy, which stood also to the east. It was here this great and good man lived, surrounded by his flock, all of whom he had converted to the faith from among the Abnaki tribes during the thirty odd years which he had spent among them.

"The lot of land purchased by the Bishop for the monument includes the whole space formerly occupied by the church, with the sacristy, and the residence of Father Rale. It consists of an acre of ground, with an outlet, of sufficient width for a carriage, to the main county road. The situation is extremely beautiful, having a delightful prospect, as well of the river as of the surrounding country.

"The Bishop was accompanied to the spot on the morning of the twenty-third, by the Rev. Messrs. Ffrench, of Portland, and Conway, of Indian Old Town, who came, accompanied with eighteen Indians, to assist at the ceremony on this memorable day, the anniversary of the massacre of Father Rale and his neophytes. The object of the Bishop was to have a Solemn Mass celebrated on the spot, and a funeral service performed for the benefit of the Indians who were slain on this day in the year seventeen hundred and twenty-four.

"The morning opened beautifully. The Bishop repaired to the spot at nine o'clock. Already an immense multitude had assembled from the adjacent country. In an hour after, there could not be less than five thousand persons present. The roads in every direction were still crowded with men, women, and children, all flocking to the same spot. At half past ten o'clock the service began. Rev. Fr. Ffrench was appointed to celebrate Mass, the Indians to perform the duty of the Choir, and the Bishop was the orator on the occasion. At this time the curiosity of the multitude assembled was intense. Some ascended the trees that surrounded the Altar, while others pressed forward, regardless of every barrier that was raised before them. Others, mounted upon wagons and vehicles of every name, drove their horses into the ranks, which were instantly filled by the people who had been displaced, in spite of every remonstrance of the proprietors. Others, again, unable to see over the immense concourse that stood in their way, which now formed one dense, consolidated mass, as closely wedged as ever bricks were in a brickkiln, endeavored to climb upon the backs of those outside, that thus they might at least be enabled to see something of what was passing at the Altar. In spite of every annoyance thus occasioned by the extreme anxiety of the people to see, Rev. Fr. Ffrench still proceeded with the celebration of the Mass. The Bishop remained during all this time in the wicker sacristy which had been constructed immediately adjoining the Altar, waiting for the end of the Gospel, that he might address the multitude. In the mean time one of the trees, into which too many had climbed, gave way, when half a dozen individuals, who had ventured too high, were precipitated into the thickest of the throng! Happily no lives were lost, nor was the least injury sustained by any from the falling of the tree. A little confusion, however, as may be conjectured, was produced by the accident, and a degree of anxiety felt for the fate of others who were similarly situated. The greatest annoyance of any that was experienced occurred on the sides and rear of the Altar. Here the Reverend officiating clergyman had much to do to keep the crowd from pressing too near him on his right and left, and to prevent their pulling the boards asunder immediately in front, in the hope of obtaining a better view. His voice was continually heard, reproving and remonstrating, but all in vain. The crowd became at every instant more and more dense, from the continued fresh arrival of others from the country, who also endeavored to press through the ranks, in order to satisfy their curiosity.

"About this time several of the respectable inhabitants of the town, seeing the impossibility of maintaining anything like order so long as the Mass was continued, from the curiosity which it excited, together with the singing of the Indians, came forward and requested the Bishop to advance into the centre of the throng, and address the multitude. The Bishop immediately assented to the proposal, and accordingly presented himself before the people. As soon as it was ascertained that the time for the discourse had arrived, each one gave away, as far as he could, that the Bishop might pass to the place assigned. Here four chairs were placed, and across these two wide boards were laid, so as to form a kind of platform from which to address the multitude.

"The Bishop, as soon as he had ascended this quasi pulpit, requested those who were near him to seat themselves upon the grass, that those who were in the distance might have a better opportunity both of seeing and hearing. This request was immediately complied with. He then called for a pole, which he observed at some distance on the ground, which was no sooner handed to him than, with this supporting himself, he commenced his discourse, in a slow and perfectly composed manner, taking for his text those words of Ecclesiastes, 'The memory of him shall not depart away, and his name shall be in request from generation to generation. Nations shall declare his wisdom, and the Church shall show forth his praise.' His address lasted about an hour, during which the greatest attention was paid by those who were within the reach of his voice. Some who were in the distance manifested their feelings at not being able to get within hearing, while others, in the hope that the voice of the speaker would at last reach them, kept them in a degree of order to the very end.

"As soon as the Bishop had concluded his discourse, the workmen were directed to proceed with the erection of the monument. The base, composed of huge blocks of granite, had been already constructed, so that nothing more was to be done than to raise the shaft, which consisted of one prodigious block, of the same material, and to place it upon its base. This was accomplished in about two hours, and without the least accident, notwithstanding the immense crowd who pressed around during its erection.

"This beautiful monument was erected over the very grave in which Father Rale was interred, and on the very spot where the Altar formerly stood at which he had so often celebrated the adorable Sacrifice of the Mass. In the form of an obelisk, it rose twenty feet from the ground, surmounted with a beautiful cross of the best wrought iron, three feet in height, and to be seen a great distance."

Church at Eastport.

The Bishop, upon his arrival at Eastport, after having visited the Indians of Passamaquoddy and Penobscot, offered the holy Sacrifice of Mass at the private residence of Mr. Kelly, July 20, 1827. In the evening of the same day, by special invitation, he preached in the meeting-house, much to the interest of the audience, principally Protestants, and delight of the Catholics, to eighteen of whom he had that day administered Confirmation.

The church at Eastport, measuring thirty-two by forty feet, was erected by Rev. Fr. Ffrench, in the year 1828, but in the absence of funds, was not completed till some time later. It was subsequently enlarged, during the pastorship of Rev. Mr. Kiernan, and was dedicated and placed under the patronage of St. Joseph at the visit of the Bishop in July, 1835, at which time he administered the Sacrament of Confirmation to fifty-seven children and adults.

Rev. J. B. McMahon, who, in 1841, had charge, and attended the spiritual wants of the Catholics at Eastport and neighboring missions, states in his report that at Eastport there were three hundred and twenty-two souls; Lubec and its environs, two hundred and ninety-five; East Machias, sixty-three; West Machias, one hundred and thirty-nine; Columbia, thirty-five; Prescott, sixty; and at Calais, seventy-seven souls.

The CHURCHES at NEWCASTLE or DAMARISCOTTA, and WHITEFIELD, were built somewhere in the years of 1818 and 1820, and are stations particularly mentioned in the mission days of Right Rev. Dr. De Cheverus. The Rev. Denis Ryan, who seems to have been the first priest appointed, apart from the occasional visits of Father Romagné, was ordained in Boston, May 21, 1817.

CHURCH AT PORTLAND.

In the first tour made to the eastern portion of his vast diocese, during the summer of 1827, Right Rev. Bishop Fenwick offered the holy Sacrifice of the Mass in this city, August 9, in the upper room of a house adjoining the Museum, where the faithful, to the number of one hundred and twenty-five souls, were accustomed to assemble on Sundays for prayer, pious reading, and mutual edification. Edified and encouraged by the lively faith and fervent zeal of this infant congregation, which reminded him so much of the first Christian assembly in the upper room at Jerusalem, he remained here several days, saying mass, preaching, hearing confessions, and instructing those who had never received the Sacrament of Confirmation, to whom, thirteen in number, he subsequently administered it.

Rev. Father Ffrench having been appointed, in connection with other stations attended by him, to look after the spiritual welfare of these devoted Christians of Portland, commenced "questing" for the purpose of building a church, and receiving every encouragement from the Catholics of the place, according to their means, as well as from their fellow-citizens, though not members of the Church, and from Catholics abroad, he began the Church of St. Dominic, a stone building measuring forty by forty-five feet, which was dedicated August 11, 1833, at which time the congregation had increased to the number of two hundred and sixty members. The holy Sacrifice of the Mass was offered by Rev. Fr. McNamee, and the dedication performed by the Bishop, who preached on the occasion, selecting for his text, "I have chosen and have sanctified this place, that my name may be there forever, and my eyes and my heart may remain there perpetually."

The morning services over, Rev. Fr. Ffrench conducted the Bishop and clergy, and particular friends whom he had invited, to a bower in the garden, where dinner was served up, his house being too small to accommodate all invited guests.

In consequence of the small number of priests at

the Bishop's disposal, and Rev. Fr. Ffrench having left for Europe, Portland had a succession of pastors to attend the spiritual wants of the faithful, among whom, in the year 1848, was Rev. Fr. Maguire, who, to accommodate the increased numbers of the congregation, was authorized, by the successor of Bishop Fenwick, Right Rev. Bishop Fitzpatrick, to enlarge the church, which he did by the addition of forty feet.

Previous to his leaving for Europe, Rev. Fr. Ffrench acknowledged his grateful thanks to the generous benefactors of Boston, from whom he had received two thousand nine hundred and twenty-six dollars, which he distributed towards building the church at Dover, eight hundred dollars, Portland, one thousand two hundred and seventeen, Eastport, five hundred and nine, and for land at Saco, four hundred.

Church at Bangor.

The Catholic residents at Bangor and its neighborhood, who, in 1833, were attended by Rev. James Conway, and who at the time numbered one hundred and forty, were accustomed to assemble for divine worship in a hired hall. A lot having at length been secured, the Church of St. Michael, Archangel, was commenced, under the pastorship of Rev. Edward Lynch, in the year 1837, and was dedicated November 10, 1839.

The report of Rev. Thomas O'Sullivan, who was pastor of the congregation in 1842, gives the census of the Catholics at Bangor as one hundred and thirty-five families, at Ellsworth, thirty, at Bucksport, ten, and as scattered, or living in other places, twenty.

Church at Augusta, Hallowell, and Gardiner.

The faithful residing in these towns were, as early as 1836, attended by Rev. Fr. Curtin. Two years later, under the superintendence of Rev. Fr. Ryan, a very respectable building, with its tower, bell, and clock, was erected at Gardiner, and by the Bishop blessed, August 4, 1838, who, at the same time, administered the Sacrament of Confirmation to eighteen persons. In 1841, Augusta and Gardiner were attended by Rev. John O'Beirne.

Church at Augusta.

We learn from the Catholic Observer of July, 1847, that Rev. P. Caraher has erected a beautiful church in Augusta, Me. The building, which measures upwards of sixty feet in length, is of a simple, yet chaste and classic style of architecture, and does much honor to both pastor and people; that the Governor of the

State, the President of the Senate, the Speaker of the House, and many members of the legislature subscribed liberally towards its erection.

Church at Whitefield.

The small frame building, which years previously had been erected for the purpose of divine service, becoming too small for the increased numbers of the faithful, a new brick structure, measuring eighty by fifty feet, was erected by the venerated pastor, Rev. Fr. Ryan, on an elevated site in the centre of the town, and dedicated to God, under the invocation of St. Denis, August 12, 1838, on which joyful occasion the Bishop administered the Sacrament of Confirmation to eighty persons.

Benedicta. — Houlton.

The churches of St. Mary and St. Benedict were erected about the same time, 1835, and were attended successively by Rev. Messrs. Tyler, Conway, and Dougherty.

Church of Claremont, New Hampshire.

The first church in this State was erected by Rev. Virgil Horace Barber, at Claremont, in 1823, and so constructed as to serve the twofold purpose, for divine service and a study hall above, where were taught the higher branches of education.

Rev. Fr. Barber had been a minister of the Protestant Episcopal Church, but, by the grace of God, he, with his wife, son, and daughters, were, in 1816, converted to the One, Holy, Catholic, and Apostolic Church.

Subsequent to their conversion, this devoted couple, actuated by the purest religious motives, and under the impression that they might, for the greater glory of God and welfare of their neighbors, do a large amount of good individually, if at liberty, in imitation of those of whom we read in the early ages of Christianity, after due reflection and mutual consent, separated, the father to prepare for Holy Orders, which he received at the hands of Bishop De Cheverus, December 1, 1822, the mother and daughters to seek in retirement all the spiritual delights of religion; while Samuel, their son, evincing a disposition for religious life, entered Georgetown College, where, having completed his studies, he was ordained, and after years of usefulness, died a holy priest in the Society of Jesus. The mother, Mrs. B., having edified the Community by her exemplary piety, was elected Superior of the religious Order of the Visitation, into which Society one of the daughters equally entered; while the others became members of the Ursuline Community, and were among those who had to fly for their lives at the midnight hour, August 11, 1834, when the infuriated mob destroyed their peaceful home at Mount Benedict, Charlestown, Mass.

The father of Rev. V. H. Barber, Daniel, had also been for many years a Protestant Episcopal minister; he too, with his aged wife, daughter, Rachel, and second son, Israel, were, upon their conversion, received into the Church.

The sister of Rev. Daniel, Mrs. Tyler, and her family, were equally favored about the same time, and to their conversion the Diocese of Hartford became indebted for its first Bishop, Right Rev. William Tyler, and the Sisters of Charity at Emmettsburg for an accession to their numbers in the daughters, who felt called to forsake all else and devote their lives to the care of the poor, the sick, widows, and orphans.

Besides these, there were several other devout converts, who swelled the congregation of the unpretending little church at Claremont; among them, Misses Chase and Alden, who subsequently entered the quiet home with the Misses Barber already mentioned; and one other name we will add, that of Captain Bela Chase and family, whose conversion was prompted by that clause of New Hampshire legislative exclusiveness that forbade a Catholic holding any office, however menial, in the State. Their commendable curiosity to learn the faith and principles of a Church so looked down upon, of a people so despised, led them to look into the approved and authenticated works that teach the true doctrines of Catholicity, and the result was, their discovery of what they were to believe and what to practise, with infallible certitude, to save their souls.

The conversion of Rev. Fr. Barber, we may add, was not without producing the happiest results otherwise, as it led the way to the conversion of Rev. Dr. Keeley, an Episcopal clergyman, and rector of St. George's Chapel, New York, and of George Ironside, a member also of the Episcopal Church, of Rev. Calvin White, of Connecticut, and others.

At the first visit of Bishop Fenwick to Claremont, in 1826, he administered the Sacrament of Confirmation to twenty-one individuals, mostly converts, at which time the little church was crowded to excess, the greater part present on the occasion being Protestants from the church on the opposite side of the village, of which Rev. Daniel Barber had formerly been pastor, and by whom he had been deeply beloved, and to whom, in his valedictory at parting, he said, "I now retire to the shades of poverty; may the faults which I have committed while among you be written on the sands of the sea-shore, that the next returning wave may wash them into oblivion."

Church at Dover.

The Right Rev. Bishop having learned the anxiety of the faithful, who were for the most part operatives in the factories at Dover, to share the advantages of their religion, commissioned Rev. Father Mahony, January 15, 1827, who had been lately affiliated to the diocese, to visit them, which he did, heard the confessions of all who were prepared, said mass, and preached in the Court House to a very respectful audience, composed for the most part of Protestants.

Towards the close of the same year, December 19, the Bishop visited Dover in person, said mass at the house of Mr. Byrne, and administered Confirmation to two individuals. Learning that there were between forty and fifty adult Catholics living there, he encouraged the purchase of a lot whereon they might build a small church. This intimation of the Bishop, small as were their numbers, was so cheerfully complied with, that at his next visit, September 25, 1830, they had a very neat church erected, measuring fifty by thirty-six feet, which he dedicated to God under the title of St. Aloysius.

A convenient house was also built for the pastor, and occupied by those Reverend Fathers whom the Bishop endeavored to supply, till the ordination of Rev. Path. Canavan, in 1832. He was appointed pastor of Dover, July 25, 1834, and in the summer of 1849 made an addition of thirty feet to the church, and toiled on indefatigably for those intrusted to his care till declining health called for a successor. Rev. Fr. Canavan died in Boston, April 26, 1870. R. I. P.

In connection with the introduction of Catholicity, into what is now the State of Maine, by those pioneer Missionaries of the sixteenth century, as seen in the early pages of these Sketches, cheering is the progress that it has made, and is making, since having been erected into a Diocese, in 1855, and confided to the watchful care of its devoted Bishop, Right Rev. Dr. D. W. Bacon, and his Reverend co-operators, a faithful and zealous clergy.

In addition to its former solitary church, Portland, at this day, has its Cathedral of the Immaculate Conception, with its Calvary and St. Aloysius Chapels, its Academy and parochial schools with their thousand pupils, while Bangor has its spacious church, its boarding and day schools, and, without particularizing, throughout the State its twenty odd other churches and schools connected, where called for; and in New Hampshire, its twenty and more additional churches, with its flourishing Academy, its boarding and free schools, and its Asylum at Manchester! Cheering, indeed, and every way encouraging is the extension of the Holy Church in the Diocese of Portland. Laus Deo.

DIOCESE OF SPRINGFIELD.

Comprising the Counties of Berkshire, Franklin, Hampshire, Hampden, and Worcester, Massachusetts.

This Diocese was established in 1870. Right Rev. P. T. O'Reilly, D. D., its first Bishop, was consecrated September 25, 1870.

Church at Worcester.

New Haven and adjacent towns having been confided to the care of Rev. James McDermott, and Hartford blessed with a devoted pastor in Rev. John Brady, our Missionary was allowed leisure to look after the spiritual interests of the faithful dispersed over the easterly part of Connecticut, and of those in the central and western portions of the State of Massachusetts; hence he selected, in 1837, Worcester as his headquarters.

The village, as it was then called, had a population of seven thousand inhabitants, of whom four families, eighteen unmarried men and a single lady, were members of the Catholic Church, who had received the consolations of religion from time to time, as it had been found convenient to visit them.

The first mass offered at Worcester was in the room of a private house, occupied by a worthy mechanic, by name of McKillup, on Front Street, as was the custom over the entire mission, wherever a Catholic family was found to reside. The first discourse in public, in the absence of better accommodations, was delivered in the dining hall of a tavern, then located near the Common. Quite a respectable audience were present, composed for the most part of those to whom the doctrines of the Church were a novelty, but who, to their honor be it said, notwithstanding the place, evinced as much decorum as if it had been a consecrated house of prayer. The Baptismal Register, previous to 1834, records the names, in different parts of the county, of thirty-five children and three adults, converts to the faith, who had received the Sacrament.

The great Western Railroad, then comparatively an infant enterprise, had been commenced, and its industrious mechanics and laborers, with their wives and little ones, leaving Boston in the distance, and moving onward farther and farther from the Church and the consolations of their religion, as well as being liable to the many casualties incident to the excavation of banks and blasting of rocks, suggested the propriety of erecting a small church at Worcester. The project was looked upon at the time as rather quixotic; but the Missionary, who received from his venerated and beloved Bishop permission to do as to him seemed best, fancied he saw, with one point of the dividers on the village as the centre, and the other encircling the many mechanical and other perspective privileges in its surroundings, a population of thousands in the future, commenced, July 7, 1834, a small frame building, sixty-two by thirty-two feet, on land then mapped out for building purposes, and which, in honor of the enterprise, was named Temple Street.

The first year saw the foundation laid, the following saw the building up and roofed, and within two years completed and paid for. In 1841, August 22d, it was dedicated to God under the title of His Divine Son, Christ's Church, at which time the congregation had so far increased, that one hundred and eighteen children and adults, many of whom were converts to the faith, received the Sacrament of Confirmation.

In the meanwhile several stations, from Suffolk County, Mass., to the border lines of New York and New Hampshire, and to New London, Conn., were to be attended, and Rev. A. Williamson was appointed pastor; but his health declining, and having left for Baltimore, where he subsequently died, Rev. M. Gibson was appointed to the charge at Worcester, April 2, 1845. During his administration a more extensive church edifice was projected, there being, as estimated, seven hundred English-speaking and six hundred French Canadians demanding church accommodations. This edifice, a substantial brick structure, was, June 24, 1846, dedicated to God under the title of St. John the Evangelist, by Right Rev. J. B. Fitzpatrick, in presence of Right Rev. Bishop Fenwick and the Rev. Professors of the College of Holy Cross.

Rev. Father J. Boyce, who succeeded Father Gibson, March 20, 1848, converted the former church building into spacious school-rooms, ample ground having been originally secured for church, school, and parochial purposes.

College of the Holy Cross.

Contemporary with the erection of the church at Worcester, our Missionary purchased between fifty and sixty acres of land on the hill-side, rising on the south part of the town, known by the name of Bogachoag, which years previous, when it formed a part of the principal settlement of the Indians, was called Packachoag. He here erected buildings for educational purposes, known as St. James's Seminary, which was generously patronized by students from several States of the Union.

The location having proved so very healthful, and in every way so well adapted for the purpose intended, apprehensive that at death the Institution might be blotted out, it was, in 1842, deeded to Right Rev. Bishop Fenwick, with the express understanding, that it should be maintained for educational purposes. The offering accepted, the annexed notice, which appeared in the public press of the day, tells the result, and the interest manifested on the occasion.

"*Grand Celebration of the Laying of the Corner-stone of the College of Holy Cross, in Worcester, Mass.*

" On Wednesday morning, the 21st of June, the festival of St. Aloysius, 1843, the new College was commenced by laying the corner-stone. Right Rev. Bishop Fenwick, Rev. C. Constantine Pise, D. D., accompanied by Rev. Mr. McCloskey, of St. Joseph's Church, New York, Very Rev. W. Tyler, of the Diocese of Boston, Rev. Messrs. Hardy and Roloff, of the Cathedral, Rev. Mr. Flood, of St. Mary's, Boston, Rev. Mr. Goodwin, of Charlestown, Rev. Mr. Lynch, of Roxbury, Rev. Mr. Fitzpatrick, of East Cambridge, Rev. Mr. Conway, of Lowell, Rev. Mr. Strain, of Waltham, and Rev. Mr. Wiley, of Providence, all departed in a special train of cars for Worcester, accompanied by a large concourse of the citizens of Boston, and several distinguished strangers.

" On the arrival at the railroad station in Worcester, a band of music was in attendance, together with the Catholic Temperance Society, the Young Men's and Young Ladies' Societies attached to the Sunday school, with their appropriate banners, and a crowd of the inhabitants, who all enthusiastically greeted the Right Rev. Prelate and his Rev. associates. The day was beautiful, the sky clear, the atmosphere refreshing and invigorating, and the sun shed his noonday lustre over every hill and valley for miles around.

" The order of the procession formed, all moved in

the direction of the College site, distant about two miles. The band played *Adeste fidelis* and Hail Columbia, and the star-spangled banner of America could be seen in the distance waving triumphantly on the Alpine like heights of the romantic site, and the roaring noise of the cannon was heard through the town and adjacent country for almost an hour, during the progress of the procession. The procession was nearly one mile in length, and the ladies of Worcester graced the moving throng with their lovely presence. On arriving near the brow of the College ground, the superintendent had already constructed arbors and shady groves for the accommodation of the visitors and youth now assembling. In the residence attached to the former Seminary, the Right Rev. Bishop and clergy arrayed themselves in surplices, the Bishop wearing his mitre and crosier. Here the most imposing and sublime part of the procession was formed, and as the glorious banner of the effulgent cross appeared in front of the ecclesiastical body, and as the sacred notes of a solemn chant echoed along the breeze of the emerald-like valley, amid the sound of artillery, and beneath the stars and stripes of our beloved country, I felt proud of the magnificent scene, and I felt proud of the worthy occasion of laying the first corner-stone of the first Catholic College in New England.

"After laying of the corner-stone, and depositing several coins and newspapers of the day, together with a record of the names of the officers of the State, the procession moved around the foundation walls of "The College of the Holy Cross," and the Bishop blessed them in the usual manner. After the *Veni Creator*, Rev. Dr. C. C. Pise, of New York, ascended the platform erected for the occasion, and beautifully decorated with evergreen boughs. At this moment thousands of spectators gathered around the orator's stand, and covered the neighboring heights, in vehicles and on foot, in order to hear the Rev. Orator pour forth his lofty strains of eloquence."

"*Address by the Rev. C. Constantine Pise, D. D.*

" The object for which we have convened, on the present memorable occasion, is of such a nature, that it cannot but excite profound attention in the public mind. It is a great national and religious object, the effects of which are to be experienced, far and wide, not merely by the present generation, but, likewise, by posterity. The ceremony of laying the corner-stone of a new College must be regarded as peculiarly solemn and sacred : perhaps, after that of an edifice dedicated exclusively and immediately to the services of divine worship, the most solemn and sacred that can be imagined. I know of no building more deserving of veneration from the good citizen and genuine patriot — after a Church — than a Seminary of Education. A Church is consecrated to the tenets and rites of religion ; a College to the arts and sciences, to literature and the muses. The latter may be considered the offspring of the former. For they guide and direct to the knowledge of Truth, which can be attained only by patient research and laborious industry, which require the aid of the sciences and letters. The prosperity and glory of a nation may, therefore, be estimated in proportion to the increase of such edifices as the one of which the corner-stone is, this day, placed on this beautiful and romantic spot: the natural retreat, it would seem, of the Virtues, and the congenial haunt of the Muses, which flourish and rejoice most in the shades and solitudes of the country.

"In any part of the civilized world, such a ceremony would not fail to command attention, but nowhere as much as in our own republic. Young though still she be, her happy soil is already dotted and variegated with houses of education; and the genius of Liberty never more triumphantly exults, in the midst of the glorious institutions of this favored land, than at beholding seminaries of this character springing up, and promising to spread abroad the blessings of knowledge and intellectual cultivation, without regard to differences of religious opinions, and without any distinction of creeds or forms. Yes, this is the boast, and may this ever be the glory, of our republic; in fact, it must be, as long as the republic subsists. For, the moment any attempt were made to give the preference of one mode of worship over another, that moment the brightest prerogative of our constitution is extinguished, — the happiest boon bequeathed to us by the Fathers of our Country is destroyed: — I mean the most unrestrained and universal freedom of conscience.

"This being the case, I feel convinced that the ancient and venerable State of Massachusetts — always famed for patriotic virtues and enlightened views — will greet the erection on her soil of another seminary of learning, no matter under what religious influence it may arise. She will perfectly understand, that where there is right education there is no danger to be apprehended; but, on the contrary, the soundest principles of liberty, the sublimest precepts of Christianity, the purest maxims of morality and national fraternization, will be taught and inculcated. And if the spirit that presides over and pervades the whole be Catholic in name, it will be truly so in effect: worthy, indeed, of its appellation, embracing all our fellow-citizens, and all our institutions, with the same impartial affection and heart-felt interest, laboring in the common cause of disseminating knowledge among all classes, and deserving well of our beloved country, which we prove to be the more dear to us, the more idefatigable we are found in administering our aid to the promotion of the general good.

"The fact of a Catholic College, under the management of the Jesuits, about being established in this place, has, no doubt, already spread throughout the length and breadth of this State; and I feel confident that intense curiosity, as to its character and destination, must have been excited in the minds of thousands. Not having enjoyed the opportunity of making themselves acquainted with the spirit of our Church, and the Institute of the Society of Jesus, it is possible that certain misgivings, not to say misapprehensions, may be entertained regarding the one and the other. And it is incumbent on me to impart correct information on both, to all those whom I now have the honor of addressing.

"The Catholic Church has always cherished within her bosom a sacred and undying solicitude for the education of the people. To many, who have not paid sufficient attention to the history of past times, this proposition may appear extraordinary. But it is, nevertheless, a fact, to which the whole world, in all preceding centuries, will bear witness. The germ of knowledge was implanted in the dogmas of Christianity, and it expanded and flourished in the same proportion as they were developed and extended among men. Wherever, in ancient days, a temple consecrated to religion was constructed, hard by there was always sure to spring up, as a necessary appendage, some school of learning, some seminary, within the walls of which the study of letters was pursued with unremitting attention, science, both sacred and profane, was fostered with untiring diligence and enthusiastic care. Universities were founded and endowed, under the shadow of whose walls the inspired volume was transcribed by the skilful craft of the monastic inmates, and the classic authors, whose elegant productions we now enjoy were rescued from destruction, and preserved for the benefit and delight of succeeding generations.

"It was the Church that stood between the deluge of barbarism that inundated Europe and the venerable monuments of ancient literature. She sustained them with the power of her arm, whilst, in dread confusion around, all other monuments of architecture, taste, and glory lay crumbled on the earth, cloven down by the irresistible and unsparing stroke of Vandalism. In the midst of the desolation which swept over the civilized world, she supported, firm on the basis round which everything else was convulsed, the HOLY CROSS; and under its heavenly protection, sheltered and sustained the asylum of the arts and sciences, which, otherwise, must have been confounded with the general wreck, leaving hardly a melancholy vestige behind.

"The history of the revival of letters, under the pontificate of Leo X., is familiar to every reader, and has been encircled with a never dying halo by the genius of Roscoe. From the testimony recorded in its annals results the glorious evidence, that it was the light of the Church breaking in on the deep and dreary clouds of ignorance that hung over Europe, which dispersed the intellectual night, and revealed anew to the admiration of the world all the treasures, and gems, and ornaments of mind, talent, and learning which had long lain buried under the rubbish of years. The sovereign Pontiff was the first to give an impulse to the magnificent project. Catholic Rome became the metropolis of letters. The Muses, so long banished from the earth, returned to their ancient seat at the invitation of Religion. Once more were the groves of Egeria made vocal with their classic lays, while the voice of Eloquence resounded again through the long-deserted Forum. Thus may it be said that Liberty was restored to the earth by the Church. For Liberty is the sister of letters, and Religion is the parent of both. Inspired by this conviction, the fancy of Pope could not but break forth into these well-known lines : —

> " 'But see each muse in Leo's golden days,
> Starts from her trance and trims her withered bays;
> Rome's ancient genius o'er its ruins spread,
> Shakes off the dust, and rears his reverend head.'

" The idea that Catholic education is adapted only to certain quarters of the world, and not to others, is incorrect and unfounded. For it adapts itself, with singular felicity, to all governments ; it flourishes in every hemisphere. Like Christianity, it is intended for every people and for every clime. To every legitimate form of civilized government Christianity is congenial. Its universal and beneficent character is not affected by the people among whom it resides ; on the contrary, it tends to refine the ferocious, enlighten the ignorant, and impart order and inspire virtue among the heterogeneous constituents of human society. The same may be affirmed of Catholic education. In monarchical governments, it tends to regulate and define the relations between the throne and the subject ; in a republic, it fosters liberty, and restrains licentiousness. It inculcates the necessity of virtue, morality, and charity towards all mankind. It breathes an inextinguishable spirit of patriotism into the ingenuous bosom, and bids the American youth remember and be grateful for the inestimable privileges he is destined to enjoy under the freest and happiest government on earth; privileges which he would not sacrifice to any foreign authority; a government, in defence of which he would regard it the noblest act to die, if necessary, at the cannon's mouth.

"Thus far I have spoken of this College as Catholic; but, as it is to be intrusted to the care of the Jesuits, it is requisite that something touching that renowned order, especially as relating to education, should now be added. The founder of this extraordinary society, which has filled the whole earth with its fame, was, as you well know, Ignatius of Loyola. 'His object was,' in the language of one of his own members, and an eloquent historian, Orlandinus, 'to leave nothing untried by which to promote the greater glory of God, and the salvation of souls, having before his eyes no prospect of earthly rewards.' *Denique nihil intentatum relinquant, quod vel ad maximam Divini nominis gloriam, vel ad animorum salutem senserint expedire, nullis ante oculos præpositis præmiis.**

"One of the principal ends of this society was to devote its members to the education of youth, to establish schools in all parts of the world, the gates of which should be thrown open, as far as practicable, gratuitously, to the children of the poor as well as of the wealthy; for the purpose of imbuing the tender minds of youth with a relish for the cultivation of the liberal arts, and the practice of Christian virtues. *Proprium item, toto terrarum orbe, expo-*

* Hist. Soc., lib. ii. 25.

sita gratis habere gymnasia ad instituendam, non modo liberalibus disciplinis, verumetiam christianis moribus juventutem.*

"We behold here the disinterested motives by which, from its earliest institution, the Society of Jesus has ever been actuated. It originated in the desire and intention of diffusing knowledge and virtue through all classes of society. It is established on a basis of sublime Christian charity. And, whether we contemplate the unwearied perseverance and zeal of its members in the great cause of education, in all its branches and varieties, or in the laborious but triumphant missions among uncivilized and unexplored nations, it is impossible not to acknowledge that the original object of its founder has been carried out to an extent which commands the admiration, not only of Catholic, but likewise of Protestant authors. 'The Founder of this Society,' writes Mr. Carne, 'was a man of no ordinary mind and character. He has been represented, *by his enemies*, as an impostor and fanatic, before his conversion. It is not too much to say, that Loyola was not a fanatic, and far less an impostor. His mind was too powerful to condescend to the former ; and who that reads his Spiritual Exercises will venture to say he was the latter? It was his passionate desire that Christ might be preached to the utmost ends of the world, and that all nations might know the Lord and call him blessed. His was not the ambition of worldly honor and glory. It aimed at a loftier flight. The enthusiasm of Loyola

* Hist. Soc., lib. i.

was in admirable keeping, and did not war with his cold and clear intellect. His was not a fiery zeal. There was a spiritual composure in his actions, nor do we find wild imaginings and extravagant fancies, either of heart or mind, in his maturer years. There was evidently in him a singleness of disposition, that does not warrant the idea that this Society was instituted for those worldly objects which have formed the burden of the accusations against him.*

" This elegant writer, although, by no means partial to the Church, of which the Jesuits have ever been, and still are, the most able vindicators, and the noblest apostles, still could not restrain the almost involuntary emotion of admiration which was awakened in his breast, at the consideration of the labors of this wonderful Society. 'Are not theirs,' he cries out, 'the greatest number of martyrs in the cause of Christ among the heathen. Is not the most brilliant, the most varied, the most extensive talent to be found among the Sons of Loyola? Even their most bitter enemies, who abused the Jesuits as a body, were often found to praise them individually. Pascal wrote against them, Voltaire and D'Alembert accused them of crimes, but Cardinal Fleury confessed their value, Bossuet praised them, and Lord Bacon applied to them these words: "*talis cum sis utinam noster esses.*" Leibnitz indignantly defended them, Montesquieu, Buffon, and Haller honored their labors, and witnessed to their virtues.'

* Lives of Eminent Catholic Missionaries, by Rob. Carne, Esq., London, &c.

"As a proof of the zeal which the Society displayed in the cause of Education, we find, that in less than half a century upwards of fifty Colleges were established in the various capitals of Europe, in China, and in Brazil. Of these the principal were those of Rome, Palermo, Paris, Louvain, Naples, Oporto, Cordova, &c.

"In the United States, the Jesuits have several flourishing and celebrated institutions, particularly the Universities of Georgetown and St. Louis. The former was founded by the immortal John Carroll, afterwards Archbishop of Baltimore, more than sixty years ago, and has stood before the country pre-eminent for the learning of its professors, distinguished for the advantages of location, and honored for the numberless illustrious personages educated within its halls. Among whom it can point, with proud complacency and merited exultation, to such names as Judge Gaston, of North Carolina, and the venerable Bishop of Boston, under whose patronage, and by whose liberality, this edifice is to be erected. That University, situated within sight of the Capitol at Washington, under the eyes of Senators and Judges, and Members of Congress from all the States of the Union, has not only been able to stand their closest scrutiny, but has won them general admiration. The spirit that animates the whole body is of the loftiest, and, at the same time, gentlest character. It has thus nothing but the love of letters, of virtue, of religion, of patriotism. And I think I may venture to assert, that in no other such Seminary in the Union have there been exhibited more frequent or more unequivocal demonstrations of love of the Republic, and enthusiasm for its institutions, than under the turrets of Georgetown College. In confirmation of this, I appeal to the annual celebrations of Washington's Birthday and the Fourth of July, on which national festivals addresses are delivered by some of the young alumni, which would do honor to the youth of Rome or Sparta. Many of these addresses have been published, and thus have given evidence of the adaptation of the educational system of Ignatius to the genius of republicanism as well as the ancient governments of Europe.

"The same profound attachment to the institutions of our beloved country, the same genuine tokens of patriotic conviction, characterize the inmates of the University of St. Louis. This now most flourishing Seminary of learning may be regarded as the daughter of that of Georgetown. It sprang out of its bosom, and was originally composed of its members. It will not, therefore, surprise us if it has inherited its spirit. Witness the following passage, extracted from an oration delivered on the Fourth of July, by the President, the Rev. J. Vandevelde: 'Our country has incontestable claims upon every one of her citizens. Whatever profession we may have embraced, whatever station we may hold in society, we owe ourselves to our country. We are bound to watch over her safety and prosperity — to fly to her aid when she is exposed to danger, and to promote her internal peace and happiness by contributing to establish concord and harmony among all our fellow-citizens.'

"I make this extract, in order to satisfy those amongst my audience, who have not had the proper opportunity of informing themselves on the subject to which their attention is now directed. Jesuitism is a word which has been strangely distorted from its proper signification. I know it. I am convinced of it. For, having had the honor of receiving my education under the shadow of Georgetown College, I can speak from a long and thorough acquaintance. And I cannot conceal that the affection I formed in my childhood for that my venerable *alma mater*, has only strengthened and become more deeply rooted at the present period of my existence. And I am proud to exclaim with St. Francis Xavier, 'If I forget thee, O Society of Jesus, may my right hand forget its cunning!'

"I have before me another testimony in favor of the character of Jesuit education, which must be considered as valuable as it is impartial. It is taken from the 'Daily People's Organ,' edited at St. Louis, by one not belonging to the Catholic Church. 'Since the Jesuits,' he writes, 'first established their excellent university in this city, they have been under the observing eye of New England Protestants of several different denominations, and during these years have discovered little that allowed even of exceptions. cavil, or doubt. Instead of being opposed to civil liberty, their scholars have been so well taught its true, generic, and philosophic principles, as to have been able to deliver orations at the court-house of the county of surpassing eloquence. Instead of being enemies to unlimited freedom of conscience, they are distinguished over all clergymen in the State for their systematic observance of the rule never to introduce in their intercourse with society any subject whatever that is calculated to wound the feelings of the humblest person present.'

"The College, of which the corner-stone has just been placed by the Right Rev. Prelate, will rear up its walls for the grand and noble purposes of education : and education proper to the soil and constitution of the State in which it is situated. This is another munificent deed among the many which have already rendered dear his name to the Catholic Church of America. Trained up himself under the instruction of the Jesuits, he knows that he could not perform an act more advantageous to his diocese, or more serviceable to his country, than to place this new College under their jurisdiction. Sprung from an American ancestry in Maryland, which traces back to the days of Lord Baltimore, and never having breathed the atmosphere of Europe, he feels himself, by nature as well as by preference, eminently devoted to the interests and happiness of our native land. And he may rest consoled, and amply remunerated, in the reflection, that his efforts to extend abroad the blessings of Education will be duly appreciated by our Church, and justly applauded by our common country.

"The Rev. Gentleman, to whose superintendence and charge the College is intrusted, derives his origin from the State of the 'Old Dominion.' The free mountains of Virginia have given him birth, and his soul is as free as his native hills. Whilst he prides himself in the name of a Jesuit, he glories in the title and privileges of an American. To no one, in my opinion, could the interests of this embryo establishment with greater advantage be committed. He brings with him no ordinary experience. During several years he presided, as Rector, over Georgetown College; and occupied, moreover, for a time the highest post to which any member of the Society can be elevated in Maryland.

"Under such auspices we cannot but augur well for the future prosperity of this Institution. The youth who will here be formed to letters, will, also, be moulded into true Christians and sincere republicans. They will be taught first the necessity of religion, the practice of virtue, the maxims of charity; afterwards, an entire devotion to the glorious institutions of our country. They will be instructed to recognize no temporal power over this free land in any foreign authority, whether secular or ecclesiastic. They will be taught that even the sovereign Pontiff, whose spiritual jurisdiction, as Catholics, we admit and revere, possesses and claims no right to exercise any sway over us as citizens of this great republic. That they must be ready to defend the prerogatives and liberties of their country against any aggressor, no matter who he may be. And while we constitute but one Church, in dogmatical tenets, we are bound to embrace all other communions in the universal national tenet of equal liberty. They will be taught, within these walls, to give to God the things that are

God's, and to Cæsar the things that are Cæsar's. And the eternal truth of this maxim will be deeply inculcated: that he who is not faithful to his country, will not be true to his God.

"I rejoice in the occasion which has assembled us here to-day. It has afforded me a favorable opportunity of bringing before an enlightened and numerous audience topics which may be new to many, but must be interesting to all. This is a bright day for the diocese of Massachusetts. It will be long remembered and commemorated. In future years, when the walls of the College shall have grown sombre with age, it will afford matter of exultation to some youthful orator, when he will refer to the peculiar period and circumstances which mark and characterize this ceremony. 'Only a few days elapsed,' he will be able to say, 'between two ever memorable events: the first and more important, the celebration of the Bunker Hill Monument, the second, the laying the corner-stone of the first Jesuit College in the State of Massachusetts.' The one, the mighty obelisk of Liberty, which is destined to endure, more imperishable than bronze, throughout all time; the other, a noble temple of the arts and sciences, of virtue and patriotism, which will, we trust, send out into the ranks of life Christians, scholars, freemen, worthy the shrine at which they were reared, and the republic to which they belong.

"All hail, then, to this beautiful spot, around which are blended the quiet shades of the country, and the busy population of the town! Upon this chosen earth, the spires of a new college will peer on the traveller's gaze, as with the speed of the wind he is hurried, by the vehement power of steam, along those mighty railroads, which, passing through this town, join together, and, as it were, annihilate, distances the most remote. May the eternal eye of Providence watch over its fortunes. Under His omnipotent protection it is commenced: '*Unless the Lord build the house, in vain do they labor who build it.*' May the hopes of the Right Rev. Prelate, under whose generous auspices it is to be completed, be fully and happily realized. May it be an enduring monument of his zeal and disinterestedness, as well as a signal ornament to the beauteous and thriving town of Worcester. In a word, my fervent aspiration, in concluding, is, QUOD FELIX, FAUSTUM, FORTUNATUMQUE, ET NOSTRIS, ET POSTERIS, SIT."

"At two o'clock P. M. the Bishop and clergy, together with several distinguished strangers from Boston and Worcester, sat down to a collation prepared for the occasion by the worthy and zealous pastor of the Church in Worcester. It was truly a feast in the evergreen bower. At the conclusion, three enthusiastic cheers were given for the Bishop and Orator of the day."

The College completed, and students assembled, the beneficial result of the enterprise was soon acknowledged, as will be seen in the following article, which appeared in the public press of 1847:—

"The College of Holy Cross has been in operation about three years, and now numbers one hundred and thirty students, and has progressed in prosperity beyond the expectations of its most ardent friends. It is designed for Catholics only, and is calculated for a thorough mercantile, classical, or theological education; each of these may be had separately, or any two or more combined, according to the wishes of the parent or abilities and vocation of the pupil. Each department is under the superintendence of a Prefect of superior education and great experience, scholars themselves inferior to none in this country, and what is of greater importance, they are divines, indefatigable sons of Saint Ignatius Loyola.

"The course of studies and discipline followed in this institution is based upon a system which has been in successful operation for three hundred years, and has proved the most effectual, moral, and intellectual plan of education ever devised by man. The devoted Fathers of the Society of Jesus are celebrated the world over for their learning, wisdom, and piety; it is one of the principal objects of their vocation to educate the young, and by their long experience and eminent abilities they are most happily fitted for the task.

"Since the first opening of the College, the pupils have rapidly advanced in the various studies to which they have been devoted; some are fitting for the counting-house, others for more learned occupations, and again others for the holy ministry; everything relating to the temporal as well as spiritual welfare of the students receive the strictest attention. At all hours, night and day, the vigilant eye of the Prefect is upon them, and his ears open to detect any improper discourse or behavior, as also to guard them against imprudence and accidents; he is their spiritual guide, their master in studies, and their companion in recreation, everything being admirably calculated to gain the respect of the students, and secure their happiness.

"Quarterly reports of the conduct and studies of each scholar are sent to the parents or guardians, and yearly exhibitions given, at which appropriate premiums are awarded to the most deserving.

"This College is quite unlike most of our modern educational establishments, got up for private interest, or for promoting selfish notions of Christianity; its professors have no family cares or expenses, they have no anxiety about this world's goods, for they have embraced the state of voluntary poverty, therefore all their time and care is spent upon the youth intrusted to their direction.

"What parent is there who will not rejoice that there is such an institution in this diocese, and that can, for a small pension, place his son in charge of these devoted teachers, whose only ambition is to promote the greater glory of God, the good of others, and their own salvation?

"To witness the serious devotion of these young men and boys at their religious service, to hear the solemn chant of their sweet voices, to see them at their sports of fishing and bathing in summer, or skating in winter, their cheerful and healthy aspect, and their habits of easy and respectful submission to their superiors, one cannot but feel that true piety is the foundation, and parental care with filial obedience the superstructure of this institution."

Mission Stations.

While the railroad was in progress, our Missionary, at that time still guardian of the interests of the Seminary, in which were students from Texas to Maine, had frequently to offer the holy Sacrifice in shanties, where the largest number of workmen could be accommodated, or in the absence of such, under some wide-spreading tree of the forest.

The most numerous congregation of resident Catholics in any one town east of Worcester, attended at the time, were at Waltham, where there were about three hundred. Saxonville, the next important station, where several were employed in the factories, had mass once every two or three months, the liberality of the citizens allowing the use of the schoolhouse on such occasions till land was secured for a church and cemetery. Westboro', Grafton, and Millbury were the next principal stations, where, however, there were very few resident members of the Church, save those employed at Millbury. The rest, with their families, were employed either as farm laborers or brogan makers, to whom for the pegging of five pairs, considered enough for a day's work, one dollar was paid, the average income for house rent, fuel, clothing, support of wife, and, generally speaking, a goodly number of healthful little ones, who, by the by, with simplicity of early diet and regimen have, with time, advanced to manhood, and are now combined with the thousands of boot and shoe manufacturers who make up the flourishing congregations of Milford, Marlboro', Hopkinton, Natick, and neighboring towns.

Accompanying the building of the railroad from Worcester west, stations were held at Spencer, Brookfield, Warren, Palmer, and so onwards wherever laborers and their families had taken up their residence for the time being. Clappville, where a few Catholics were employed in the mills, whether of cotton or woollen, Ware, Barre, Templeton, Thorndike, Springfield, Chicopee, Hadley, Thompsonville, Westfield, Northampton, Amherst, Barrington, and other towns east and west of the Connecticut River, had been frequently visited by the Missionary, both previous to leaving Hartford, and after having selected Worcester as his headquarters, as in most of those places, where there are now churches and large congregations, Catholics had already found employment, and had settled with their families, and needed the Sacraments and holy Mass, and their little ones, particularly, catechetical instruction.

After the example of the primitive Christians, the few who were found at these several stations met together for divine worship and reception of the sacraments in private houses, as their numbers were yet too few and their means too limited to contemplate the erection of churches; since which days, however, of simplicity and fervor, and with increased numbers, many are the churches that have been erected, and among them are many beautiful, extensive, and even magnificent, — the spacious, ornate, and Gothic stone edifice at Pittsfield, by Rev. Fr. Edward Purcell; that at Chicopee, by Rev. Fr. W. A. Blenkinsop; and without attempting an enumeration, the Church of St. Michael, at Springfield, which was erected by the devoted zeal and indefatigable energy of the lamented Fr. Gallaher, seconded by a united congregation, by whom he was beloved, — and which, at this day, is the Cathedral of the Diocese.

Church at Springfield.

The present large and influential body of Catholics at Springfield were represented, in 1830, by three families and a few unmarried men, who were visited by the Missionary, in connection with the few living at Thompsonville, Westfield, Chicopee, and other river towns, once every two or three months, as circumstances permitted, when Mass was offered, and the Holy Sacraments administered, in whatever house was found to be the most convenient.

Springfield, which had always been one of the most flourishing towns in Massachusetts, where the

Armory of the United States has been established as early as 1795, and where many elegant private residences, as well as public buildings, highly creditable to the tastes of its inhabitants, had been erected, like Worcester, with the construction of the Western Railroad, received a powerful impetus, and from its delightful, pleasing, and village-like character became in a few years the mart of commerce, assuming the business-like proportions of a city.

The faithful, whose numbers increased with the prosperity of the place, and whose spiritual wants had been hitherto attended from Hartford, — the cradle-Church of the Connecticut valley, — concluded, with the approbation of the Bishop, to provide themselves with a more convenient place to assemble for divine worship than they had previously had in private houses. Fortunately, about the time when their numbers had so far increased as to warrant the undertaking, the Baptist society proposed the sale of their frame building, which was in excellent repair, measuring seventy by forty-five feet. The Bishop, upon invitation, visiting Springfield October 15, 1846, approved the purchase, and selected a site to which the building might be removed, appointing Rev. George T. Riordan to superintend the alterations necessary for the purpose of Catholic worship, and act as pastor to the congregation.

Lieutenant Scammon, of the U. S. army, a convert to Catholicity, with several of his brother officers, who, while students at West Point, were taught to accept of no mathematical problem that admitted not of demonstration, with judgment matured, and in manhood, sought for the evidence and divine proofs of Christianity. Perceiving that "prayer and searching the Scriptures," as counselled by ministers of the day, led invariably to sectarianism and diversity of opinion, and having learned that there was but "one church, one faith, one baptism," they were prompted, in connection with prayer and reading the Scripture, to trace the history of the Christian religion to its fountain source, and, discovering that the Catholic Church of to-day taught the same doctrine as in the apostolic age, and had every demonstrative evidence of its divine authenticity, they joyfully embraced it. About the time of which we write, there were between forty and fifty gallant officers of the army and navy, many among them converts to the Church, who were united in the Sodality of the "Sacred Heart," of which General Rosecrans was Promoter.

The sanctuary of the late purchased church edifice, with its altar and tabernacle arranged with taste and beauty, after the design of Lieutenant Scammon, having been completed, the church was dedicated to God by Rt. Rev. Bishop Fitzpatrick, under the patronage of St. Benedict, February 14, 1847. Rev. Fr. Ryder, President of Holy Cross College, preached on the occasion to a large audience, drawn together either from curiosity to witness what they had never had the opportunity of looking upon before, or to give grateful thanks to God for the blessings of a house of worship they could count their own, and where they might assemble, after their weekly toil, to hear the word of God, and bow in adoration at the mystic sacrifice of Calvary, the Holy Mass.

The following, which appeared in the public press, tells the joy evinced on the occasion: —

"SPRINGFIELD, February 15, 1847.

"Last Sunday was a proud day for the Catholics of Springfield. Though numbering about four hundred, hitherto we had no home for the worship of our faith. At one time in an humble cabin, at another in the common town-hall, we assisted at the holy mysteries, praying for the day when our means would enable us to raise aloft the banner of the cross, and under our own roof to sing the praises of God. Like the Israelites of old, we wept in the land of exile, and sighed for the termination of our bondage. And now that day has come, and for the first time a permanent altar has been erected in our midst, and we raise our eyes with gratitude and love to behold the cross, the emblem of our redemption.

"The church where now we worship, originally a Protestant meeting-house, was yesterday solemnly dedicated to Almighty God, under the invocation of the blessed Mother of God, and St. Benedict, by the Rt. Rev. Bishop of the diocese. . . . Our Protestant neighbors never before had seen a Catholic dedication. They mingled with us, and by their respectful demeanor, showed that they partook of our joy. Rt. Rev. Bishop Fitzpatrick officiated, assisted by Rev. Fr. Riordan, our estimable Pastor, and Rev. Messrs. Brady, of Cabotville, and O'Brien and Williams, of Boston. The solemn chant of the Miserere, the invocation of the blessed Saints of God, the presence of the Pontiff, the solemn benediction, not only of the place, but of the assembled people, have made here a deep and vivid impression. And this feeling of respect for our faith, of awe and love for sacred mysteries, was increased by the eloquent discourse of Very Rev. Dr. Ryder, President of the College of Holy Cross. The learned divine chose for the subject of his sermon the Sacrifice of the Mass, proving from the Scriptures the necessity of a sacrifice in worship, as ordered by Almighty God; showing also, from moral and theological reasons, that the whole ceremony of the Christian religion demands a sacrifice, and that the prophecies can be verified only by admitting in the Mass a true, though unbloody sacrifice, wherein Jesus Christ, God and man, offers himself anew to the Father, a victim of propitiation for the sins of men.

"The singing was conducted by Rev. Mr. O'Brien, assisted by Rev. Messrs. Riordan and Williams, and a young gentleman of the College of the Holy Cross, named Crowley. It would be difficult to find a better choir."

Church at Chicopee.

The early Church history of this, like that of many towns and villages of New England, commences with the toil and untiring industry of Ireland's exiled sons, who were employed at the excavations of canals, and other important labors that have since brought wealth and prosperity to thousands. The few Catholics who were employed in the construction of the canal, of what is now the flourishing manufacturing town of Chicopee, were attended by our Missionary as early as 1830. The boarding-house, a temporary building, which stood near to the river bank, where the dam is now constructed, — the only building in the place, save the grist-mill and home of the miller, — served for chapel, and all other purposes. The Cabot Manufacturing Company being incorporated in 1832, an impetus was given to the erection of mills, and dwellings for the operatives, and soon a beautiful, flourishing town arose, giving employment to its thousands of mechanics and mill operatives.

The faithful, who in 1830 numbered thirty souls, having in ten years increased to two hundred and fifty, a church was projected for their accommodation. Rev. John D. Brady, who then attended this station, in connection with Pittsfield and other towns west of the Connecticut River, encouraged by the promised assistance of this noble little band, commenced in 1841 the erection of what subsequently was St. Matthew's Church, which was blessed by the Bishop, September 29, 1843. Rev. B. O'Cavanagh was appointed as an assistant to Rev. Fr. Brady in 1845, and these gentlemen continued to attend alternately Chicopee and other stations till 1848, when Rev. Fr. Strain was appointed to the pastoral care of the rising congregation.

Church at Northampton.

The earliest reminiscence we have of the rites of religion being performed in the western part of the State of Massachusetts, was within the prison walls of Northampton, where two young men therein confined were doomed to execution. Among the papers of Cardinal Cheverus, writes his biographer, Rev. J. Huen Dubourg, there are letters in which these young men say, " We adore, in the judgment of men liable to be deceived, the decrees of Providence. If we are not guilty of the crime imputed to us, we have committed other sins, and to expiate them, we accept death with resignation. We are solicitous only about our salvation; it is in your hands; come to our assistance." It being then the custom to conduct convicts to church to hear a funeral discourse immediately before their execution, a second letter was addressed to M. Cheverus, praying him to deliver this discourse. " It will be a painful task for you," said they to him, " after the fatigue of a long journey, and especially after the sad impression made on your heart by the sight of two young men about to die, in the bloom of youth; but you will not refuse us this favor, and reduce us to the necessity of listening, just before we die, to the voice of one who is not a Catholic." However painful this twofold duty might be to the feeling heart of M. Cheverus, he did not hesitate to undertake it, and promptly acceded to their request. Hatred to the Catholic religion was carried to such an extreme in Northampton, that it was with the greatest difficulty he could find lodgings, no one being willing to receive him. He passed many days in the prison with the condemned; he compassionated their condition, and persuaded them to look on death in the light of the gospel, as an entrance upon a better life, and the gate of true happiness. These instructions, and the sacraments which he administered to them, inspired them with such holy dispositions of soul, that the last moments of life lost, in their view, all the terrors with which they affright unassisted nature; and they looked on the approach of death not only without distress, but with calmness, serenity, and celestial joy. M. Cheverus alone was overcome with grief, his heart overpressed with pity; and those whom he had come to console became themselves his comforters. "O father," said they to him, "moderate your grief, or it will make you ill." At length the fatal day arrived; and, as this day seemed to these men so full of faith, like the dawn of a festal day, they wished, at the time of their execution, to appear clean and decent, and asked for a razor, to shave themselves. It was, at first, refused them; but, upon M. Cheverus's pledging his word that they should not attempt their lives, their request was granted. At the hour appointed, M. Cheverus went with them, and all the funeral train, to the church. There the Protestant ministers wished to pronounce the usual discourse; but M. Cheverus opposed this with force and energy. "The will of the dying," he said to them, "is sacred; and they have desired to have no one but myself, and I alone will speak to them." He immediately ascended the pulpit, and, casting his eyes upon the immense crowd that surrounded him, and beholding a great multitude of women, who had come from every direction to be present at the execution, he felt himself animated with holy indignation against the curiosity which had attracted to that mournful scene such a crowd of spectators. "Orators," cried he, in a loud and stern voice, " are usually flattered by having a numerous audience, but I am ashamed of the one now before me. . . . Are there, then, men to whom the death of their fellow-beings is a spectacle of pleasure, an object of curiosity! . . . But you, especially, O women! what has induced you to come to this place? Is it to wipe away the cold damps of death that trickle down the faces of these unfortunate men? Is it to experience the painful emotions which this scene ought to inspire in every feeling heart? No, it is not for this. It is, then, to behold their anguish, and to look upon it with tearless, eager, and longing eyes. Ah! I blush for you; your eyes are full of murder. . . . You boast of possessing sensibility, and you say it is the highest virtue in woman; but if the sufferings of others afford you pleasure, and the death of a man is an inviting entertainment for your curiosity, I can no longer believe in your virtue. You forget your sex; you are a dishonor and reproach to it." The execution took place immediately after the discourse, but not a woman dared to appear at it; all retired from the church ashamed of themselves, and blushing for the inhuman curiosity that had brought them there.

The audience, being much interested in the discourse of M. Cheverus, wished to hear him again; and he yielded to their wishes. He preached several times in public; he conversed with them in private, and took advantage of every opportunity to remove their prejudices against the Catholic religion, and to show them how reasonable were its doctrines, and how holy, pure, and lovely was its morality. Many among them, struck by the touching spectacle presented by the holy resignation of the two young Irishmen, when about to be executed, and thinking it incredible that guilty men should possess such a modest and calm assurance in the presence of death, begged M. Cheverus to tell them, as in confession he had acquired a more perfect knowledge of the facts, whether these two young men were really innocent. M. Cheverus promised to give, in his next discourse, the only reply it was possible for him to make to this question; and, in fact, happy in the opportunity of speaking in defence of Catholic truth before a large concourse of hearers whom curiosity had collected, he developed, with force and clearness, the doctrine of the Church respecting confession; spoke of its divine institution, its important advantages, and the inviolable secrecy imposed upon the confessor, which he cannot break, even to save a kingdom. The Protestants were so much pleased with this discourse of M. Cheverus, and with the interesting character of his private conversation, that they wished him to remain with them; and he found almost as much difficulty in parting from them, as he had in procuring a shelter on his first arrival.

We have taken the liberty to transcribe this incident in the mission life of Cardinal de Cheverus, in corroboration of the fact that the life of many an innocent man has been sacrificed upon mere circumstantial evidence; that many a good and honest man has been condemned upon mere surmise of ignorance, prejudice, or malevolence. We knew in boyhood days, and in our childish heart sympathized with, the widowed mother of one of these young men, whom we often saw kneeling at the foot of the cross, in the Cathedral of Franklin Street, where she often went to pour forth the sorrows of her heart, and seek consolation in her declining years. She has long since left this world, to meet in heaven, we trust, her dearly-loved boy, the support of her declining years. Long years after the above sad event, while a Missionary in the same part of the State where the execution took place, we heard, " as murder will out," of a certain native-born, who, when dying, confessed that he was the murderer of the " mail carrier," for whose death the two young Irishmen were executed at Northampton. We called upon the jailer, an aged man at the time, to learn whether he had heard of the circumstance, and his reply was, quite unconcernedly, " Yes, he had heard something about it."

And this reminds us of another event, which shows how very cautious we should be in speaking or judging of what we consider the faults of others, and especially in condemning others on mere hearsay or circumstantial evidence. Four laborers were employed ditching the swamp meadow of a Protestant minister. After their day's labor and supper were over, one of the four, examining the roll of bills he had saved, — eighty dollars, — the result of his hard toil for months on the Western Railroad, where the four had last worked, and finding all safe, put the amount, nicely rolled up, into his watch-pocket. All retired, at bed time, to sleep in the same room. To their alarm, next morning the money was missing. The minister, much disturbed in mind that he should have harbored thieves in his house, had the four arraigned for examination, and the theft, upon mere surmise, was fastened upon one of the four, and he consequently was condemned. We visited him in his prison cell, and he declared his innocence. We saw him on his dying bed, and he still protested his innocence. Time passed on, and what was our surprise to learn, twelve months after the death of the one suspected and condemned, that the money counted on the table, in the face of all in the room, was purloined that night by one who knew the chamber well where the laborers slept, and who, in the dead of night, had been the thief! — a young man of eighteen, the son of the minister.

Let us be slow to hear, and slow to speak of each other's faults, lest, erring in judgment, we falsely suspect, rashly judge, and unjustly condemn our innocent brother.

The lot upon which the church at Northampton

was erected by Rev. John D. Brady, in 1844, had been secured by the Missionary as early as 1834, at which time the faithful were so very few, that they were accustomed to assemble for divine worship in the private house of a very worthy Catholic family by the name of Foley, at a place called Straw Hollow, now Leeds, a small manufacturing village, midway between Northampton and Williamsburg. The congregation now at Northampton, with its surroundings, Hatfield, Hadley, and Florence, numbers about one thousand souls. The present zealous pastor of Northampton, Rev. P. V. Moyce, with the assistance of his devoted people, has erected two very neat and commodious churches, one at Haydenville, another at Easthampton, and a third at Amherst, where the Missionary, in his day, had three families only to attend.

Such has been the cheering increase of the true faith in the Connecticut Valley! If we were not confined, as we are in these Sketches, to speak only of the early establishment of the Church, we might add some description of the many beautiful and commodious edifices, with their crowded congregations, that have since been erected, and we might speak of the thousands who are now enjoying the blessings of religion, from Saybrook, at the mouth of the river, to the border line of New Hampshire and Vermont; of such are the churches at Portland, Windsor, Thompsonville, Deerfield, Enfield, Hadley, Holyoke, Longmeadow, Mittineague, and others; but these we leave to the future historian, while we confine ourselves to the small beginnings of other days.

Churches West of the Connecticut River.

The excavation of the Westfield Canal, which was made between 1828 and 1830, added materially to the population of the town. A number of mechanics and laborers having been employed upon the above work, a majority of whom being Catholics, were attended by our Missionary. There being neither house nor shanty capacious enough to accommodate the congregation, the holy Sacrifice of Mass was offered on a temporary altar, erected under the shade of the trees, the nearest residence serving the purpose of confessional. The canal completed, there remained but few Catholics in the village, and these were attended from time to time, when Mass was offered and the sacraments administered at the private residence of some one of the early settlers. Accessions in time being made to the few, who found ample accommodations for divine worship in the room of a private house as mentioned, when attended by Rev. W. Blenkinsop, pastor of Chicopee, in 1854, it was suggested that they should build a small church for themselves, where they, and such as had families, might assemble on Sundays for mutual edification and prayer, even in the absence of a clergyman. To which suggestion Messrs. P. O'Keefe, J. Phillips, P. Reilly, C. Donevan, W. Sullivan, and others cheerfully corresponded, and a frame building was commenced, and so far completed as to serve the purpose of divine worship the year following.

Rev. Fr. Gallaher, of Springfield, the distance between the two places being more direct, succeeded Father Blenkinsop, visited Westfield monthly, and encouraged the interior finish of the church. The first reverend gentleman appointed as resident pastor was Rev. M. X. Carroll, in 1862. He was succeeded, in 1868, by Rev. D. Miglionico, who enlarged the church, introduced a sweet-toned organ, and otherwise beautified the building, and added a very convenient and comfortable parochial residence.

From Westfield to the State line there were very few Catholics previous to the construction of the railroad, though Mass had been said by our Missionary as far west as Great Barrington, and the villages of Berkshire County, as early as 1832.

The only church, previous to 1855, claimed by the Catholics, as a place of worship, between Westfield and the State line, and that a very small frame building, was at Pittsfield, which was built in 1845 by Rev. J. D. Brady, of Chicopee, but since which time, however, Catholicity has spread over mountains and valleys most wonderfully, as will be seen by the subjoined condensed report of Rev. Frs. P. Cuddihy and E. H. Purcell, who have been specially blessed in their untiring efforts for the greater glory of God and spiritual welfare of those intrusted to their care.

The church at Pittsfield, in 1853, about the time these Reverend Fathers entered upon their labors, appeared to be large enough for some years to come; but soon an emigration set in, and so much so that Rev. Fr. Cuddihy was obliged, the second year of his pastorship, to enlarge the church. About the same time the Catholics of North Adams purchased the church formerly belonging to the Methodist society for their special use. The next Church or congregation was formed at Great Barrington, about the year 1855. The church at North Lee was built in 1856. The church at Hinsdale was built in 1859, and that at Stockbridge the same year. The church at Mill River was built in 1866, and the new church at Pittsfield, a splendid stone edifice, was erected by Rev. Fr. Purcell in 1867. The church at North Adams — another beautiful church — was built in 1868, and the church at Williamstown was purchased in 1869. The church at Cheshire was built in 1869, and the church at South Adams was purchased and dedicated in 1870, and the church at West Stockbridge was completed in 1871; all which gives us a partial view how our holy religion has flourished during the past twenty years, there being now, as we perceive, twelve churches, where a few years ago there was but one.

The towns north and south of Worcester, in their growth and temporal prosperity, have been also blessed spiritually. In the Observer, of March 15, 1848, we learn that "the Catholics of Fitchburg, under the guidance of Rev. M. Gibson, have bought a lot of land, whereon they intend to erect a church. The lot, which is one hundred and fifty feet square, commands a view of the whole town. Their means not permitting them as yet to erect a brick building, they have determined for the present to put up a frame church. Mr. Cahill, with his usual generosity, has kindly given for that purpose ten thousand feet of lumber. Messrs. Crocker and Mansur, both Protestants, have also contributed very liberally to the good work." We learn from the same paper that " the corner-stone of the new church, under the invocation of St. Bernard, was laid the 8th of October, 1848; on which occasion a choir from Boston sang one of Demonti's Masses, and the sermon, appropriate to the occasion, was preached by Rev. N. J. O'Brien."

Uxbridge, Blackstone, Waterford, Woonsocket, and other manufacturing towns were attended from Worcester, both previous to and after the construction of the railroad to Providence. This latter enterprise gave an impetus to mechanism in many a village, and Catholics found employment, and were very generally esteemed, not precisely because they were attached to their religion, and were up long before bell hours when they had opportunities for mass or confession, but because they were always at their post, and prompt in the discharge of their several avocations.

Among the female operatives, in particular, it might happen, if a day's rest was thought needful, or a little recreation necessary, there was aunt Mahitable not far off, or cousin Matilda, to be visited, and the loom was left idle; while the Catholic girl, far from home, had none to associate with save those who, like herself, were at their daily toil from Monday morning till Saturday night. The proprietors of the factories, as a matter of course, knew and felt where their interest lay; and the result is seen in the crowded congregations of the Blackstone Valley.

Prejudice there was, and deep, before this was accomplished. To illustrate: An additional canal was to be opened at a certain factory village where a Catholic had never been seen, and the agent, in pursuit of laborers, introduced two hardy sons of old Ireland, who took their meals at the ordinary boarding-house table, but when night came, not a place was there for them to sleep; and the reason assigned by the landlady was, when questioned by the agent, who knew that there were ample accommodations, that they were filthy. They travelled two miles after their day's labor, that night, to find a lodging-place. Prejudice alone was the cause. They were Irishmen and Catholics; and that was sufficient for the landlady and her Protestant fellow-boarders, who, as it was learned, threatened to leave if Irishmen were admitted. But now to the sequel. Two years from that day the factory was completed, and in full operation, and the Missionary, learning that a few Catholics were there employed, deemed it advisable to stay over night, and give them Mass the next morning. So he commenced, as usual, hearing confessions, after the bell had rung, and the day's work over, and continued his labor till the last penitent was heard, when, thinking it was time for supper, he was quite surprised by the good Catholic housekeeper's saying, if he intended having Mass before it was time for the boys and girls to go to work, that he had better wait a little longer, as it was midnight — past twelve o'clock! Such has been the spread of Catholicity in many a factory village.

Churches at Millbury and Grafton.

The churches in these towns were commenced by Rev. M. W. Gibson, in July, 1850, and dedicated the following year. He was succeeded by Rev. Frs. L'Eveque, E. J. Sheriden, and J. J. Power, who enlarged both churches considerably. The successor to the last named Reverend gentleman was Rev. M. J. Doherty, who, in addition to the erection of a very convenient and comfortable parochial residence, beautified the above churches interiorly, and encouraged the formation of several religious associations and confraternities to the greater glory of God and to the spiritual welfare of the congregations.

The Church of St. Paul, Blackstone.

Years previous to the erection of the church in this town, the faithful assembled, as often as the Missionary found time to visit them, in some one of their private houses, or came together when Mass was offered, at the residence of Mr. McCabe, of the adjoining factory village of Waterford, till the church was erected in the neighboring town of Woonsocket.

Their numbers at length warranting the undertaking, they requested the Bishop's permission to build a church; which, being obtained, a public meeting was held, and a generous subscription on the part of all told their unanimity of feeling in the enterprise. Mr. Welcome Farnum, a resident of the place, though not a member of the Church, generously contributed not only an ample lot ·for the contemplated new church, but liberal funds towards its erection.

The church was commenced in the autumn of 1850, and dedicated by Right Rev. Bishop Fitzpatrick, in 1852. It is a plain Gothic edifice of stone, and, though it lacks the ornament of many other churches, there is perhaps no church in New England capable of seating so many, or that was built at so small a cost.

Rev. Charles O'Reilly, who was appointed to the spiritual charge of the congregation, held the responsible trust till removed by death, in September, 1857. He was succeeded by Rev. E. J. Sheriden, who fulfilled all the duties of a zealous, devoted pastor till transferred to the charge of St. Vincent's Church congregation at Boston, in 1867. Rev. T. H. Bannon was then appointed; but in the summer of 1870, in consequence of ill health, resigned his charge, and, in a few months after died in Boston, of consumption. In the month of October, 1870, Rev. W. A. Power was installed pastor of the congregation, which appointment was one of the early blessings conferred on the faithful of Blackstone by Right Rev. Dr. O'Reilly, the newly-appointed Bishop of the diocese.

Such is an authentic, though brief account of the introduction of Catholicity into what is now the Diocese of Springfield, Mass., with its sixty odd churches, convent schools, and hospital. Though we have mentioned a few of the churches erected since the death of the illustrious Bishop Fenwick, we leave to the future historian the pleasing labor of writing the history of the numerous churches erected during the administration of his worthy successors, the late deeply lamented Bishop Fitzpatrick, and the present apostolic laborer of the Boston Diocese, Right Rev. Dr. J. J. Williams.

In concluding these brief Sketches of the introduction and progress of the Church in New England, it is cheering to note, that where but fifty years ago there was but one Bishop and three Priests, there are now six Bishops, over four hundred Priests, upwards of three hundred and fifty churches, with a Catholic population of near a million souls! *Magna est veritas, et prevalebit. Si Deus pro nobis, quis contra nos?* "If God be for us, who is against us?" (Rom. viii. 31.)

CONCLUSION.

Claims of the Catholic Church.

"He that heareth you heareth Me; and he that despiseth you despiseth Me; and he that despiseth Me, despiseth Him that sent me. — Hear the Church, and if a man hear not the Church, let him be held as a Heathen and a Publican. — He that believeth shall be saved; he that believeth not shall be condemned."

These are texts from the Sacred Volume, and are to be found in the Protestant as well as Catholic editions of that Book of books. If the Bible be the word of God, then it is certain that our blessed Lord established a Church, and commanded all men to unite themselves with it under penalty of eternal loss. As guardians and teachers of this Church, He appointed certain men invested with peculiar powers, and made their office perpetual. *Lo, I am with you all days, even to the consummation of time.* To these men He gave a solemn commission to *teach. Go teach all nations.* Proclaim to all men the words of instruction and the precepts that I have given you. The Father sent me with authority to teach you, and to present to you the conditions of your eternal salvation. *As the Father hath sent me, so I send you.* Go, therefore, to all nations and tribes of the earth and teach them, and enjoin upon them *to do and observe all things whatsoever I have commanded you.* If they listen to you and believe, they shall be saved; if they do not believe, they shall be condemned. *Go and preach, saying, The kingdom of heaven is at hand. — Whosoever shall not receive you, nor hear your words, going forth out of that house or city, shake off the dust from your feet. It shall be more tolerable for the land of Sodom, on the judgment-day, than for that house or city.*

What do we learn from all this, but that religion, true religion, is not a matter to be trifled with; that it is an affair of awful moment the search for truth; that the present happiness and eternal destiny of men are at stake upon the issue. But what was true religion in the days of our Lord and His apostles must be true religion now, for truth is like God, the same yesterday, to-day, and forever. Truth, then, as revealed by Christ, and enjoined upon His apostles, the full belief, public profession, and faithful practice of which were the conditions of salvation, must have always existed, and must still exist, entire and uncorrupted. It is of infinite importance then to us, as immortal beings, to examine diligently and see that we possess it. It is the *pearl of great price* spoken of in the gospel, to obtain which a man would do well to sell all his possessions and purchase it.

But how are we to make this search? Where shall we seek it? The world is full of sects, each claiming for itself the high prerogative of truth, each claiming to have emanated from God, each to hold the doctrine of the Son of God! Must we examine them all? Must we investigate the claims of each? Must we search all religions? It were a task beyond the powers of the human intellect. No. We are not bound to examine all. But we are bound to examine the claims of one. That one is the religion of Catholics.

There are reasons, in our search after truth, for investigating the claims of the Catholic Church, that do not hold with regard to the numerous sects around us. She alone retains the name of *Catholic*, — a title always accorded to the Church of Christ, and by which it was always distinguished from rebellious sects. She alone hath converted the nations of the earth, and thereby fulfilled the commission of Christ — *Go teach all nations.* She alone hath proved the validity of her claims by an uninterrupted succession of pastors, from the days of Christ to the present. She alone hath demonstrated her divine origin and guidance by a constant series of miracles. She is the oldest of all Churches, for she is the first of all. She existed in all her vigor and beauty and full development long before any of the sects were born. Full of years, she is nevertheless still vigorous and beautiful as when she started into life. She has existed in every age, she still exists in every clime. From the rising of the sun to the going down of the same the incense ascends from her altars, and the clean oblation is made in her sanctuaries. Thrones have crumbled, dynasties have ceased, busy cities have become deserts and deserts busy cities, old worlds have been forsaken and new worlds peopled, many nations have apostatized from the truth, and many more have been converted and embraced the truth, but the Catholic Church hath stood, like the rock of ages, unchanged, unchangeable, and indefectible.

These are some among the many reasons why a sincere inquirer after truth is bound to investigate the claims of the Catholic Church. These are some of the reasons which will render men inexcusable before God, should they unhappily live and die without the fold. O, that men would but feel the importance and appreciate the grandeur of this search after true Wisdom, " whose ways are beautiful ways, and all whose paths are peaceable," — " who, in her right hand, offers length of days," — eternity; "and in her left, riches and honors," — celestial treasures, an immortal crown.

The increase of Catholicity in the United States will be seen in the following table, wherein is given the number of bishops, churches, literary institutions, &c., at the opening of the present century, and in any one of the ten years since, say from 1840 to 1850: —

CONCLUSION.

Year,	1808	1840	1841	1842	1843	1844	1845	1846	1847	1848	1849	1850
Dioceses,	1	16	16	16	16	21	21	21	23	27	27	27
Apostolic Vicariates,						1	1	1	1			
Bishops,	2	17	17	21	18	17	25	25	26	27	26	27
Priests,	68	482	528	541	561	617	683	737	834	890	1000	1081
Churches,	80	454	512	541	560	611	675	740	812	907	966	1073
Stations,		358	394	470	475	461	592	560	577	572	560	595
Ecclesiastical Inst.,	2	13	14	17	18	19	22	22	22	22	25	29
Colleges,	1	9	10	11	11	11	12	14	14	14	15	17
Female Academies,	2	47	49	49	48	48	63	63	63	74	86	91

Anecdotes.

Strange were the ideas that many non-Catholics formerly had of a Catholic priest! They viewed him as something singular and unearthly, wholly different from any other mortal. He was generally called, however young in years, "the old priest," or "the paddy priest." Others again, after having satisfied their curiosity upon seeing him, were heard to remark, "that he was no great show after all!" Scarcely need be mentioned the annoyance that had to be contended with in by-gone days. We will, by way of amusement, mention one or two instances, which, however, by those whose constitutional gravity may deem out of place in a work like this, may pass over in silence.

On a certain occasion the Missionary happened to be the only gentleman passenger in the stage-coach, the rest being ladies, among whom was one, evidently "Miss Somebody," a Sabbath school teacher, probably, or the maiden aunt of a minister, for to talk religion seemed her hobby. Having learned from the coach-driver, at one of the way stations, the vocation of the taciturn gentleman passenger, she promised her travelling companions, it is presumed, in the ardor of her zeal, a display of her controversial powers, for scarcely had the gentleman returned to his seat, and the coach got fairly under way, than every eye was fixed on the discovered "popish priest," and the lady commenced: "Pray, sir, do you think man can forgive sins?" "Most assuredly I do, madam," replied the priest, "most assuredly I do, and ladies too, I trust." This was more than anticipated, and the good-natured smile among her companions seemed to intimate, take care; you may have awaked the wrong passenger! However, not to be silenced in this summary way, "Pray, sir," resumed the lady, "please explain; I don't understand you; how can man forgive sins?" "Why, madam," replied the priest, "suppose a neighbor had calumniated you, or unkindly censured your motives, and upon reflection had repented of what she had done, and came imploring forgiveness, could you not, and would you not forgive her? Assuredly you would. Yes, you would pardon her sin; and if ladies have such power, why not gentlemen?"

This good-natured reply was thought quite sufficient under the circumstances, for had religious discussion commenced, the poor horses themselves would have tired, in all probability, long before it had ended. From tea-party theologians and dyspeptic religionists, O, deliver us!

Early Impressions.

Travelling at another time in the coach, one of the passengers, a gentleman who had lived long enough to discover that it was not all gold that glittered, perceiving, towards evening, a new moon, "There," said he, "there is a new moon; now, when I was young, I was told if, when I saw a new moon over my right shoulder, and I had a penny in my pocket, it would be a lucky month for me. Now," continued the old gentleman, "I have outlived that foolish notion, and I know it is all superstition, prejudice, and not a word of truth in it; but positively, I acknowledge it, even to this day, whenever I see a new moon, I always think of my pocket."

Better informed than the Preacher.

Stopping at a certain town in L—— County, our Missionary was invited to preach to an audience composed of the representatives of the varied shades of Protestantism. Agreeably with custom, he invited any one present, if so disposed, to select a text or subject for discourse. None having been proposed, the Missionary went on to illustrate from Scripture, history, and tradition, a succinct account of certain doctrines and teachings of the Church, particularly on the necessity of heart-felt sorrow for sins committed, without which there was no power on earth able to forgive them. Respectful was the attention of all present, and by no one more so than a venerable, and to all appearance, worthy gentleman of threescore and ten, who, at the conclusion, rose up to say, that all they had listened to "was mere gammon; that he had read, and *he knew* the Catholic religion better than that."

Small Beginning — Happy Result.

In the town of P——, in the heart of a neighboring State, there formerly lived a solitary Irish Catholic, who, prompted to walk in the footsteps of others, did a thriving business. He was a pedler of small wares. He was conscientious, loved his religion, and was, we trust, or tried to be, an honest pedler: be that as it may, in his rambles from house to house he at length found a young woman of marriageable age, apparently to his liking, and whom he proposed should be his wife, provided she would be of his religion, " as fish and flesh should never be allowed on his table on days forbidden by the Church, much less would he be married like a heathen."

To the country town of his intended, most pressingly invited, the Missionary must go and preach, and a " blind set they must be," intimated our pedler, if, after hearing the plain truth, they were neither convinced nor converted! Away then goes the priest in the pedler's wagon, and at the district school-house the crowd are gathered, — as they had heard of his coming, — both to see, and hear, and judge for themselves. The evening passed away quite pleasantly, so much so, that an invitation was extended to hear the preacher the following evening, in the adjoining school-house. The invitation accepted and the audience assembled, strange to say, there is no entrance! The door is locked, and no one knows what has become of the key! Prejudice and bigotry, however, at length yield to curiosity, and the key is found! At this there is a rush for the seats, and, by certain outsiders, a rush for sticks and stones; and then came the contest between might and right. A few stones were thrown, and some drumming on the clapboards. Upon this the Missionary stepped out, and politely invited all to walk in and listen, and then, if necessary, demonstrate. The deliberate good sense of the turbulent triumphed over prejudice. "Hear him; let us hear what he has to say, and what he can prove." Order established, there was pretty good attention to the end; and, while the majority came through curiosity to see and hear for themselves what they had never looked upon before, — "a popish priest," — there were those who really appreciated the truth, and were prompted to inquire further; and of this apparently mixed crowd, five were subsequently, after due instruction and probation, admitted to the Sacrament of Baptism. At this day, within a radius of ten miles of this very town, where a priest was such an object of curiosity, there are six thousand Catholics.

Truth Triumphant.

We will mention another little incident which occurred at a certain sea-port town, where, at this day, there are upwards of two thousand Catholics.

The Missionary was called to administer the rites

of religion to a dying Christian. The call being fifty miles distant, he carried, as usual, his valise, which contained the vestments and all else requisite to offer the holy Sacrifice of Mass. There were in this town a few Catholic, hard-working sons of the Emerald Isle, who no sooner heard of the priest's arrival, than they came, as usual, to bid him a thousand welcomes. Learning that he was to remain over night, they rejoicingly carried his valise to a house in another part of the town, near to where they lived, that they might have Mass before going to their day's work the following morning. With the arrival of the stage-coach there came, the same evening, a schooner from New York, with a lady passenger on board, who, when about to disembark the following morning, found, to her great disappointment, that her trunk and wearables were missing. The police were soon on the alert, and Irishmen were reported to have been seen the evening previous, hurrying through the street with one trunk, for certain, if not two. They were soon ferreted out, and the Missionary had just finished Mass, as the force entered, to seize the surmised thieves, trunk and all. The little valise was scrutinized and examined thoroughly, but however turned or twisted, it would not swell into anything like a decent-sized travelling trunk, anyway! There was mystery, however, somewhere. The officers were puzzled, and left for consultation. To be outwitted by "a popish priest, and ignorant Irishmen," was too bad. By and by others came, and lest there might be some legerdemain or trickery in transforming the trunk into a valise, everything had to be opened out and displayed, that they might testify, as one of the officials remarked, "that there were no female wearables about it."

The place where this little incident happened was found to be rather hard soil, and the hatred of Catholicity intense. It was therefore deemed advisable to visit it, from time to time, which was done; and through notoriety, which little annoyances like the above, and occasionally stonings and hootings by unruly urchins for being a popish priest, Catholicity gained ground. A vacant lot of land, located between two fine frame buildings, was very quietly purchased, and, to the alarm of the neighbors, who could not conveniently burn it down, without considerable inconvenience to themselves, a Church and Cross arose in their very midst.

We relate little anecdotes like these to show the feeling formerly created by bigoted preachers and prejudiced writers upon the minds of otherwise earnest, sincere, and benevolent souls.

Faith in the Preachers.

Catholics have been often credited, and as often smiled at, for "pinning their faith to the priest's sleeve." The following little incident will show that credulity of certain non-Catholics are not always faultless. The old adage, "that they who live in glass houses should be careful how they throw stones," is worth remembering.

At the interment of a young man at C——, where the cemetery was a very dry, sandy soil, as the corpse was laid beside the grave for the funeral service, probably from its weight, or friends standing around, a small portion of sand caved in, and it was thought well to remove it before lowering the coffin to its destined resting-place, — a very simple occurrence, and not uncommon under similar circumstances. What was the surprise of the Missionary to learn, in less than forty-eight hours after the occurrence, that a certain travelling preacher regaled his hearers, at an evening lecture, with what he knew for truth, " as he was passing through the village at the time it happened," to wit, " that several poor, superstitious, benighted Irishmen were burying one of their countrymen who had died at C——, and so heavily had they loaded the coffin with candles and specie, quarters and halves, to get his soul through purgatory, that the coffin burst, and all present saw it!"

By no means is it surprising that many otherwise well-meaning, simple-minded souls should be prejudiced against Catholics, their practices and religion, when thus hoodwinked by those whom they pay so well to pray and to preach the word.

At the next interment in the same place the calumny was alluded to, and those present who were not Catholics requested to observe everything well; that if any one felt curious to know the name of the detractor, he might hear it privately, after the service. One gentleman remained to learn the name of the preacher; and when informed, replied, "I know him. It sounds just like him, the old ——."

Answer a fool, it is said, according to his folly. That was a droll incident where the priest, while travelling, reading his Breviary, was accosted, when through, by an itinerant preacher, who, peering over his shoulder, and guessing whom he addressed, said, "Sir, do you understand what you were reading?" The priest, looking up with the air and tone of one apparently deaf, re-echoed, "Sir!" "Do you understand," repeated the minister, in a clear, ringing voice, "do you understand, sir, what you have been reading?" "Sir," again replied the priest, putting his hand to his ear, as though still not understanding the impertinent question. The inquisitive divine, concluding he was trying to talk with the deafest man ever met in all his travels, had no more to say.

www.ingramcontent.com/pod-product-compliance
Lightning Source LLC
Chambersburg PA
CBHW020234240426
43672CB00006B/525